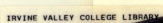

CHILDREN
OF THE LAND

CHILDREN OF THE LAND

Exchange and Status
in a Hawaiian Community

Jocelyn Linnekin

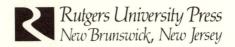
Rutgers University Press
New Brunswick, New Jersey

Library of Congress Cataloging in Publication Data

Linnekin, Jocelyn, 1950–
  Children of the land.

  Bibliography: p.
  Includes index.
    1. Hawaiians—Social life and customs.   2. Ceremonial
exchange—Hawaii—Keanae.   3. Social status—Hawaii—
Keanae.   4. Keanae (Hawaii)—Social life and customs.
I. Title.
DU624.65.L56   1984   306′.0969′21   83–24673
ISBN 0–8135–1052–X

Jacket and frontispiece illustrations courtesy of Jocelyn Linnekin.

For all my teachers

CONTENTS

LIST OF
MAPS AND FIGURES

MAPS

FIGURES

ix

LIST OF TABLES

PREFACE

The title of this book is a translation of the Hawaiian word *kama'āina*, which means old-timer, a long-time resident of a place. *Kama'āina* appears often in nineteenth-century land records; Hawaiians justified their claims to the land that they cultivated and lived on with phrases such as "I am a son of the land." The word is still in common use in Hawaii today to refer to a long-time resident. This study is about a community unique in modern Hawaii: a village of *kama'āina*, of Hawaiians who can boast of uninterrupted residence on the land of their ancestors.

During the summers of 1972 and 1973, I worked for Marshall Sahlins on his ethnohistorical project dealing with the Hawaiian kingdom. The background and the inspiration for this study stem from that apprenticeship. Fieldwork in Hawaii was conducted from October 1974 to October 1975. The ethnographic present used in the text refers to that period. My research was funded by a National Science Foundation Field Sciences Grant (GS-39667) and a National Institute of Mental Health predoctoral fellowship, and I gratefully acknowledge the support of these institutions.

I owe thanks also to many individuals for their support and encouragement. Dorothy B. Barrère shared with me her expert knowledge on all things Hawaiian; she and Professor Sahlins graciously lent me historical materials from their own collections and helped me to clarify aspects of the research. For friendship and hospitality while I was in the field, I thank Dorothy and Weas Barrère, Poppy Buser, Duane and Elaine Carlsmith, Mei-Ling Chang, Arthur and Ellen DePonte, Cynthia Gillette, and David and Elizabeth Marciel. My gratitude of course also goes to the people of Keanae for their tolerance and to Aunty Louise Akiu for her wisdom and aloha. I wish particularly to thank

Raymond C. Kelly for his interest and his conscientious reading of and thought-provoking suggestions on earlier drafts, and Professor Sahlins for an invaluable critical reading of an earlier version. Thanks also go to Aram Yengoyan, Michael Taussig, and L. A. Peter Gosling for their comments.

Finally, there is the category of persons without whom this book would never have been written: my friend and colleague Aletta Biersack, whose encouragement came at a critical time; Professor Sahlins, who first pointed out to me "the watered flats of Keanae"; and my husband, William Fay, whose unflagging support kept me going.

ABBREVIATIONS
AND SYMBOLS

AH	Archives of the State of Hawaii, Honolulu
E-0000	Hawaiian Court of Equity case number; originals in AH
F.O. & Ex.	Foreign Office and Executive File; originals in AH
HMCS	Hawaiian Mission Children's Society Library, Honolulu
HSB	*Honolulu Star-Bulletin*
LCA	Land Commission Award
NT (vol.:page)	Native testimony given before the Commission to Quiet Land Titles, Kingdom of Hawaii, 1846–1854; translation on microfilm in AH
OL	Older
PCA	*Pacific Commercial Advertiser*
P-0000	Probate Court case number: First Circuit Court unless otherwise noted
UH (vol., part:page)	University of Hawaii (see references in Works Cited)
YO	Younger
1st c.c.	First Circuit Court (Honolulu)
2nd c.c.	Second Circuit Court (County of Maui)
□	Male or female
○	Female
△	Male
⌀	Deceased
=	Marriage

≈	Common-law marriage
≠	Divorce
│	Parent/child relationship
┊	Adoptive parent/child relationship
—	Sibling relationship

Chapter One

PRIMITIVE EXCHANGE
AND MODERN HAWAII

I went to Keanae to investigate a paradox of sorts: the persistence of tradition in a highly acculturated society. I did not expect to find precontact customs somehow surviving in this rural village, but I believed that Hawaiian culture must possess a certain resilience, even in the face of a devastating history of foreign contact. This study describes a contemporary community but takes cues from traditional materials. My goal has been to analyze the situation of modern Hawaiians in light of cultural precedents—to arrive at a meaning of *Hawaiian* that clarifies the present and also helps us to understand the past.

Located on the windward side of Maui, Keanae is a postcard-pretty village that calls to mind the travelogue's "here people live as they have lived for centuries." The quilt of watered taro fields is broken by clumps of banana trees; sugar cane grows on the banks between the patches. The casual visitor might feel transported back to the time of Captain James Cook but for the automobiles parked in front of the residents' houses. Keanae is significant to students of Hawaiian culture because it is one of the few places in the islands where Hawaiians have retained ownership of their lands and where they still grow taro, the Polynesian staple. For the same reasons, Keanae has special meaning to modern Hawaiians in search of an elusive cultural identity; for them the village represents life in "the real old style," a link to an essential Hawaiianness.

Yet in spite of its popular image, Keanae is still a modern American community, tied into the market economy and participating in the social distinctions and political developments of the larger society. In Hawaii today, tradition is a political symbol (Linnekin 1983a). Taking cues from Ameri-

1

can ethnic politics, Hawaiian nationalists and cultural re-
vivalists variously define their identity in terms of Polynesian canoe voyaging (Finney 1979), love of the land (*aloha
'āina*[1]), and Hawaiiana, a category that comprises traditional crafts and performance arts such as chanting and the
hula. Does Keanae represent a more authentic tradition
than the somewhat eclectic version promoted by Hawaiian
nationalism? Yes—to the extent that many cultural practices in this community have demonstrable links to the
past. But Keanae does not exist in a social or political vac-
uum; the village is remote by today's standards but not isolated from the society outside.

Hawaiian tradition as experienced in Keanae is not unselfconscious. Villagers are fully aware that they represent
a traditional Hawaiian lifestyle to islanders of all ethnic
backgrounds as well as to tourists. The village is marked as
an attraction on the maps distributed by car-rental agencies, and an official Hawaii Visitors Bureau marker used to
stand alongside the highway above Keanae with the legend "Hawaiian Village." Travel writers of the nineteenth
and early twentieth centuries found the community remote and picturesque. Today, Keanae's relative isolation is
popularly assumed to indicate a pristine folk heritage. The
modern perception of the village's Hawaiianness is intrinsically linked to the premise that this community has a
privileged relationship to the past. A Honolulu journalist
(Lueras 1975) described Keanae as "the Hawaii that used to
be." As I will show, Keanae does represent Hawaiian tradition but not a naive or unchanging heritage.

Except for the taro patches, Keanae presents few overt
reminders of early Hawaiian society. The Hawaiian religion
was abolished over a hundred and sixty years ago; other
formal institutions—most notably, the chieftainship—have
long since disappeared. All Keanae residents are inextricably dependent on the external economy. Yet there are still

1. Diacritics and glosses for Hawaiian words are taken from Pukui and
Elbert (1971).

qualitative social differences between Keanae and other small American communities. Hawaiian culture does persist in Keanae—not in formal institutions but in the symbols, categories, and structure of relationships. That Keanae villagers grow taro seems to be a holdover from the past. The resemblance is superficial in that taro is grown for the market rather than for subsistence and provides only supplementary income for most householders. Nonetheless, the symbolic value of taro and the ethic of distributing it are distinctively Hawaiian and can explain why some residents of this taro-growing community rarely eat the traditional staple. What is most traditional about Keanae is not so much that women salt and dry fish but that they give those fish to relatives and friends in carefully measured portions. Keanae's Hawaiian heritage is exchange—and exchange here means much more than the mere transfer of goods. In Keanae, gifts are not solely economic commodities "but vehicles and instruments for realities of another order" (Lévi-Strauss 1969a:54).

EXCHANGE

The anthropological literature on exchange has focused on stateless, kinship-ordered societies. To stress gift giving in modern Hawaii may seem inappropriate. The setting is, after all, an industrial nation-state, and the market economy inevitably pervades every community within its political boundaries. But the colonial expansion of Western society has fostered a problematic category for anthropology: the non-Western cultural groups that have been incorporated into nation-states. Newly defined as peasants and wage laborers, these converts to Western civilization may retain a decidedly non-Western cultural identity for some time. Where external economic relations are impersonal and commercial, internal social relations may be qualitatively different. Yet anthropology still tends to dichotomize acculturated communities (where it is appropriate to study market relations, political maneuvering, or the psychological impact of Westernization) and pristine, primitive societies (where one looks for symbols and structures). The primitive society is increasingly becoming a mythical category.

Viewing Hawaiians as just another minority within the industrial state ignores their cultural past and their unique history. Keanae villagers are Hawaiian-Americans who participate in national political and economic institutions, but they also have a non-Western heritage. My method has been to integrate historical and modern materials in order to portray both dimensions of their lives. I will discuss wage labor and the market, and I will also discuss structures and symbols. I freely draw parallels between what Keanae villagers do today and descriptions of early Hawaiian society. The analogues to non-Western cultural institutions, such as exchange-in-kind and big-men, are quite intentional and are not inappropriate here. Relations between Keanae and the larger society are conditioned by the political and economic characteristics of an industrial nation, but relations within the village and within the wider community of Hawaiians are qualitatively different—as the villagers themselves recognize.

The Hawaiians of Keanae depend on the cash economy for their livelihood but simultaneously engage in a form of exchange that recalls the "archaic" societies described by Marcel Mauss and Claude Lévi-Strauss. Within the village and with relatives and friends, Hawaiians carry on exchange-in-kind with Polynesian commodities: food, land, service. This commerce is not a trivial aspect of social life in Keanae; relationships between families and individuals are played out in long-term cycles of gift giving. Implicit distinctions between relatives, affines, and non-relatives are revealed in acts of exchange. These social categories are neither static nor discrete; they refer to differing expectations and obligations in exchange. With nonrelatives particularly—friends and neighbors—exchange may be fraught with status rivalry and manipulation. Ties are initiated, elaborated, tested, and broken as the parties strive for an elusive symmetry.

In Keanae, as in many non-Western societies, exchange is a total social phenomenon. There is the same pervasive idea of "the power inherent in a thing" (Mauss 1967:49) to command a return payment. The unrequited gift "'creates a something between people'" (Sahlins 1965:165). The gift is productive of further gifts; it embodies the potential in human relationships. But this productivity also makes the gift, in Mauss's words, "dangerous to accept" (1967:58). The gift can create a difference in status between donor and recipient. The "calculated generosity" (Sahlins 1965:162) of Melanesian big-men succeeds precisely because gifts must be repaid, lest the recipient suffer a permanent loss of status. Open-ended indebtedness is to the giver's advantage, for the return may be demanded at any time. In Keanae, Hawaiians carry on an exchange of food, services, and commodities that is theoretically voluntary and spontaneous—out of the goodness of one's heart. But the underlying motives for such gift giving range from love for a relative to self-interest. Some people manipulate the etiquette of reciprocity to create indebtedness. Internally, the village remains an egalitarian society; age is the only ascribed basis of prestige. Personal prestige must be created but without appearing to violate the egalitarian ethic of social relations. Local big-men must overcome this paradox to gain influence over others.

The dynamic of creating and avoiding indebtedness impels interpersonal relations in Keanae. But short-term cycles of gift giving are only one form of reciprocity. Exchange describes not only the movement of commodities but also the movement of people—a form of exchange between groups. Marriage and adoption join Hawaiian households and localities in long-term cycles of exchange. The reciprocal movement of people between local groups can be demonstrated in genealogies going back several generations and in the family histories of living Keanae residents. I am not suggesting that Hawaiians today act out an unconscious structure when they decide whom to marry or when they entrust the care of their children to others; but as I point out in later chapters, marriage and adoption create alliances between households and local groups. These ties are crucial to local-level social organization and are intelligible only in that wider context.

INSIDE, OUTSIDE

The limits of reciprocity are the boundaries of the Hawaiian social world. The difference between the society of Hawaiians and the society dominated by foreigners is in part a difference in transactional rules. Within the village and with friends and relatives, gift giving prevails. Relations with the outside are commercial, indifferent, and perceived to be mutually exploitative. Keanae Hawaiians distinguish their rural heartland from the alien town society with the terms "inside" and "outside." The opposition has both social and geographical referents; the contrast is country as opposed to city, Hawaii as opposed to foreign, west (toward the industrial town of Kahului) as opposed to east (toward the old Hawaiian town of Hana) (see Map 1). Inside and outside are metaphors for contrasting spheres of social relations, in which different kinds of transactions are expected. The terminological contrast describes a scale of social distance and provides an extraordinarily apt model of society as perceived by Keanae Hawaiians.

The opposition between inside and outside contrasts the solidarity and egalitarianism of social relations within the village with the impersonality and hierarchy of the larger society. The key to Keanae's present-day significance, for both scholars and Hawaiians, is the fact that most Hawaiians live outside and have long been alienated from the land and the rural lifestyle. Hawaiians have historically been the least powerful group in island society, although they are attempting to change that status through political mobilization. An island aphorism states that the Japanese

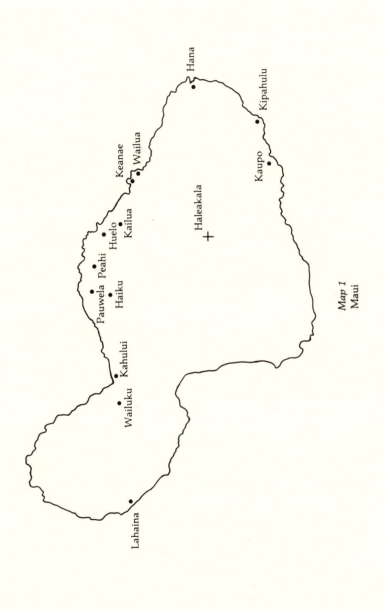

Map 1
Maui

have the politics, the Chinese have the money, the haoles (whites) have the land, and the Hawaiians, in the words of a popular song, "get plenty not too much of nutting." Hawaiians are disproportionately represented in public assistance rolls and juvenile courts (Howard 1974:x). In the national political context, they are an impoverished minority in search of their cultural roots. This search has accentuated Keanae's importance for Hawaiians and has enhanced the villagers' own awareness of their symbolic status.

Tradition is both lived and invented in Keanae, as rural Hawaiians conform to their own and others' expectations of what that tradition comprises. In contrast to the outside society, where foreigners are more numerous and more powerful, the inside has come to represent the Hawaiian identity and a link to an authentic cultural past. When villagers represent their lifestyle to outsiders, such as haole visitors, they speak of fish and taro, the Hawaiian staple foods, and they explicitly link their identity to exchange-in-kind: "In Keanae, you *give*, don't sell." A practice with referents in the past has thus become a marker of Hawaiian identity. Keanae villagers have chosen a life that they recognize as traditional in some sense. The fact that the content of this tradition has altered significantly over time does not detract from its present-day meaning for Hawaiians. The definition of authenticity always reflects the current social context; authentic is not synonymous with unchanging.

TRADITION IN THE
POLITICAL CONTEXT

Keanae's modern significance for Hawaiians is defined within the national context. Outside political models have become part of the self-perception of the people inside. The objectification of tradition in Hawaii today reflects a major trend in American politics, where both ethnicity and tradition have proved to be effective means for mobilizing groups to demand political power. Whether it is because of their material success or because of their self-perception, Hawaii's other ethnic groups have not mobilized in specifically nationalist movements. For political models, Hawaiian nationalism has looked outside the islands, to the movements of other colonized and dispossessed peoples: Native Americans, Puerto Ricans, Micronesians (see Protect Kaho'olawe 'Ohana 1981:17). Human groups from ethnic nationalists to academic disciplines (see Cohn 1980) use a conscious model of tradition to differentiate themselves from others. Ethnic groups searching for their identity tend to idealize their folk, rural, and Old Word origins, and it is by now a truism that nationalist movements create, at least in part, the cultures they claim merely to discover (see, e.g., Linton 1943). The tendency to objectify culture in the definition of group identity has become an international political phenomenon, particularly among indigenous peoples trying to overcome their subordinate status. When Melanesians sit and discuss *kastom* (see Keesing and Tonkinson 1982) and when Hawaiian nationalists wax poetic over love of the land, culture has been externalized and made into a thing to be consciously shaped.

Hawaiian nationalism began as an urban movement, primarily attracting young part-Hawaiians who did not speak Hawaiian and whose families were long separated from rural life. In the late 1960s, the University of Hawaii became the center for the resurgence of interest in Hawaiian culture. A Hawaiian studies program was started, and courses in the Hawaiian language and Hawaiiana became popular all over the islands. The Hawaiian renaissance looks partly to communities such as Keanae for cultural models and partly to accounts of early Hawaiian society— most of these written by foreigners. The resulting version of Hawaiian culture could be termed inauthentic in that the relationship of its focal symbols to the Hawaiian past is variable. Ben Finney (1979) has related the conflicts that plagued the voyage of the double-hulled canoe Hokule'a from Hawaii to Tahiti in 1976. The Hokule'a project was originally conceived by haole scholars as a refutation of the accidental-voyaging theory of Polynesian migration. But the voyage became a rallying point for the Hawaiian cultural renaissance, with inevitable clashes between the canoe's haole sponsors and the part-Hawaiian crewmen. The Hokule'a project illustrates how tradition is reconstituted in the process of political and ethnic differentiation. The objective relationship of tradition to past lifeways is always equivocal because the selection of what constitutes tradition is made in the present. Isolated facts may be seized upon and accorded a significance without precedence in the aboriginal society. The Hokule'a's designer, a half-Hawaiian reared and educated in the Midwest, proclaimed the canoe to be "the central artifact of Polynesian culture" (ibid.:29). This position is not intrinsic to the canoe nor taken over from precontact Hawaiian culture. Conceivably, other artifacts might have served just as well as focal symbols.

Nonetheless, the construction and launching of the Hokule'a became a celebration of Hawaiian tradition, involving the participation of Hawaiians on several islands. As the Hokule'a project spawned several other canoe-building ventures, scores of Hawaiians who had never previously been active in the cultural revival or nationalist movement sought to contribute to some part of the enterprise: the lashings, the wood, the preparation of food for the crew. For the meaning of Hawaiian tradition in the present, it does not matter that the voyaging-canoe projects embodied a number of borrowed elements. For the Hokule'a's journey to Tahiti, a Micronesian navigator was recruited because no Hawaiians could be found with experience in deep-water canoeing. The launching rites for the canoe attempted to recreate ancient Hawaiian ritual, with chanting and the throwing of foods into the sea as a sacrifice. But after the canoe's first interisland cruise, a kava ceremony modeled on the kava ritual of Samoa was incorporated into the rites (Finney 1979:31). Hawaiians drank an intoxicating brew made from the *'awa*, but the details of the ceremony are lost (see Kamakau 1961:119).

Inevitably, the version of Hawaiian culture espoused by the essentially urban-based nationalist movement contains some consciously constructed elements. But the Hawaiian cultural revival is not concerned only with rituals and voyaging canoes. There has been an ongoing conjunction of the nationalists' idea of tradition and Hawaiian tradition as experienced in rural communities such as Keanae; the content of both versions has been modified in the process (Linnekin 1983a). The nationalist and the rural experiences of tradition converge in a focus on the land. The *'āina* has become a potent political symbol for the nationalist movement, which has demanded reparations for the lands that commoner Hawaiians lost during the last century. The movement's slogan, *aloha 'āina*, evokes the identification of the Hawaiian people with the land (see Protect Kaho'olawe 'Ohana 1981:1–2). The barren island of Kahoolawe, used as a bombing target by the U.S. Navy since World War II, has become the archetype of the despoiled Hawaiian landscape. There have been occupations of the island, arrests, and the accidental deaths of two young men in the waters offshore. Occupiers subsisted as much as possible on gathered foods, thus representing Hawaiians as people who make their living from the land and sea (Ritte and Sawyer 1978).

The concept of *aloha 'āina* underscores the importance of Keanae: the survival of this taro-growing community proves, to many Hawaiians, their historic link to the rural lifestyle. This has become a public perception in the islands. Taro and other Polynesian plants are cultivated on the grounds of the University of Hawaii. The taro plant has become an iconic symbol for the *aloha 'āina* movement and is frequently represented in their publications. At Keanae, the state maintains an arboretum with an extensive range of native cultigens and nearly twenty varieties of taro. Many urban-born nationalists have attempted to live their Hawaiian identity by starting taro farms and establishing settlements in remote areas of the islands.

Hawaiian nationalism has also looked to the rural community for models of interpersonal behavior. A key concept in the organization of the cultural revival is that of *'ohana*, a term for extended family (see Handy and Pukui 1972:40ff.). *'Ohana* appears rarely in texts and archival materials from the nineteenth century, but today it refers to an idealized version of the Hawaiian family unit, characterized by cooperation (*kōkua*), internal harmony, and aloha (love, affection). The word evokes Hawaiian kinship and solidarity and has been incorporated into the names of protest groups such as the Protect Kaho'olawe 'Ohana. Within this putative family, it has become obligatory to call all older males "uncle" and older women "aunty." As will be shown, the casual use of these terms is indeed customary among Hawaiians, but here the custom has become a model for behavior, a practice to be consciously emulated. *'Ohana* also describes an ethic of egalitarianism and thus represents the rejection of certain historical aspects of Hawaiian society. The crewmen of the Hokule'a claimed that not having anyone give orders was "the Hawaiian way." Yet Hawaii was a hierarchical society, both in the ranking of chiefs over commoners and within the family, where junior siblings owed service to their elders.

The egalitarian ethic does have a correlate in rural society, although aloha and *kōkua* represent the ideals rather than the reality of village social relations. Keanae Hawaiians identify themselves as the descendants of the common people, and this is demonstrably true. Informants express hostility toward the Hawaiian chiefs, whose origins were foreign (Sahlins 1981:29–30) and who were wanderers without fixed residence on the land (Kamakau 1961:376). The chiefs and their agents were outsiders, although, as I will show, some of the latter settled into the rural community and became residents on the land. The society of Hawaiian commoners was egalitarian, as is village society today: ideally egalitarian, but not free from conflict and competition.

The nationalist and the rural conceptions of Hawaiian-ness mutually influence one another. The nationalist model draws on the rural lifestyle selectively and idealizes it for political ends. The cultural revival has in turn affected the way that Keanae villagers perceive and represent them-selves. Hawaiian children are taught chanting, the hula, and the Hawaiian language at Keanae School. One village woman has become a specialist in Hawaiiana. She learned the traditional arts partly from family members and partly from elderly neighbors and hones her skills by attending Hawaiiana workshops in the city. A Keanae boy was one of the Kahoolawe martyrs, lost at sea in an attempt to rescue occupiers of the island. His father has eulogized him as "brought up cultivating taro and passion fruit" (Ritte and Sawyer 1978:xix) and has himself become active in the Kahoolawe movement since his son's death.

Few Keanae villagers participate directly in either the cul-tural revival or the nationalist movement, and many scoff at such activities. For most, the effect of the external political context is rather more subtle: a growing awareness of Keanae as a special place, a heightened self-consciousness when using the terms "uncle" and "aunty," a tendency to say, "We Hawaiians do this." Villagers now reflect on the characteristics that differentiate the inside from the outside and attempt to behave in accordance with this categorical distinction. The differences correspondingly become more salient, more apprehensible. Exchange-in-kind becomes an explicit norm of behavior within the community: the Ha-waiian way. Residents who claim to live by fish and poi are making a statement about their Hawaiianness, not giving a factual description of their mode of subsistence. When young Hawaiians choose to live in Keanae, they are choos-ing to embrace that identity.

Chapter Two

THE TARO PLACE

K eanae's identity as a Hawaiian place is intrinsically linked to its relatively remote location and to the history of its lands and settlement. Keanae is an ancient community, notable for its unbroken occupation by Hawaiians and for the long history of taro growing in the area. Unlike other Hawaiian communities described in the literature, Keanae is distinguished by the historical depth of the present population. The villagers are *kama'āina*, long-time residents or "children of the land." They are descendants of the common people, the *maka'āinana*, and most of them live in Keanae because of a relationship to someone who held the land in former times. This chapter describes the locale, the settlement history, and the people of Keanae.

THE ETHNOGRAPHIC SETTING

Although I have called Keanae a village, the name has two referents. Keanae proper is the *ahupua'a*[1] of Keanae, the ancient land division stretching from the mountain to the sea. Lower Keanae is a flat, lava-rock peninsula jutting about a half mile into the sea. Keanae Valley, behind it, is part of the Koolau Gap, one of two major fissures in the rim of Haleakala, the dormant volcano that forms the land mass of East Maui. Although the lower reaches of the valley are relatively flat, farther upland the gap becomes an impassable rain forest, eventually meeting the lava flows that spilled anciently from the crater floor.

1. The *ahupua'a* was the most important Hawaiian land division, in its ideal form a valley running from the mountain to the sea. Usually the province of a single chiefly owner, the *ahupua'a* was a unit of tribute collection in precontact times and an administrative and tax-collecting unit under the state. The *ahupua'a* was also a customary prize given by a ruling chief to a subordinate as a reward for loyalty and service.

Keanae in general denotes the peninsula and its environs, including the neighboring valley, Wailua, and it is in this sense that I refer to Keanae as a community (see Map 2). Lower Keanae and Wailua Valley lie at a lower elevation than the state highway connecting them and are the primary taro lands. Sheer rocky cliffs abut the coast between them. The soil of Keanae Peninsula is only a thin layer over jagged rock, but its productivity was famous even in the days of the chiefs. E. S. Craighill Handy and E. G. Handy (1972:500–501) recount the legend of the origin of Lower Keanae's taro lands:

> Anciently . . . the peninsula was barren lava. But a chief, whose name is not remembered, was constantly at war with the people of neighboring Wailua and was determined that he must have more good land under cultivation, more food, and more people. So he set all his people to work (they were then living within the valley and going down to the peninsula only for fishing), carrying soil in baskets from the valley down to the lava point. The soil and the banks enclosing the patches were thus, in the course of many years, all transported and packed into place. Thus did the watered flats of Keanae originate.

Only eight families live on the peninsula now; there were more before the 1946 tidal wave. (For an account, see Shepard et al. 1950:436.) While some residents waited for their homes to be rebuilt on the peninsula, others settled permanently along the highway. Keanae is the most populous settlement between Haiku and Hana, the nearest small towns. Kahului, the major industrial and shopping center, is about thirty-five miles from Keanae; experienced drivers can make the trip in an hour, if driving conditions are good. Canefields and pasture lands lie between Kahului and Pauwela, where the improved highway ends and a sign warns: "Narrow winding road next 30 miles." When I returned for a visit in 1981, the word "bumpy" had been added to the sign's legend. The beginning of the bad road is the approximate frontier of the inside, or the country.

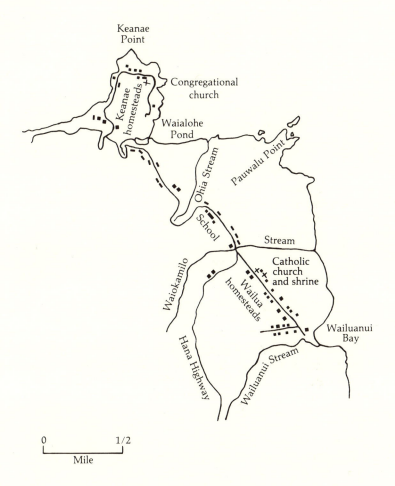

Keanae
Point

Congregational
church

Keanae
homesteads

Waialohe
Pond

Pauwalu Point

Ohia Stream

School

Stream

Catholic
church
and shrine

Waiokamilo

Wailua
homesteads

Wailuanui
Bay

Hana Highway

Wailuanui Stream

0   1/2
Mile

Source: U.S.G.S. 1:24000 Series

Map 2
Keanae and Environs

From here to Hana the road snakes through a tropical rain forest, past a series of narrow gorges cut by innumerable streams. Hana is "all the way inside." A popular song claims that there are "fifty-four bridges to Hana town." The inside is a lush, wet land that was nearly impassable in former times. The outside is barren and dry by comparison, and is inhabited by many Portuguese and young haoles, whom the locals call "hippies." Older residents sigh with relief when they reach the shade of the first gulch: "So nice to be inside again."

A history of isolation preserved Keanae's identity as a reservoir of tradition. Such a place was called the *kua'āina*, the back land, the out-district. The Hana region was known as "one of the most isolated places in these Islands, remote and difficult of access" (Sereno Bishop, 1861. Report to Board of Sandwich Islands Mission. Original, HMCS). Because of the many treacherous ravines and unpredictable flooding, travelers usually rode on horseback to a point before Keanae, then completed the journey to Hana by canoe. The wild middle stretch of the Hana coast belonged historically to Koolau District. This section of the windward coast was impassable, except by footpath, until 1927, when the belt road was completed to Hana. Over land, Keanae was inaccessible—at least to haoles—from both Hana and Wailuku (D. T. Conde to Titus Coan, c. 1845. Original, HMCS). Mission duty in Hana District was one of the most severe in the islands and took a heavy toll on the missionary families who served there. Before the Hana station was founded in 1837, missionaries reached East Maui no more than once or twice a year (Anonymous, 1837. Wailuku Station Report. Typescript, HMCS). Koolau was visited even less frequently than Hana.

Although the difficulty of land access to Keanae was a formidable obstacle to haoles, it would have been no barrier to Hawaiians in ancient times. Both Keanae and Wailua had harbors for small vessels. Traveling wholly by canoe, one could make the trip from Wailuku to Hana in only five and a half hours, as opposed to two days by land

and sea (D. T. Conde to D. Baldwin, 7 February 1844, and to L. Chamberlain and S. N. Castle, 26 December 1838. Originals, HMCS). Keanae is still noted for its rough water. During the winter, waves break over sections of the road encircling the peninsula, and even Hawaiians must at times have been prevented from reaching the area in bad weather. Before the highway opened, travelers to Hana might be 'delayed up to a week until the seas calmed sufficiently for them to pass Keanae. Interisland shipping began to prosper in the 1880s, and a steamer touched at Hana once a week until the road was completed (Wenkam 1970:67). The steamers refused to call at Keanae, however. In 1901, a Chinese merchant began running a junk from Keanae to accommodate the Chinese planters who had leased taro lands for growing rice (*PCA* 2 September 1901:11).

Overland communication improved somewhat after 1876, when the Reciprocity Treaty with the United States was signed and central Maui began to fill with sugar plantations. After Claus Spreckels secured the water right to the Hana coast, a vast irrigation network of flumes and ditches was constructed in the uplands to tap water for the canefields in the dry isthmus. The Koolau Ditch Trail, built for the maintenance of the irrigation system, became the only overland route to Keanae (Judd 1938:6). The ancient Hawaiian trail and later horsepath followed the coast, but the Ditch Trail lies far upland of the village. The Hana Highway was the first major improvement in access to Keanae. By 1941, Hana had telephone service, a monthly steamer visit, mail three times a week, and bus service every other day (Yamamura 1941:9). Electricity was provided to Keanae in 1960 (UH 1967 I:12), and today mail is delivered five days a week, although public transportation no longer serves the area. Keanae is remote by modern standards, but there are no longer any physical barriers to travel. A few times during the winter rainy season, floods or landslides may block the road outside temporarily, but the time involved is actually the only hindrance to travel.

The Hana road effectively ended Keanae's isolation and may have jeopardized its future as a Hawaiian place. Although the amenities of country life have improved in the past forty years, the population has steadily declined. Since the mid-nineteenth century, Hawaiians have steadily left the country for the towns and cities. In 1930, the Secretary of the Territory estimated Keanae's population as 527, with 2,210 in Hana District, which encompasses the eastern half of East Maui, including Keanae (Clare and Morrow 1930:14). Keanae School had sixty-three pupils then, compared with forty in 1965 (UH 1965 I,2:47) and thirty-one in 1975. The 1970 census gave 459 as the population of Hana village, with 510 in the rest of the district (State of Hawaii 1974:17, Table 7). This represents a decline of almost 10 percent from the 1960 census. By my field census, the resident population of Keanae in 1975 was 148, compared with 195 reported in a 1959 study (Forster 1959:50). Tables 2.1 and 2.2 describe Keanae's Hawaiian population in 1975. The three localities are Keanae Peninsula, Wailua Valley, and the upland along the highway. The unbalanced age structure, with twice as many adults as children, does not seem auspicious for Keanae's future. Of fifty-one Hawaiian households, 65 percent are presently childless, and 27 percent are occupied by single persons. But, as I will show, this population structure is a response to limited opportunities for schooling and working inside and does not necessarily portend the community's demise.

Formerly, the area of populous Hawaiian settlement extended beyond Hana, to Kaupo on the leeward side of Maui. Now the coast between Hana and Kaupo is almost deserted; a rough unpaved road connects them. Although all the remote areas in the islands have suffered depopulation, the dry side of Maui has been particularly hard hit. Kaupo is dry, marginal land, unsuitable for wet-land taro. Residents lived primarily on sweet potatoes in precontact times and traded actively with communities on the windward side. Social and material exchange relationships broke down as Hawaiians drifted away from the land, and Kaupo

Table 2.1
HAWAIIAN POPULATION OF KEANAE, 1975:
NUMBER OF HOUSEHOLDS

Locality	Full-Time Resident Households	Part-Time Resident Households	Total
Lower Keanae	7	1	8
Wailua Valley	24	2	26
Upland	17	0	17
Total Hawaiian households	48	3	51

Table 2.2
HAWAIIAN POPULATION OF KEANAE, 1975:
NUMBER OF RESIDENTS

Locality	Adults (18 and over)	Children (under 18)	Total
Lower Keanae	17	6	23
Wailua Valley	44	18	62
Upland	39	24	63
Total population	100 (67%)	48 (33%)	148 (100%)

became even more isolated. Ranches hastened the process of attrition by swallowing up Hawaiian lands in Kaupo and turning them into pastures. Always a long journey from any sizable town, Kaupo today is accessible only with a four-wheel-drive vehicle, and few Hawaiians remain there.

The rural heartland between Pauwela and Hana is sparsely inhabited now. But except for a sprinkling of young haoles returning to nature, those who remain are Hawaiian. Tourists come in queues of rented cars to admire the exotic tropical beauty, but most non-Hawaiians consider the windward coast too wet for permanent residence. Long-time Hawaiian residents of the country consider themselves fortunate to live "in the old style," in spite of the relative isolation. Hawaiians living outside often express regret at their alienation from the way of life that Keanae represents. Many say that they would live inside if not constrained by economic considerations. There is a sense that Hawaiians are quite literally out of place in the towns; to use a traditional phrase, they "belong to" the country, not to the outside. Undoubtedly such sentiments are partly an idealization of the past and the Hawaiian identity; perhaps few would actually choose the rigors of the Keanae life if they had the opportunity. Nevertheless, when Hawaiians come inside, they recognize that they are returning home, not only to a close-knit set of relationships but to a lifestyle that has something "real Hawaiian" about it. To residents and visitors alike, the first gulch is the physical symbol of this enveloping identity. "You feel those cool breezes," as one informant expressed it, "you know you close to home."

Although Keanae's population is about a quarter of its 1930 size, the community's vitality belies the attrition of residents. Tranquil in appearance, Keanae hardly resembles a dying village, particularly on weekends, when visitors from outside fill every available bed. Despite the population's skewed age structure, the community of Hawaiians survives. Keanae represents as traditional a lifestyle as can be found in the islands, except perhaps on Niihau.[2] Ease of access has not altered Keanae's fundamental identity as a Hawaiian place nor its symbolic value to Hawaiians.

SETTLEMENT HISTORY

In the history of its lands and settlement, Keanae is inherently different from other Hawaiian communities described in the literature. Many villagers can boast of an unbroken link with the land of their ancestors. In the estimation of Hawaiians as well as other islanders, the tra-

2. Lying to the lee of Kauai, Niihau is owned by a haole family determined to maintain a pristine Hawaiian community. Access is restricted, and residents grow up speaking the Hawaiian language in school and at home.

ditional Hawaiian lifestyle is represented by small rural communities that survive on Maui, on Niihau, in eastern Molokai, and in Kona on the island of Hawaii. There are a handful of such settlements left in remote areas of the islands, in locations that have an undesirable climate, are difficult to reach, or are simply "too rocky and barren to attract Western industry or agriculture" (Lind 1959:6). Andrew Lind called them "Hawaiian subsistence communities." These settlements and Keanae "have developed spontaneously among the native Hawaiians" (ibid.:6).

In contrast, urban Hawaiians, whose life was described by Ernest Beaglehole (1937), have been displaced from the land. Others have been resettled in artificially created Hawaiian homestead communities. These modern Hawaiians are best known from the University of Hawaii studies of Nanakuli, a Hawaiian homestead community on the leeward coast of Oahu (see Gallimore and Howard 1968; Howard 1971, 1974; Howard et al. 1970); Felix Keesing's (1936) early work concerned Hawaiian homesteaders on Molokai. But homestead communities such as Nanakuli lack the time depth of Keanae, many of whose residents are demonstrably descended from Hawaiians who received land in the Great Mahele, the land division of 1846–1854. Applicants with diverse origins settled in the homestead communities individually over time as they met the requirements of the Homes Commission. By the terms of the Hawaiian Homes Act of 1920, those who could prove at least 50 percent Hawaiian ancestry were entitled to apply for ninety-nine-year leases on lots set aside for Hawaiian homesteads. As is typical of reservation-type programs, these lands were "among the poorest in the islands," some lacking water and most unfit for agriculture (Howard 1974:3–4). Nanakuli was chosen for house-lot homesteads only because the land was admittedly "completely unsuitable for farming." The area had never been occupied previously and remained unsettled and without water until 1929. The majority of lease applications were filed after World War II. Nanakuli is a much larger community than the remote subsistence villages, with a 1960 population of

2,745 and 394 households (ibid.:xiii, 14). Given this recent and artificial association of residents, one might expect more social problems than in a small, continuously occupied village such as Keanae (cf. ibid.:x).

The earliest land titles in Keanae—and in the Hawaiian Islands—date from the Great Mahele, when the king divided the lands of the kingdom among himself, the government, and the chiefs. These three parts became known as crown, government, and *konohiki* (landlord) lands, and all were subject to the rights of native tenants (Revised Laws of Hawaii 1925 II:2152). Before the Mahele, private land titles did not exist in Hawaii. The Board of Commissioners to Quiet Land Titles was appointed in 1846 to hear the testimony of Hawaiian commoners, who had previously lived as tenants under the chiefs. The Land Commission Awards, or *kuleana*s, were meant to establish the commoners' title in fee simple[3] to the lands that they had long cultivated and lived on (Territory of Hawaii 1929:x–xi). There were twenty-one Land Commission Awardees in Keanae, and thirty-nine in Wailua. In most areas, the small parcels awarded to the common people were taken primarily from the *konohiki* lands, the one-third apportioned to the chiefs as landlords (ibid.:vii). Keanae and Wailua had belonged to the ruling family and were classified as crown lands during the Mahele, meaning that the king retained ownership of all the lands not apportioned to commoners as Land Commission Awards—that is, a considerable amount.

The Mahele proved not to be the last opportunity for Hawaiians to acquire land. Royal Patent Grants, which originated after the Mahele, were sales of crown lands to individual applicants, with no restrictions on the buyer's identity. Beginning in 1855, Keanae Hawaiians began to

3. Fee simple is ownership in the Western sense, implying absolute and unqualified possession, and the right to alienate. It conveys a property right that belongs to the owner and his heirs forever, unless they convey it to someone else.

acquire Royal Patent Grants, either individually or as a cooperative group, or *hui* (see Linnekin 1983b). Between 1855 and 1906, twenty-one such awards were made in the Keanae area, involving a total area of 769.35 acres. As an indication of the significance of this figure, the area represents 58 percent of the total land acreage in Keanae, as computed from the Maui County tax records. All but one of the Royal Patent Grants went to Hawaiians.

The four Royal Patent Grants issued to *hui*s of Hawaiians have created a quandary for their owners' descendants, many of whom still reside in Keanae. By definition, *hui* land is owned communally by all members of the group, each of whom has a fractional share of the whole (Watson 1932:9–10). No one member, however, has the right or title to any specific parcel within the total land area. A *hui* member claiming an interest of two acres, for example, actually owns only a general share equivalent to that area; he cannot legally alienate any particular acreage, although he may sell his share. The Keanae *hui*s are relatively small in size and membership. Two of the *hui*s originally had seven members; the other two had fifteen and nineteen shareholders. But with the division of estates over time, particularly when an owner died without a will, the number of interest holders in the *hui* lands has increased geometrically; today some hold fractional shares as small as 1/240. Small *hui*s such as those in Keanae were often dissolved by partition deeds executed by the original owners or their heirs; these subdivided the land held in common and established the owners' particular shares. Alternatively, the grantees often agreed to a de facto division of the land, in part or as a whole. Other, larger *hui*s in the islands have been the subject of exceedingly lengthy and complex litigation. None of the Keanae *hui*s has been formally subdivided, either by suit or by partition deed. There has been some de facto occupation of specific parcels, but this has been undertaken by individuals; there is no consensus in the community as to the disposition of these lands. For the most part, current shareholders do nothing with their claims and complain about the uselessness of "undivided land."

The third type of land grant found in Keanae derives from the Land Act of 1895, the first homestead act (Territory of Hawaii 1895:49–62). This act combined the former crown and government lands into a category of public lands, to be administered by a board of commissioners. The act instructed the commissioners to survey and open for settlement "suitable portions of Public Lands . . . selected only from agricultural and pastoral lands," to be laid out in lots containing not more than an acre of irrigated land. Certificates of occupation were to be issued to any applicant who met the following qualifications: "Under no civil disability for any offense, who is not delinquent in the payment of taxes, who has not made a false declaration in applying for land . . . who is not the owner in his own right of any land . . . not classed as wet land" (ibid.:62).

The act seemed designed to ensure that land would go to those who had no holdings or had only small holdings, for disallowed was any married person "whose wife or husband owns land other than one acre of wet land in her or his own right." After the certificate of occupation was issued, the applicant had a probationary period of six years before a 999-year lease was issued. Within the probationary period the occupant was required to build and maintain a house and to cultivate at least 10 percent of the land. If the occupant did not meet these conditions, the certificate would be canceled and the land returned to the public domain.

Figure 2.1 clarifies the land types in Keanae today, according to their historical origin. Unlike the 1920 Hawaiian Homes Act, the law of 1895 did not require Hawaiian ancestry, although in practice the great majority of the homesteaders in Keanae were Hawaiians. The Hawaiian Homes Act had the effect of assembling persons who were for the most part unrelated and who originated in different places. The 1895 Land Act attracted primarily local residents who had little or no land. In Keanae, many of the

Figure 2.1
Origins of Land Titles in Keanae

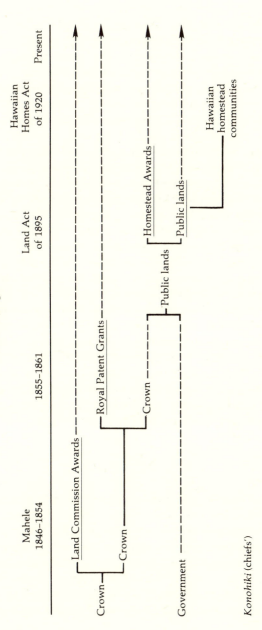

Note: Underscored titles denote land categories represented in Keanae.

applicants were relatives or descendants of Land Commission Awardees. Others resided in Keanae before the Land Act was passed. In the late 1920s, several homesteaders came to Keanae from Kaupo on the dry side of Maui, an area which has a history of exchange relations with Keanae dating from ancient times. Most of the Kaupo settlers were already related to Keanae people through marriage or putative cousin relationships.

Table 2.3 graphically illustrates the difference between Keanae homesteading and the settlement of Hawaiian homestead communities. Of fifty-one Hawaiian households in Keanae, thirty-one are homesteads created under the 1895 law. The remaining twenty households are situated on Land Commission Awards or Royal Patent Grants. Only one homesteading family is of nonlocal origin, a retired Chinese-Hawaiian couple who began leasing in 1972. *Local* denotes persons who, if not born in Keanae, are reputed to be "long time from 'round here" as opposed to from some other locality. In nearly half of the homesteads, both husband and wife are long-time Keanae residents. If one considers the origins of all householders, the *kama'āina*, old-timer, nature of the current population is similarly evident. In 32 percent of all households, both spouses are from Keanae. Only two Hawaiian homes in Keanae are occupied by outsiders. Of the one hundred adult residents, sixty-seven are reputed to be of local origin.

THE CHINESE

The largest group of outsiders to settle in Keanae was the Chinese. There are as many Chinese-Hawaiian as Hawaiian surnames on the mailboxes lining the road. Yet the community's cultural identity has remained Hawaiian, partly because of the nature of the Chinese immigration. Beginning in 1852, Chinese were brought into Hawaii as coolie labor for the plantations. Until 1876, the average rate was about a hundred Chinese immigrants a year, nearly all

Table 2.3
ORIGINS OF MARRIED HOMESTEADERS

	Local Man	Nonlocal Man
Local woman	14 (45%)	8 (26%)
Nonlocal woman	8 (26%)	1 (3%)
Total = 31 homesteads (100%)		

of them male. The largest influx occurred from 1876 to 1886, with a smaller wave between 1890 and 1897 (Adams 1937:32). The Chinese signed five-year labor contracts, and most left the plantations after completing their terms to initiate a variety of mercantile and entrepreneurial activities (Lorden 1935:454). In Hawaiian villages, Chinese storekeepers and rice planters became an integral part of the local population. Because of their skewed sex ratio, the Chinese immigrants usually married Hawaiian women, who regarded Chinese men as being better providers than Hawaiians (Adams 1937:48–49). In the 1878 census, there were 1,990 Chinese on Maui (*The Friend* January 1882:4).

The rice industry in Hawaii grew concurrently with the Chinese immigration, which provided both demand and labor for the crop. Despite a short-lived and enthusiastic introduction in 1861, rice growing did not become extensive until after 1876 (Kuykendall 1953:150–151). Between 1876 and 1900, rice was second only to sugar in exports, even though much was consumed in the islands by the immigrants (Kuykendall 1967:47). Chinese dominated the Hawaiian rice industry throughout its peak period. In rural Hawaii, the Chinese most commonly organized their enterprise in a corporation, or *hui*, of ten to twenty men, who financed the business with their savings from plantation work (Coulter and Chun 1937:18). Hawaiians were generally quite willing to lease their lands to the Chinese, and the rentals were high as long as rice remained a profitable crop (Cross 1912:345). Some Keanae Hawaiians insist that all the present taro land was once in rice, with "no taro here at all." One informant, a woman of about sixty, related the modern version of Keanae's origin myth:

> Before the Chinese came, Lower Keanae was all barren lava. The Chinese brought the soil from upland in buckets and made the paddies to plant rice. The Hawaiians didn't like rice, though; they would rather eat poi,[4] so after the Chinese died they started planting taro. That's how there is taro here today.

Keanae and Wailua were the major rice-growing areas on Maui (Coulter and Chun 1937:20). The first leases of land to Chinese in Keanae date from the early 1880s. In nearly every case, a Hawaiian leased his land to a company of Chinese. Between 1884 and 1894, there was a flurry of conveyances involving Chinese, with various rice-planting companies leasing, disbanding, changing hands, or mortgaging their property to raise more capital. The area listed as rice land in the 1890 tax rolls was 67.84 acres, compared with 95.482 acres of taro (Real Property Tax books. Originals, AH). For 1892, John Wesley Coulter and Chee Kwon Chun (1937) list 75 acres of rice in Keanae. Leases to Chinese continued through the early 1900s, with mention of rice mills and warehouses on the wharf at Keanae. In 1901, the *Pacific Commercial Advertiser* (2 September:11) announced that a merchant sampan crewed by Chinese and Hawaiians had fetched five tons of rice from Keanae.

Yet the period of Chinese commerical activity in Keanae was relatively brief, and the cultural impact of the Chinese

---

4. Poi, the traditional staple food of Hawaii, is a paste made by boiling and grinding the taro root. In early times, the taro was pounded smooth with a stone pestle in a trough. Nowadays, taro growers have grinding machines for the job. Commercial poi is sold in island supermarkets in plastic bags holding one or two pounds. At the time of fieldwork, a one-pound bag cost sixty cents. When I returned in 1981, the price was twice that. Food coloring is added at the factory to make the poi a reddish color in imitation of the prized *lehua* variety of taro. The natural poi served in Keanae is from the *moi* and *ha'okea* varieties, however, and is grayish white.

on Hawaiian village life was minimal. About forty thousand Chinese men came to Hawaii in the nineteenth century, but half of them had returned to China by 1900 (Adams 1937:145). Immediately after Hawaii was annexed by the United States in 1898, the Chinese Exclusion Act put a stop to further immigration and contributed to the demise of the Hawaiian rice industry. Local demand for Chinese-style rice diminished, while competition from the California rice crop largely cut off the Mainland market (Coulter and Chun 1937:22). The Hawaiian rice industry, interest in which resembled a speculative fever in the beginning (Thrum 1877:48), declined precipitously in the early years of this century. In Keanae, land was leased to a Chinese for the purpose of growing rice as late as 1926, but the conveyance also mentions taro growing on the land. It is likely that taro gradually supplanted rice in the 1920s, concurrent with the general decrease of rice lands in the islands.

The cultural identity of villages such as Keanae remained distinctly Hawaiian; any cultural adjustments were made by the Chinese men, who "learned the Hawaiian language, ate the Hawaiian food, and in other respects followed the Hawaiian manner of life" (Lorden 1935:455). The Hawaiian wife "continued to live in her native village, according to her native customs," often preserving her relationships with native men (ibid.:456). Hawaiian ethnicity is apparent in the phraseology used to describe the arrangement: The women "took men from outside." The Chinese are Hawaiians who "have a Chinese father." The frequent practice of adoption also encouraged the maintenance of Hawaiian identity, for children given away to Hawaiian families were raised like any other native children.

The offspring of these unions are nowhere called Chinese and rarely Chinese-Hawaiian except by outsiders. In a 1904 letter to the Chinese consul, a major rice planter in Keanae, Cheong Chong, petitioned for a reduction in rent on his lands, on the following grounds: "Married to a native woman for 20 years. He has 8 children and a resident of Maui for about 14 years [*sic*]. . . . He claims that his children are Hawaiians and they are entitled to the same rights as the Hawaiians do" (Extracts of Letters, Lands File, F.O. & Ex., 28 December 1904. Typescript, AH). Long after the foreign husbands departed or died, Hawaiians remained: "The children reared in this type of family differed from Hawaiian children chiefly in the fact that one parent was Chinese. . . . The traditions and habits of life were Hawaiian" (Lorden 1935:457).

ETHNICITY

I consistently refer to Keanae as a Hawaiian village, but it should be apparent that this designation has little to do with biological parentage. Hawaiians have a historically high rate of marriage to non-Hawaiians, and Keanae residents are no exception. Villagers represent the range of ethnic mixtures found in the islands. Only one family in Keanae—a large sibling set now ranging in age from their late thirties to about sixty-five—is reputed to be pure Hawaiian. Most other residents will admit to being Chinese-Hawaiian, with the usual admixture of Filipino, Portuguese, and Japanese. Seven households are occupied by haoles, either the "hippy" variety or older weekenders; these have been excluded from all population and household statistics because they are marginal to the Hawaiians' social world. For the most part, Hawaiian villagers successfully ignore the haoles and do not initiate contact with them, except for one young man who farms taro and occasionally hires out to other growers. The designation of "hippy" reveals that he is still very much an outsider, although some villagers have relented in their opinion enough to call him "half hippy, that."

Ethnicity is a matter of orientation, identification, and personal choice. As Ronald Gallimore and Alan Howard (1968:1) rightly point out, Hawaiian does not denote "a racial group but rather a culture." The 1960 census listed only ten thousand pure Hawaiians left in the islands, and ninety thousand part Hawaiians (UH 1965 I,2:33, Table 28). When the 1970 census revised the definition of Hawaiian to be by "self-identification by race of father," the figure became 71,274 Hawaiians (State of Hawaii 1974:28, Table 11). Keanae is culturally a Hawaiian village. Residents identify themselves as Hawaiian, regardless of their percentage of Hawaiian ancestry. The village was identified as the "most Hawaiian in the Islands" in 1957; a state population survey then showed Keanae to have the "greatest concentration of Hawaiians" of any community in Hawaii, with 94.8 percent of the residents having pure- or part-Hawaiian ancestry" (Lueras 1975:A3).

Keanae people customarily call almost anyone with part-Hawaiian ancestry "Hawaiian" if they are friends or kin, if they are country dwellers, or, quite simply, if they act Hawaiian. Residents may add the qualifier "Chinese-Hawaiian" when describing the make-up of the village to an outsider, but usually this designation is an indicator of social distance from the speaker. An illustration of the cultural definition of Hawaiianness is provided by the case of a young woman who married into the village from Honolulu. Her father was Portuguese, her mother a Portuguese-Hawaiian who claimed *ali'i* (chiefly) blood. During the wedding preparations, while the groom's relatives labored to make the luau, the bride's kin held apart without working, even eating separately in their guest quarters. They became the butt of jokes and deprecatory comments during and after the festivities. The Keanae Hawaiians always referred to the outsiders as "Portuguese," sometimes, eyebrows raised, adding the qualifier, "They *say* they get Hawaiian blood." Several characteristics marked these people as not Hawaiian. They came not only from outside but from Honolulu, the epitome of the alien town society. The consensus was that they "acted high" by holding apart and not helping. The bride and her relatives also spoke with no trace of island dialect. Popular opinion in the village was quite sympathetic to the bride, however; as her father-in-law commented, "She's one of *us* now." Her relatives and guests received no quarter and were the subject of "talk stink" (censorious gossip) for many months afterwards.

In contrast, some of the individuals who behave most Hawaiian are *hapa* haoles, meaning half white. They are accepted as Hawaiian because they are kin and friends and behave according to the Hawaiian expectations of those relationships. One *hapa*-haole woman is well known in Keanae because she accompanies the crew of fishermen who come inside for *akule* (mackerel). Despite mixed ancestry and a haole father, she speaks Hawaiian more fluently and uses the language more often than most Keanae residents; her everyday dress and dialect would not distinguish her from any pure Hawaiian. She is also a font of Hawaiian folklore, exhibiting proper awe for the spirits of the dead and the guardian gods, or *'aumākua*. Most importantly, the fisherwoman actively participates in reciprocal social relations with Keanae people, exchanging favors, food, and visits.

TRADITION

The people of Keanae identify themselves as Hawaiian. How traditionally Hawaiian is their lifestyle? In many obvious ways the villagers are undeniably modern. Anyone who comes to the community looking for a precontact cosmology or the sort of cultural elaboration found in less acculturated Oceanic societies is likely to be disappointed; this is, after all, Hawaii. Taro is now far more important symbolically and as a market commodity than as a food staple. Although some villagers wax poetic over fish and poi, the outside monetary economy provides the staff of life, not taro. Keanae villagers are not subsistence planters. All but one of the taro farmers are part-timers, holding full-time salaried jobs. Of forty-eight household heads, eight men commute daily or weekly to jobs outside in construction or road work. Over half of the households in

Keanae are occupied by retirees who rely on pensions or social security for their livelihood.

For most villagers, Keanae's isolation is also more symbolic than real. As much as residents may complain about the inconvenience of traveling, most go outside regularly, and there is a remarkable degree of visiting by friends and relatives from town. Women, who do most of the day-to-day taro-patch work, and wage earners employed inside, such as by the state road crew or East Maui Irrigation Company, have no necessity to go out often but usually find a pretext to drive out at least once a week. Older residents go out less frequently. Some have no choice in the matter; those without automobiles or unable to drive must rely on others to take them. Chauffering is thus a valued and weighty service, and "going out" figures in cycles of reciprocity. One trip a month is almost mandatory as the minimal contact with the outside. Retirees must cash their monthly checks, pay utility bills and debt installments, and buy specialty items. But if it were not for financial transactions, going outside regularly would not be absolutely necessary. Fuel, oil, and gas are delivered. Groceries, dry goods, and a vast array of sundries can be ordered from Hasegawa's General Store in Hana, which makes a weekly supply run to Keanae. Most trips outside, of course, are made for reasons other than necessity. Keanae residents retain the Hawaiian penchant for travel and visiting that chiefs and missionaries bemoaned in former times.

Although they are able to eat fish and poi more often than Hawaiians living outside, Keanae residents have come to rely on store-bought foods for most of their diet. On the open market, poi has acquired the status of a luxury item, and Hawaiians who do not grow taro seldom buy it at the supermarket price. Even in taro-producing households, rice is as much a staple as poi, and both are generally served at every main meal. The daily diet of Keanae people is better than that of a city-dwelling Hawaiians but still includes a large proportion of sweets, packaged cereals, snack chips, Vienna sausage, and highly sugared drinks.

The knowledge and use of the Hawaiian language in Keanae varies directly with age; the older the person, the more he or she will use the language and with greater fluency. Most residents in their mid-thirties to early forties can understand and speak a limited Hawaiian but rarely use the language unless conversing with an older person. Knowledge of Hawaiian diminishes considerably among those under thirty. Most young adults understand little and can speak only a few sentences. Parents often express regret that their children have almost no comprehension of Hawaiian except for some frequently used words and idioms. Even in Keanae, one rarely hears sustained conversations in Hawaiian except among the elderly since only they have sufficient command of the language. One young man in his twenties is fluent, but he worked to perfect his knowledge; none of his contemporaries has comparable proficiency.

The Hawaiian spoken in Keanae is a diminished language. Both vocabulary and syntax have suffered incursions of island dialect and other tongues (see Carr 1972). The trend is for fewer words to encompass a wider range of meanings. The word *hemo*, for example, originally meant to loosen or unfasten (Andrews 1865:157–158), but it is now used for every kind of opening action, from opening a tin of sardines to shredding a piece of cloth. "*Hemo* the *kūlolo*" refers to opening the five-gallon cracker tins in which *kūlolo*, a taro-coconut pudding, is baked. The word for harvesting taro is properly *huki*, to pull or draw (ibid.:223), but *hemo* is now more common since pulling taro involves forcibly loosening the corms from the mud. *Hemo* in the sense of cutting also denotes the act of slicing off the stalk end of the taro corm for shoots.

The rules of syntax have likewise broadened over time. The expressions *hana pa'a* and *hana pio*, for example, have come to mean to close a door and to put out a light. This pidginized usage derives from *hana* (to do, to work, to make) plus the adjectives *pa'a* (closed, tight) and *pio* (extinguished). Most older Hawaiians are aware of correct usage and will argue over original pronunciation and meaning. When Hawaiian is used in everyday speech, however, the pidginized expressions predominate. Similarly, although they know Hawaiian kinship terms, many older persons rarely use them. This reflects an attrition of the language even since Yamamura's (1941:40–41) study in 1940, when the terms *makua kāne* and *makuahine* were in common use, the former denoting a male parent, either father or uncle, and the latter a mother or aunt. English words have now replaced most Hawaiian terms, but, as will be shown, this does not mean that they have the same content as American kinship terms.

To all outward appearances, Keanae Hawaiians are thoroughly Christianized—as one would expect in light of Hawaii's 160-year history of missionization. The Hawaiian religion was overthrown in 1819. The first missionaries to take advantage of the spiritual hiatus represented a stern Calvinist brand of Congregationalism (see, among others, Kuykendall 1938:61–70, 100–116 for an overview of the encounter). The Protestant Mission Station of Hana was established in 1837 (HMCS 1969:16). According to the Hana Station Reports, the present stone church at Keanae was built between 1856 and 1863. Local lore alleges that the Keanae church was founded in 1840 and that the original Protestant church was in Wailua, but the ruins in Wailua are probably those of a meeting house built from 1862 to 1863 (Sereno Bishop, 1862 and 1863. Station Reports. HMCS). The first attendance statistics for the Keanae church were reported in 1866.

There is still a Congregational church in Lower Keanae, and a Catholic church in Wailua. Both have illustrious histories, but the heyday of church activity in Keanae appears to have passed. In 1871, reported membership in the Protestant church reached a peak of 318, but steadily decreased thereafter, to 136 in 1875 and 81 in 1877 (S. K. Kamakahiki, Keanae Church Reports. Originals, HMCS). Although membership declined more gradually in the next hundred years, the official congregation of the Keanae Congregationalist Church has remained at nine since 1963 (Hawaiian Evangelical Assn. Reports. Originals, HMCS). Today the church is supported primarily by four households, and two of those are composed of elderly widows. The overgrown ruins of another Protestant church stand amidst the taro patches in Wailua, and there is an abandoned Mormon meeting house on the Hana road above Keanae. Only one couple in Keanae is reputed to be Mormon today, and I do not believe that they attend meetings.

The first mass was said in St. Gabriel's, the white coral church at Wailua, in 1860 (*HSB* 13 September 1941, Supplement). When the present wood-frame structure was built, St. Gabriel's was rededicated as the Shrine of Our Lady of Fatima. In this incarnation, restored and repainted, it is Wailua's main tourist attraction. The Catholic church is far better attended than the Keanae Protestant church. Mass is said twice weekly by an itinerant priest, in contrast to Keanae's twice-monthly services. About fifty individuals attend at least occasionally. The congregation averages about twenty-five at the main Sunday service; about half the attendees are children. The most devout members are several elderly women who attend both weekly masses and see to the maintenance of the church building and grounds.

In both the Catholic and Protestant churches, women are the leaders of the congregation. The spiritual head of the Congregational church is an elderly woman, one of the oldest and most respected residents in Keanae. Her son mustered the labor and materials to restore the stone structure in 1968. Since then, he has been treasurer and caretaker. At the time of fieldwork, his wife was the deacon of the church and was studying for the licentiate, which would give her the authority to give sermons. In this case religious leadership was passed down to a daughter-in-law. In the Catholic church, a few older women alternate as readers of the gospel.

From my observation, church activities are incidental to the lives of most Keanae villagers today. In each congregation, a few families are active in maintaining the property and looking after the pastor's comfort, but only about 25 percent of the adult population attends regularly. Religion is not often discussed, nor does it appear to define social boundaries; friendship and marriage cross-cut denominational lines.

The Hawaiian religion is recalled by isolated prohibitions and tales of the goddess Pele. Certain areas in Keanae are considered to be holy: a *heiau* (ancient temple) site, a sacred watercourse, a place frequented by the dead. Many villagers will not venture in these places for fear of spirits. As is common in coastal Hawaiian villages, several residents claim a special relationship with the shark, as their *'aumakua*, or guardian spirit. According to Kamakau (1964: 78), "the people of Maui worshipped sharks." In return for protection at sea, the Hawaiian fisherman "feeds" it by throwing back part of his catch.

Keanae Hawaiians retain considerable respect for the power of unseen forces. Even young adults warn against carrying bananas in a boat when fishing: "You no catch nothing, for sure." It is also said that one cannot take pork out of Keanae. Keanae Valley is popular with pig hunters, and Keanae is locally called "the pig place" as well as "the taro place." Hawaiians and Portuguese come from outside to hunt in the forested ravines and plateaus above the Hana Highway. Villagers say that if one tries to carry raw pork outside, spirits will stop the car. They cite incidents where the driver was able to proceed only after he threw the pork away. The Portuguese foreman of the state road crew was an avid pig hunter. As he prepared to return home after a successful hunt, a Keanae woman repeatedly warned him not to take the pig outside. He drove home without incident but later found in the back of his car a cross of *ti* leaves (a plant used ritually in the old Hawaiian religion and believed to have protective qualities).

The disappearance of *kahunas* is an indication of the erosion of pre-Western beliefs. Originally meaning priest, *kahuna* came to mean sorcerer after missionization, either a healer or the evil variety who could pray people to death. There were said to be few *kahuna*s left in Hana in 1940, but Hawaiians relied on them rather than doctors during illness (Yamamura 1941:113, 121). Keanae informants insist that "the real kind" of *kahuna* has died out, "all of them." In other parts of the islands, a few individuals still claim to be *kahuna*s, but the *kahuna*s of Hana District are said to be long dead.

Hawaiian medicinal lore flourishes in Keanae, however, and herbal remedies are the first recourse for minor ailments such as boils or colds. For anything more serious, Keanae residents do not hesitate to visit the medical clinic in Hana, which provides excellent care at nominal cost. The clinic also enjoys considerable popularity as a social institution, for waiting patients have ample opportunity to exchange news with Hawaiians from Hana and other villages on the windward side. When haole medicines fail to relieve certain ills, there is still a woman in Hana who practices lomi-lomi, the ancient Hawaiian art of massage. It is said to be helpful for persistent pains or muscle aches, which she treats by first massaging with baby oil or mentholated jelly and then wrapping the limb in a *ti* leaf.

The modern surrogate of the *kahuna* is the prayer lady, usually a woman of Portuguese or Filipino origin, who dispenses holy water, blessings, and penances. Her method utilizes the props of Catholic ritual and involves probing the patient's soul and life situation for the source of trouble. Prayer ladies use similar techniques in other parts of the islands, and Hawaiians visit them when they suspect illness of a spiritual nature. Upsetting dreams, trance states, and spirit possession, called "the Hawaiian sickness," are maladies taken to the prayer lady. She diagnoses whether the cause is "outside or something inside," blesses the sufferer, and prescribes prayers and offerings at church.

It should be clear that Keanae is no pristine survivor of a pre-Western society. But neither is it an average American community. What, then, is the meaning of *Hawaiian* within this most acculturated society in Polynesia? Two tales of

the dead suggest an answer. A thoroughly Hawaiian pre-
scription for placating the spirits advises that if the dead
accost a traveler or stop one's car in a strange place, one
should invoke the network of relatedness: "If you're a
stranger in the place, mention some family names. You
never know, you might be related to somebody in that
place. You might have family there, and someone might
know you that way. You can explain to them who you are
and try to make it all right. Then they may let you go."

The dead take a special interest in their living kinfolk
and descendants and may vouchsafe gifts to younger relatives "to take care." One elderly woman said that a burial
cave opened to her husband and a few companions while
they were pig hunting. A local sage advised the husband
to leave some article "of his own, even smash a whiskey
bottle, as long as it's his," and he might be permitted to
take something. But, before he could return, his friends
divulged the location, and the cave sealed again, forever.
The story teller explained that the cave would open only to
her husband because "must be he related. You can't just go
and take any kine thing, and leave something. If you're not
related, they won't open to you. But if they show you, that
means it's all right for you to take something. They're giving it to you. But when you leave, you have to *mōhai*, leave
something of your own as an offering."

The tales of the dead reveal a set of interrelated concepts
rooted in traditional Hawaiian social relations. The meaning of Hawaiian lies in the wide and unknowable extension
of relatedness, the mutual, enduring obligation established by kinship, and the mandatory nature of exchange.

Chapter Three

WORK AND PRODUCTION

Keanae Hawaiians are able to participate simultaneously in two spheres of exchange because of their relationship with the one that is dominant; by interacting with the cash economy of the outside, they preserve their way of life inside. Keanae villagers live on the land, but they are not subsistence farmers. Although Keanae's taro fields are the most visible symbol of the village's Hawaiianness today, wage labor has long been the primary source of income for most residents. All the men now living on pensions formerly participated in salaried work as well as taro farming. Yet even wage earning in Keanae is subordinated to Hawaiian values regarding work and the distribution of its returns. This chapter describes productive activities in Keanae. Not all of these activities are purely economic in the sense of contributing to subsistence; production in Keanae is also geared toward ensuring social viability, which depends on participation in reciprocities.

THE MEANING OF WORK

The outside society perceives the Hawaiian lifestyle as "lower class" (cf. Howard 1974:x). Yet Hawaiians do not measure the quality of life by gross income. In Keanae as in Nanakuli, "there is little evidence that many Hawaiians feel deprived. In fact, the opposite is probably more accurate" (Gallimore and Howard 1968:8). The irony of our idiom "making a living" is especially apparent when applied to Hawaiians, for whom work is not the primary referent of living. In the stereotype popular in Mainland society, Hawaiians are carefree, happy, and unfettered by

financial worries. The negative version of this stereotype—
which closely resembles Mainlanders' image of Native
Americans—has a history dating back to the missionaries,
who saw Hawaiians as lazy, shiftless, and unmotivated
and unmoved by appeals to the Puritan work ethic. They
are allegedly prodigal spenders, with little ambition for
advancement.

The haole stereotype of the Hawaiian illustrates an essential truth about the cultures that confronted each other
in the islands: their priorities and values were quite different. Hawaiians do not value material achievement for its
own sake. Ronald Gallimore and Alan Howard (1968:10)
have pointed out that Hawaiians seek to nurture human
relationships rather than to accumulate material wealth.
Commitments to relatives and friends take precedence,
even though meeting these obligations may strain the
household budget. Ernest Beaglehole (1937:29) noted that
Hawaiians gave luaus with little regard to cost and would
even go into debt to finance them. A recurrent theme in
these descriptions is that Hawaiians demand a degree of
personal freedom that most workers in Western society
have learned to sacrifice. Orientals were brought to the islands as laborers because Hawaiians seemed disinclined to
plantation work. Beaglehole (1937:30) wrote: "Certain cultural ideas still have for the Hawaiian an essential value
which defies monetary estimation. . . . The Hawaiian . . .
demands more leisure from life."

Other differences are implicit in Mainlanders' comments
on the Hawaiian lifestyle. A difference in cultural definitions and goals is apparent: the terms *work*, *ambition*, and
leisure mean different things to a haole than to a Hawaiian.
In the external society, work refers primarily to salaried
employment, and leisure is the time away from that employment. What is leisure to a haole, however, is the time
that Hawaiians devote to the most important thing in a life
which is social above all: to the fulfillment of reciprocities
with other Hawaiians. No one who has witnessed preparations for a luau would ever say that Hawaiians are lazy. On

the contrary, Keanae Hawaiians, some of whom come home to work in the taro patches after eight hours of manual labor, demonstrate an almost inexhaustible capacity for industry.

It is true that prestige among Hawaiians does not hinge on material success, as it does in haole society. Success in the Hawaiian context must be measured in terms of sociability: as garnering relationships rather than garnering possessions. Obvious economic gain can result in social failure for a Hawaiian because it violates the egalitarian ethic of interpersonal relations and threatens sociability. A show of material advancement jeopardizes the continuity of relationships with other members of the community. As I will demonstrate in subsequent chapters, it is possible to be ambitious in Keanae and to succeed, but in a distinctively Hawaiian way.

OCCUPATIONS AND INCOME

Keanae workers are engaged primarily in unskilled labor. These are the occupations of forty-eight household heads (excluding three part-time residents): retiree, pension (twenty-four), wage laborer (nineteen), unemployed (four), full-time taro farmer (one). Twenty-one of the retirees and salaried workers grow taro for the market but also receive an income from outside sources. At least four landholders regularly take care of another's patches and reap the proceeds. A few other householders supply labor more or less faithfully for a taro grower but clearly work under the owner, with no say in the disposition of the crop. Since all but one of the male taro farmers have full-time jobs, the labor of women and children is indispensable for maintaining both sources of income.

Thirteen of the nineteen wage laborers work inside, ten based in Keanae and three commuting to Hana. The six men who work outside either return to Keanae on weekends or commute daily. There are three possible employers in Keanae: the state, the county, and the East Maui Irrigation Company (E.M.I.), a subsidiary of a major sugar company, which is in turn a subsidiary of Alexander and Baldwin, one of the Big Five corporations in Hawaii. Most of the jobs inside are in road labor. The County of Maui maintains side roads, and the state garage in Keanae has responsibility for the Hana Highway. Three Keanae men work for the State Forestry Division, caring for public parks and forest reserve lands in the vicinity. E.M.I. employs four Keanae men as laborers to clean and maintain the upland irrigation ditches that supply water to the sugar fields of central Maui.

Rates of pay are comparable for all these positions. In 1975, a laborer working for the state received $480 a month, with promotions possible up to $700, the top of the scale before the foreman grade. The largest annual salary of any Keanae man working inside at the time of fieldwork was about twelve thousand dollars for a top foreman with E.M.I. The other householders at this income level commute outside to construction jobs, which are considered high paying, albeit inconvenient. Normal working hours for laborers are 6:30 A.M. to 3:00 P.M., after which the men usually go into the patches to work until sunset. Men with full-time jobs rely on their wives and children for most of the day-to-day maintenance of the patches.

TARO

The traditional subsistence staple of Hawaii is now a profitable market commodity that can contribute considerably to household income. Taro, with both commercial and symbolic value for Hawaiians, is the economic bridge between the inside and the outside. About half the householders in Keanae grow taro for the market in varying degrees. Several elderly residents keep a small patch open "for poi." During the day, women and retired villagers work individually in the taro patches for a few hours. Children are a major source of labor after school and during vacations, when many growers substantially increase their weekly "order," the number of bags sent to market. Most of the daily work is maintenance: weeding and "pulling grass." Keeping the patches clean is particularly important at the beginning of the growth cycle in order not to stunt the young taro. If not given attention at this stage, all the taro will spoil. If neglected early, the undergrowth in the patch may become so thick that weeding would ruin the taro, and it must be left until it is time to harvest whatever is salvageable.

Badly overgrown patches produce recognizably smaller yields and poorer quality corms, and harvesting a grass-choked patch is a laborious task. While regular maintenance might not be critical if the taro were only for the household food supply, it materially affects the cash proceeds if the taro is marketed. Once the taro matures, the growers leave the interior of the patches unweeded to avoid treading on the full-grown corms and clean only the periphery to ensure free-flowing water.

Informants gave varying estimates of the maturation period. The taro is ready to pull in a year, but most growers leave the crop a few months longer. One farmer claims that Keanae growers leave the taro in the ground longer than those in other areas to produce larger, firmer corms. The quality deteriorates the longer the mature taro remains in the patch, but, for market purposes, the growers prefer to maximize the size of the corm; the resulting product is referred to as "junk taro" as opposed to the better, smaller corms pulled for home use.

Although growers weed the taro by hand, they spray "poison," diesel gasoline or oil, to kill the grass and weeds bordering the patches and irrigation ditches. Each landholder maintains the section of the ditch adjacent to his or her patches, a task that involves weeding approximately every other week if the ditch is to be kept clean. Most maintenance tasks are performed sporadically and casually in the early part of the week, for none is so critical as to require constant or immediate attention. Growers seldom spend more than half a day in the patches at one time, and even for a single person this would be more than ample for the everyday care required. Given the rather minimal up-keep and the high yield of taro, a single elderly person working alone could easily supply himself or herself with a staple food source. Growing for the market, however, in-troduces both a production quota and a weekly deadline. The level of activity in Keanae's taro patches thus passes through a weekly cycle, from irregular, individual labor at the beginning of the week, to intensive, collective labor at the end, when the market order is due. A reliable, stable pool of workers is most important when it is time to "pull for the order."

The farmers of Keanae and Wailua market their taro through two growers' associations, each with a resident agent who trucks the bags of corms to the harbor every weekend in time to be shipped to Honolulu on the Monday-morning barge. Thursday and Friday are the days to har-vest and bag the taro. The agent's role is more that of a middleman than a manager, although in fact the taro agents are both big-men in the community. The agent acts as intermediary between the poi factories and the growers and allocates to each grower a share of the weekly market order. The size of the total order is set by the poi com-panies; farmers cannot decide independently how much they want to sell each week, although they do negotiate their share with the agent. The agent's job is to see that the order is filled, while observing the preferences and limi-tations of his growers. In this task, the agent's power is not arbitrary. The taro growers' associations meet once a month, and their consensus is a powerful sanction on the agent's decisions. Fair and equal apportionment is the strict rule of the scheduling process, and the agent who violates this principle risks desertion by his growers. Sea-sonal fluctuations in demand can cause wide variations in the size of the total order from week to week, and the agent's job is to see that the effect is distributed equally among the individual farmers. In a week when only one barge was going to Honolulu, for example, each grower was responsible for five eighty-five–pound bags; the following week, the order was twenty-four bags each.

Besides variations in external demand, several other factors determine how much taro a farmer can supply each week: the size of his or her landholdings, the availability of workers, the amount of taro planted, and the quantity of mature taro ready to be pulled. The usual weekly order is ten to twelve bags per grower. In 1975, the market price rose to ten dollars per bag. At this rate, a household able to maintain a constant supply of mature taro could increase its monthly income by three to four hundred dollars, nearly doubling the salary of an unskilled road laborer. The farmers prefer to guarantee a year-round harvest by replanting as they pull and by moderating the size of their weekly order in order to have continuous rather than sporadic income. But this capability depends on the availability of land and workers at critical times. In reality, few growers are able to achieve an uninterrupted supply because of limited land, lack of labor, or poor planning.

Ideally, each grower is responsible for an equal share of the total order. But some farmers regularly deliver fewer bags because they have small plots, have less time to work, or are simply too old. One elderly woman pulls five bags each week in order to ensure a year-round crop; her rationale is that if she assumed a larger order, she would have to rest two or three months while waiting for the remainder to mature, and she much prefers to have a regular income. At different times of the year, however, as when schoolchildren are on vacation, certain growers offer to pull up to twenty-four or thirty bags in a week to take advantage of the sudden wealth of workers. Farmers may also increase their orders substantially when they have large crops ripening all at once. The agent deals with these individual vagaries by devising a schedule whereby the growers rotate the number of bags for which they are responsible each week. One informant described the system in this way: "If I pull twenty this week you'll get your chance next week. Everyone gets their chance that way. Otherwise it's not fair. But if all my taro is ready at once, they give me more bags, and when my patch is empty, *pau* [done, finished]. Then I don't have any more and the next guy gets more bags next time. I might have twenty this week, then nineteen, like that."

In order to maintain a continuous yield, a grower must have a relatively large amount of land and a dependable pool of workers available and must also be a skilled crop manager. The fact that only one farmer subsists solely on taro marketing suggests that in practice it is difficult to meet these requirements. Traditional kinds of mutual aid come into play. If a grower needs more assistance than the household can provide, he or she looks first to "the family," whether resident in Keanae or not. The preference is thus always to draw workers who are obligated by relatedness before recruiting outsiders, who must be paid in one way or another. As I discovered in repeated attempts to assist villagers in the patches, taro-patch work is a weighty commodity. Villagers are loath to accept such help from anyone outside the family. Relatedness permits a degree of mutual assistance that is not possible between unrelated individuals without implying the subordinate status of one of the parties.

Whether this aid materializes, however, depends on situational factors. Although it is true that kin may be recruited on the basis of aloha, there is no categorical assistance required of a relative, except perhaps a younger sibling, as will be elaborated in later chapters. In two cases, young men residing with their parents do not work their own family's taro patches but those of a maternal uncle, while their parents' fields lie uncultivated. In another instance, an adult son assumed cultivation of the homestead lands for his parents, who can no longer work in the patches. Sons and daughters living in Keanae normally assist their parents if they still grow taro. Nevertheless, each household maintains independence in property ownership and budgeting. Although related nuclear families in the village may help each other in the taro patches, they do not share the proceeds. As far as I could ascertain, there is no pooling of income or joint ownership of property by members of different households.

Relatives from outside are also recruited to work in the family patches while visiting Keanae, particularly on weekends, when guests regularly aid several households in pulling for the order. As suggested above, a taro farmer's material success depends to a great extent on the ability to recruit workers when needed, preferably without paying them. It is an indication of personal tact and influence when one can muster a labor force on the basis of relationship or indebtedness and thus avoid a monetary expenditure. Although only twenty-one of the forty-eight full-time resident households in Keanae directly market taro, many of the remaining villagers provide labor for the taro growers. A few unemployed Keanae men can be engaged in outright hire, but the rate in 1975 was fifteen dollars per day. If one man were hired for two days, this would reduce the average grower's weekly income by one-third, assuming a ten-bag order. For the elderly who require even more assistance or for small growers, such paid labor would consume most of their returns.

When the elderly give up farming themselves, save perhaps for a tiny plot for table use, they prefer to let a younger relative take care of the patches. If there is no likely candidate in Keanae, one may be enlisted from outside. One young woman purchased her father-in-law's patches and drives inside a few days each week to work them, but this is an unusual arrangement. For most, the rewards of taro-patch labor do not seem to warrant the commute. A landowner who cannot find a caretaker who is a relative may try to lease the land to another grower for taro or pasturage. The fee is customarily payable after the taro is harvested and sold, and the lessee is expected to pay the landlord the difference if the market price goes up during the period. In one such case, an elderly woman wanted to lease her three small patches for three hundred dollars a year, estimating that they would yield seven to eight hundred dollars in that time. The prospective lessee considered the fee too high, however, for the patches were located way up the valley, at some distance from the nearest access road. In this and in similar instances, the owner had no choice but to abandon the patches to grass.

Early Western observers remarked on the high productivity of taro. The missionary J. S. Emerson (in Wyllie 1855:82) suggested that an acre of wet-land taro could support twenty persons; one of his colleagues estimated twenty-five (ibid.). Certainly the potential output of Keanae's patches has not been approached in recent times, when taro production has been determined largely by market demand. Computed from Maui County tax records,[1] the average amount of taro land per household in Keanae is 1.44 acres, with a range from none to 6.712 acres. Forty-three of the fifty-one Hawaiian households own or lease some land in Keanae, ranging from 0.216 to 20.525 acres. Including all land types, the average household landholding amounts to 4.26 acres. Two brothers in the village living in separate households work their taro lands jointly; their combined landholdings total 9.226 acres, of which 4.947 acres is taro land or abandoned taro land. Their two households support five adults and two children, who also work in the patches.

These figures illustrate the potential productivity and the level of aspirations within the village rather than subsistence requirements since Keanae's taro growing is no longer geared toward production for use. But the size of the Land Commission Awards and homesteads, which were established before the advent of local wage labor, does in part reflect estimated subsistence needs. The land

1. For each parcel, the tax records give the current owner(s), recent title history, assessments, and use—house lot, pasture, taro land, abandoned taro land, or forest. Acreages cited in the text were calculated from these records.

immediately available for taro cultivation in Keanae averages at least half an acre per resident, although not all the
land so categorized is planted in taro at one time. If one
includes all the land classified in the tax rolls as "uncultivated or abandoned taro," the area potentially suitable for
taro growing is much greater and could have supported a
vastly larger population in former times. With the exception of the one grower who lives entirely on taro marketing, no household in Keanae today requires any taro land
at all, but the size of household landholdings does materially affect the potential income to be derived.

To some extent, taro growing has become an arena for
the economically ambitious. A farmer tries to increase his
or her lands and labor force not to make ends meet but to
make more money. Yet the additional profits are rarely visible as permanent improvements in the standard of living
compared with that of other villagers. The limitation on
overt economic success is the social sanction against appearing "high" vis-à-vis one's neighbors. The social fate of
the large landowners in Keanae varies accordingly from
ostracism to esteem. In order to preserve exchange relations with neighbors, the successful farmer must reconcile
very real economic disparities with the egalitarian norm of
village relations.

OTHER INCOME

In contrast to the popular stereotype of the Hawaiian,
Keanae residents are extremely industrious in pursuing
supplementary economic activities. Most of these secondary productive activities have a value for exchange that far
overshadows their contribution to household food or income. Except for taro, traditional subsistence items such as
fish, bananas, and special luau foods are given away more
often than they are consumed within the household. All
the taro growers have banana plantations adjacent to their
patches, a long-established use of land in Hawaii, and sev-

eral homesteads have banana trees growing on their lots. Of minor importance as a food, bananas are a frequent item in interhousehold exchange. Growers also periodically sell bunches of bananas to bakeries outside, at twelve to fifteen dollars a bunch. Other locally grown produce, such as mangoes, papayas, and avocados, is rarely sold but is given to relatives, friends, and neighbors.

The seasonal picking of guavas, which grow abundantly wild in Keanae, can be quite profitable if several workers are available and a household coordinates activities. As with taro growing, the capacity to supplement household income is proportional to the number of available workers. On certain days, a cannery outside buys guavas by the crate to be pressed into juice. Households that engage in guava picking have personally labeled crates for this purpose. While one member hauls a load into Kahului, the rest of the household fills more crates until the driver returns with the empties. One informant claimed that his household could occasionally earn up to one thousand dollars a month by guava picking. The figure may seem high, but this particular household belongs to a local big-man and includes five adult members. This household's ability to take advantage of a potential cash income, which is available to anyone with enough workers and a truck, affords insight into the characteristics of an important man. This form of income is obviously far less accessible to a single-person household or a family of two retirees. One of the two taro agents, this householder owns a large truck for hauling taro; he can also call on a wide range of possible helpers who are indebted to him by virtue of kinship or long-standing obligation. Chapter 8 further explores the dimensions of his position.

About 20 percent of the Hawaiian households in Keanae keep cattle, from a few head to a small herd, and one or two horses for working the stock. Cattle raising is a small-scale operation in each case but can provide additional income more or less as needed. Most of this work is done by men, and every cattle-owning family has at least one able-bodied male. For pasturage, herders use abandoned taro land or the unirrigated uplands on either side of the belt road, including the *hui* lands. They may use their own land or lease from another landowner or the state. The cattle are slaughtered at irregular intervals, no more than a few head at a time, at the discretion of the owner, who takes them outside to the slaughterhouse himself. After a week of cold storage, the meat is sold by the owner to the supermarket, with prices varying according to the grade of the meat. Since the Hawaiians haul and market the cattle themselves, they have considerable leeway in timing their sales. This flexibility is particularly amenable to the uses of meat in exchange activities. The man with cattle always has a ready supply of beef for special occasions, whether for making *laulau*s, a standard luau food, or for use as a gift.

Fishing is another economic activity that contributes more to social relations than to household subsistence. There are no physical or financial restrictions on this pursuit; anyone capable of walking, from the very young to the very old, can fish from shore. Although pole fishing is popular with both sexes, and particularly with elderly women, net fishing is restricted to men. Only a few householders own boats, and these are used infrequently, partly because of Keanae's rough seas. The scarcity of boats also reflects the solitary character of fishing. Hawaiians are extremely jealous of their personal fishing techniques and private spots and prefer to fish alone, although this is truer of men than of women. Small skiffs are most useful for laying nets and taking in large hauls, an activity requiring some cooperative labor. Communal fishing by Hawaiians has disappeared in Keanae, and deep-sea fishing is carried on only by a crew of young Japanese fishermen from outside. Individuals fishing from shore normally do not catch quantities worth marketing. Some residents gather *'ōpae*, fresh-water shrimp, and *'opihi*, sea limpets, for sale to luaus, where they are prized foods. *'Opihi* have become regarded as such a delicacy that the 1975 market price in Honolulu was sixty to eighty dollars a gallon. Since Hawaiians try to minimize apparent disparities of income, residents generally attempt to conceal such private entrepreneurial activities from fellow villagers.

Whenever there is more fish or meat than a family can immediately use, the remainder is frozen and is as likely to be given away to visitors and relatives as it is to appear on the table. For this reason, a large freezer is standard equipment in Keanae households, even those of the widowed. Great quantities of food are often stored not so much for future consumption as for future gift giving. For this kind of exchange, the deep-sea fishing carried on by outsiders is a bonanza for Keanae residents. According to Hawaiian custom, anyone who helps to load the boat or bring in the nets receives a share of the catch. Although the school fishermen of today are Japanese, they respect this tradition and distribute fish to all who have assisted them. Each person's share of course depends on the size of the catch, which may be nothing or several boatloads. Yet the lure of receiving buckets of fresh fish is irresistible. Many villagers spend all day at the landing, gossiping, commenting on the proceedings, and waiting eagerly to see the size of the catch.

The intense interest, even acquisitiveness, displayed on these occasions is far out of proportion to the role of fish in the diet. Single, elderly persons may receive more fish at one time than they could consume in months, and, during the early summer, the fishermen come to Keanae at least every few days. One widow, who covets her share as avidly as anyone, admitted to me that she does not eat fish at all; instead, in Hawaiian style, she freezes or dries the fish and ultimately gives it all away. The role that these distributions play in village social relations will be discussed further in later chapters. The point here is that certain economic pursuits have a value for exchange that transcends their contribution to household income. At the same time, Keanae Hawaiians are adept at exploiting the resources of the inside in order to increase their income from outside. In a sense, Keanae residents have learned to manipulate the external economy; their commercial relationships with the outside enable them to participate more fully in a traditional lifestyle: to travel, hold luaus, give gifts, and spoil grandchildren, as well as to pay land taxes and utility bills. The money gained from economic pursuits is still subject to a Hawaiian set of values.

Chapter Four

HOUSEHOLDS

The Hawaiian household in Keanae is both a productive and a landholding unit; its composition is determined by external economic factors and also by the nature of land succession. Superficially, villagers appear to conform to what was once the normative division of labor in the American family, with a wage-earning husband and a wife who stays at home. But in Keanae, the woman of the household is likely to be the mainstay of taro-patch work. In this chapter, I argue that marital stability and household composition in Keanae, which seem to reflect middle-class American norms more than Hawaiian cultural precedents, work to preserve a traditional pattern of landholding and property succession. The present discussion treats marriage functionally, as establishing the domestic unit and upholding the continuity of Hawaiian residence; later chapters will consider marriage as an element in exchange.

THE HAWAIIAN
LOCAL GROUP

In contrast to historical descriptions of Hawaiian marriage as casual and transitory, marriage in Keanae is a stable and enduring union, with an incidence of divorce half that of American society as a whole. Accounts of early Hawaiian society described large extended-family households, but the nuclear family predominates as an economic and residential unit in Keanae. This stable nuclear-family organization is not entirely the result of acculturation; it reflects both modern constraints and prior cultural principles.

Reconstructing traditional local-group organization is particularly difficult for Hawaii, and this problem is only partially the fault of the available sources. My statements about the early society are based on the accounts of eighteenth- and nineteenth-century observers, both Hawaiian and European, and on archival materials. Struggling with the nuances of Hawaiian society, I have often wished that I had chosen a system with clearly stated rules: a society with lineages, perhaps one of Claude Lévi-Strauss's elementary structures, where people say, "We marry our mother's brother's daughter." The fluid character of Hawaiian social organization frustrates easy conclusions: the absence of descent groups, the lack of marriage rules or ceremony, the flexibility of kinship categories all contribute to the apparent fuzziness of the system. Yet the loose quality of Hawaiian social organization is intrinsic; it is not the result of acculturation or the dissolution of the precontact society.

The previous anthropological understanding of the Hawaiian local group (Handy and Pukui 1972), as a branch of a ranked lineage on the Polynesian conical clan model, is "consistently contradicted" by nineteenth-century land records (Sahlins 1974:11–13). The Handy and Pukui model stipulates that the *ahupua'a* land section was the territorial arm of a lineage segment. They use the term *'ohana* for this landed kin group, but, in the few cases where *'ohana* appears in testimony from the Great Mahele, it refers to a domestic group. Nowhere do Hawaiian witnesses in the Mahele or in nineteenth-century court cases describe anything like a corporate kin group. Commoners had shallow genealogies and generally traced relationships back no further than the grandparental generation. The local community was not composed of descent groups or lineage segments but of overlapping bilateral kindreds. This horizontal dimension of kinship corresponds to the modern Hawaiian use of the term *'ohana*, a point that will be developed further in Chapter 5.

The most inclusive social unit at the local level was a large extended-family household. Residential options were extensive, and the domestic group could include consanguines, attached affines, distant or putative relatives, adopted children, and unrelated dependents. Nineteenth-century archival materials, as well as the statements of elderly informants, attest to the flexibility of household organization. According to early travelers' reports, Hawaiian households ranged up to twenty-seven persons (Bates 1854:246). Two- and three-generation families were common in the early contact period (Ellis [1827] 1917:53). In nineteenth-century testimony, Hawaiians use the particle *ma* to designate an individual's household group, as in "Hakau *ma*." Lorrin Andrews (1865:356) defines *ma* as "persons belonging to, or accompanying." In similar fashion, modern Hawaiians use the word "them," as in "Keola them" or "Harry them." "Them" refers not only to an individual's permanent household group but also to anyone who may be staying there at the time, as in "Go ask Annie them to come talk story."

Hawaiian household structure is inextricably tied to principles of land succession and the nature of marriage. Nineteenth-century descriptions suggest that there was no marriage at all for commoner Hawaiians, in the sense of a socially marked, lasting bond between man and woman. Western observers characterized the marital tie as ephemeral and easily broken (Campbell [1822] 1967:136; Ellis [1827] 1917:329; Mathison 1825:474–475). There are no Hawaiian words for husband and wife other than *kāne* and *wahine*, man and woman. Testifying in court in 1854 (P-805. Original, AH), a Hawaiian woman described the prevailing custom as "*moe aku, moe mai*" (sleep here, sleep there). The Hawaiians' preference for casual, nonbinding attachments was the bane of the missionaries, who labored mightily to weed out the sin of adultery among the natives. Before the introduction of Christian marriage or, in the words of the nineteenth-century witness, "before the custom of marriage became general," no formal ceremony marked the union of commoners. More recent studies (Beaglehole 1937; Yamamura 1941) also report the looseness of conjugal relationships among Hawaiians.

Although *moe aku, moe mai* was the most frequent practice among commoners, not all Hawaiian unions were ephemeral. The journalist and historian Samuel M. Kamakau (1961:347) distinguished between cohabitation and *ho'āo pa'a*, the binding form of Hawaiian marriage. In cohabitation arrangements, "men took many wives and women many husbands," while *ho'āo pa'a* "could not be dissolved" (Kamakau 1964:25–26). According to Kamakau, *ho'āo* marriage was reserved for high-ranking people: "The marriage agreement was made, and they became husband and wife in a *ho'āo pa'a* marriage until death separated them. The children born to them sealed the relationship between the two families (*puka a maka*). This was the marriage custom (*ho'āo ana*) of the chiefs and the first-born children of prominent people and family pets of *ka po'e kahiko* [the people of old]" (ibid.:26).

There is quite a discrepancy between this account and early reports of casual, easy attachments. There is a similar disparity between *moe aku, moe mai* and the infrequency of divorce in Keanae. But the apparent contradictions can be explained by differences in life cycle and by differential expectations for those who remain on the land as opposed to those who do not. The formal, binding tie may have been limited to people of importance, but some commoners also entered into lasting conjugal relationships. Although not marked by ceremony, marriage was more stable among landed commoners. *Moe aku, moe mai* was the custom unless and until one assumed a claim by inheritance or acquired land by some other means.

Until the Great Mahele, commoners did not own land privately but cared for it as tenants under the chiefs. The chief's local land agent, the *konohiki*, allocated use rights, but commoners also passed down land through the family. As long as they met the tributary and labor demands of the chiefs, commoners had the right to remain on the same land indefinitely. Within the family, control over the land's disposition was vested in a senior individual, who could apportion plots to relatives or dependants. Each landholder was considered a temporary custodian in a chain of ancestors and descendants. The bond of descent created a right in the land of one's ancestors, regardless of whether one resided there permanently or not (Kamakau 1961:376). But this theoretical right, the "belonging to" a place that gave one the right of burial there, did not necessarily include authority over the family lands. The heritable land was indivisible; disfranchised siblings were expected to marry out or to live "under" someone with land—a relative, affine, or unrelated *haku'āina* (landlord). For most consanguines, the hereditary right to reside on the family's land remained a dormant claim. In practice, impartible inheritance negated the potential claims of junior collaterals. Land most frequently passed to the eldest son's descendants, while junior siblings became wanderers unless they could acquire or marry into land. Sexual freedom was both a life-cycle phenomenon—the behavior appropriate to young adulthood and social immaturity—and a general condition for the mass of Hawaiian commoners.

A story published in a Hawaiian newspaper in 1868 illustrates the link of marriage to landholding and the ideal of deference to an elder sibling. In this passage, Kanakaiki is the suitor of Nawahineokamae, sister of the hero, Kanewailani (Anonymous, 1868):

> Because he stayed around Kanewailani's place so much he became an adopted husband (*kāne ho'okāne*) of Nawahineokamae. . . . When Kanakaiki went home to his parents he said, "I have a 'wife' and I think I shall marry her later on." His parents said, "It is hardly fit that you should marry, but let your brother have your wife." Kanakaiki was somewhat doubtful, yet he gave his consent to let the older brother have the wife. . . . Nawahineokamae . . . lived at Halauwai (Halawa) with her husband and became a native and an ancestress there.

This tale purports to be from "an old Hawaiian story" describing traditional times. Here a woman marries an older brother and becomes a "native and an ancestress" of his place. The moral is that the eldest continues his family's birthright through marriage and childbearing; the moral is also that social maturity begins with establishing a household and particularly with having children who will one day inherit the property.

Visiting the islands in 1818, Peter Corney (1896:105–106) wrote: "The young women rove about without restraint until they attain the age of twenty. They then become more steady and have children." Those who maintained a stable union in past times were progenitors. In contrast to the unmarked custom of marriage, birth was the important ceremonial occasion, the event that sealed the relationship between man and woman (Kamakau 1964:27; Kekoa 1865; Sahlins 1974:16–17).

In Hawaiian ideology, grandchildren replace their grandparents on the land. It is not children so much as grandchildren who ensure the succession of family property. Since the holder lived on the land and had authority over it until death, the child generation was effectively bypassed in inheritance. The eldest son may have been the most frequent heir, but it was his child who was destined to enjoy long-term residence on the land. The conjunction of impartible inheritance and tenure-for-life meant that the long-term holders were grandparent and grandchild. This long-established pattern of land succession can explain household structure and demographics in Keanae today.

THE HOUSEHOLD AND LANDHOLDING

I have said that the Hawaiian household in Keanae is a property-holding unit. One cannot understand land tenure in Keanae without appreciating the distinction between landowning and landholding. Tabulated from the Maui County tax assessment records, absentee owners hold 48 percent of the land parcels in the area. But this does not mean that all these lands are abandoned. Landholding in Keanae means not only having a legal share but actively managing the property—living on the land and using it. It is a well-established Hawaiian cultural principle that the right to use land is distinct from the right to dispose of it, so that landowner and landholder may be two different people. Many titles in Keanae are legal nightmares. Most lands in the area have multiple interest holders. This situation has arisen in two ways. First, the problem of undivided land, where a dozen siblings may own fractional shares, arises when a landowner dies without conveying or devising the property. The Probate Court then divides the land among all the surviving heirs. Second, in the past, some Hawaiians also sold fractional interests to relatives as well as to outsiders. Realistically, most individuals do not know how to make use of a 1/240 interest, particularly if they reside outside. Yet although land-ownership is subject to partition, landholding in practice is not. The fractional interests of other siblings become dormant claims, for only one interest holder—and not necessarily the largest—establishes a household on the property. Hawaiians use the traditional phrase "taking care" for just this sort of tenure; the sibling who remains in Keanae is seen as caretaker of the family land.

In several cases, residents who held overlapping interests in land have executed exchange deeds: one party conveys his or her share in a parcel to another title holder in return for an interest in a different piece of land. Both parties thus consolidate their titles to particular parcels and avoid a possible conflict with another villager. This sort of transaction dispels any ambiguity as to who has the right to use the land, for the individuals are left holding interests in different parcels. The exception is *hui* land, in which many Keanae residents hold fractional interests (see Linnekin 1983b). Ownership of the *hui* lands is far too complex to be clarified by deed at this point; as Keanae Hawaiians recognize, there are so many shareholders that the land is useless from a practical standpoint. Nevertheless, some individuals have asserted their claim by establishing households on the *hui* lands. Most villagers do nothing with their shares, however, for they recognize that not everyone can activate a use right to the same land.

Title to land is usually vested in one family member. Most landholders have two or more small parcels. The *kuleana*s, or Land Commission Awards, were typically composed of two or three pieces (*'āpana*): a house lot and one or more cultivation plots. Similarly, each Homestead Award consisted of a house lot and taro land. Not uncommonly a landholder may own a homestead as well as a *kuleana* and a share in a Royal Patent Grant. One villager, for example, owns four parcels, has undivided interests in eight others, and leases another small lot from the state. In a few cases, two homesteaders manage their holdings as de facto joint land to produce taro for the market. One father/son pair and two sets of brothers work taro lands jointly but maintain separate households. In the case of the father and son, neither makes any decision concerning the patches or the disposition of the crop without consulting the other. Two brothers work their father's homestead together, although most of the land is in the name of the elder, who also inherited his father's role as taro agent. While in Keanae, the brothers reside together in the family home, but only the younger, a bachelor, lives there full time. The elder's family and permanent home are outside, and he spends a few days each week in Keanae. The older brother has title to eleven parcels, and the younger to three.

The other instance of de facto join landholding involves a large set of siblings who are unusual in that nearly all have remained permanently in Keanae. Although they have all established separate households on different lands, two of the brothers have combined land and labor resources in producing taro. The county tax rolls show no taro land belonging to the younger brother; this is ironic since he is the only man in Keanae who lives entirely on taro marketing. The elder brother owns about an acre and a half of house-lot and taro land, while his wife leases another half acre of taro land from the state. The two brothers reside on neighboring parcels. Originally, these plots constituted a single house lot, in which the brothers each inherited an un-divided half interest. Rather than hold the land in undi-vided ownership, the brothers executed a set of partition deeds dividing the area between them. Their concern for an absolutely equal split is demonstrated by the fact that one brother's half-share lot lies between the two quarter shares belonging to the other.

In 23 percent of the landowning households in Keanae (ten out of forty-three), two members own land individu-ally. Seven of these are cases where both spouses have title to different parcels. In the remaining three, the coresident owners are a father and son, a pair of brothers, and a mother, father, and son. The latter is the only household with more than two resident landowners. Although the husband is usually the title holder to household lands as well as the chief wage earner, 40 percent of all resident landowners are women. Women hold some land in twenty-two of the forty-three landowning households (51 per-cent); in twelve of these cases, a woman inherited through widowhood. But these totals include ownership of un-divided interests, which are often acquired through inheri-tance and are likely to be unusable in practical terms. In the seven cases where both husband and wife own land, the holdings are of different type, suggesting an attempt to build up the household property. If one spouse owns a Land Commission Award, the other may own the home-stead or lease additional taro land from the state.

MARRIAGE AND
LAND SUCCESSION

The people of Keanae are those who have stayed on the land, and their marital stability is intelligible in the context of Hawaiian principles of land succession. Keanae Hawai-ians see household stability as crucial to the continuity of family holdings. Against external pressure on villagers to divide and alienate their lands, the domestic unit is a placeholder, keeping the property within the family in this generation and in the next. Marriage ensures the succession of family lands because it produces children, the future heirs. Most Keanae Hawaiians whose marital histories I recorded, sixty-four, or 76 percent, had married only once, eight, or 9.5 percent, more than once. Twelve adults (14 percent) had never married. By following J. A. Barnes's (1967:61–66) method, one can express the frequency of divorce as the number of marriages ended in divorce divided by the number of marriages ended in death or divorce. Using the Keanae marital histories, this ratio (Barnes's ratio B) is 3/19, or 15.8 percent. In other words, about one in every six marriages ends in divorce as opposed to the commonly cited figures of one in every three for American society as a whole.

These figures do not conflict with my earlier statements about sexual freedom as a life-cycle phenomenon. The Hawaiian attitude toward affairs among young, unmarried adults is one of amused tolerance; the unattached are expected and encouraged to enjoy their freedom. Since heirs usually take possession of their parents' land in Keanae only after the elderly owner has died, the period of sexual freedom may last well into adulthood. The practice of *moe aku, moe mai* does not preclude entering into a more lasting relationship later on.

The normative attitude of villagers accords with the low incidence of divorce. The break-up of a marriage is heavily censured and is considered a source of personal shame for the parties involved. Marriage establishes a tie that is expected to endure until death. Divorce provokes a sense of shock, where cohabitation, illegitimacy, and minor adulteries do not. Informants convey the feeling that divorce is almost unnatural. Public opinion chooses sides in divorce cases and usually portrays the partner who left Keanae as irresponsible and no good. In the retelling, the most disturbing aspect of divorce is that the dissolution of a marriage breaks up a property-holding unit and can lead to land alienation. One oft-cited example involves a local man and woman whose divorce resulted in the sale of homestead land to a haole. The husband owned land inherited from his father, while the homestead where the couple resided belonged to the wife. The divorce resulted from mutual adultery, first the husband with his wife's sister, then the wife with a "boyfriend." The husband, who still lives in Keanae, is rarely blamed for the break-up; in fact, he is generally esteemed and is a village big-man. The wife afterward sold her land to a haole and left Keanae, and she is heavily criticized for doing so; in the public version of the story, it is she who left him. The divorce is a far more serious social offense than the adultery that precipitated it.

Despite the disapproval of divorce, the husband/wife relationship among Keanae Hawaiians is not particularly solidary. The tie is often strained. One spouse may be clearly subordinate, the other dominating; or long-standing quarrels over money, relatives, drinking, or land may burden the marital relationship. Another case of a marriage effectively dissolving, although it did not end in divorce, illustrates how the destiny of a marriage is linked to the destiny of the family lands. A Keanae man often called "*pilau*" (rotten) by his neighbors was suspected of having *kahuna*'d[1] his wife because he coveted her lands. After years of ill treatment at his hands, she developed a psychogenic paralysis and by 1975 had been institutionalized for several years. Their son was given legal control over her property, and the husband continued to live on their homestead in Keanae. Few villagers associated with him, and he was criticized for consorting with a "hippy lady" and her friends. Residents frequently expressed the fear that these haoles were persuading him to hand over his land to them.

---

1. In pre-Christian Hawaii, *kahuna* meant priest. After missionization, the word came to be used for a sorcerer, either good or bad. Nowadays, *kahuna* means a practitioner of Hawaiian healing arts or, more generally, an expert. In this case, *kahuna* was used in the sense of causing misfortune by means of ill will, similar to our idea of putting the hex on or giving the evil eye. The weapon is psychological. Here the husband was not suspected of actually practicing sorcery against his wife but of directing evil thoughts and wishes against her. Hawaiians believe that such evil thoughts are extremely potent.

Villagers say that the eldest should inherit the family lands, but modern constraints have interfered with the realization of this norm. Pragmatic and situational factors enter into the decision. The parents' tenure-for-life and the limited number of jobs inside often combine to discourage elder siblings from assuming their inheritance. When the time comes, the intended heir may have a job and a home outside or on another island. The work of a taro farmer is hard labor, and the schedule kept by the Keanae men who also have salaried jobs is grueling by any standard. Nowadays parents often leave their land to the child who is willing to live in Keanae. When a couple has no children, they will adopt a child or convey the property to a younger collateral relative—perhaps a favorite niece or nephew. Alternately, couples who own several parcels in Keanae may try to give land to each of their children: the homestead to one, a Land Commission Award to another, a share in a Royal Patent Grant to yet another. Landholding is indivisible in practice, but this does not mean that adult siblings never live in the same community, only that they reside on different lands. Several members of the same family may—and do—live in Keanae but in separate households. Homesteads and individual parcels are rarely subdivided, but the tax records show that Keanae landowners are increasingly trying to accommodate all their prospective heirs when they have enough property to do so.

Individual landowners often execute deeds conveying property from the grantor to the grantor and spouse. Husband and wife then become joint owners of the property with right of survivorship. While the parents are alive, their children remain scattered over the islands and on the Mainland. A common convention is for an elderly Hawaiian couple to convey land "for one dollar and aloha" while reserving a life interest in the estate. This is effectively a bequest before the fact; the grantors ensure that their wishes will be carried out, while the actual succession occurs only after the death of both man and wife. To ensure that the intended heir will take up the family land, the owner may give him or her a small parcel for a house lot, thus enabling the heir to establish a home in Keanae before the holder's death.

If such a bequest is not made, the youngest child may be the only sibling left in residence when the parents die and may inherit "care" of the land, if not legal ownership, by default. There is cultural precedent for this alternative—for the youngest child's offspring to inherit rather than those of the eldest. The youngest of the family, the *pōki'i*, is the parents' sentimental favorite and "was playfully called *haku* or family head" (Goldman 1970:214). Hawaiians say that the youngest should stay at home and care for the aging parents after older siblings have left, thus creating the possibility that the "baby" will in some cases supplant the eldest. A younger sibling will sometimes take advantage of the elder's absence by attempting to win over the elderly parents. In lieu of the *pōki'i*, a grandchild is often given to the grandparents, either informally or in *hānai* (adoption), to help with household tasks and taro-patch work. This child is not necessarily destined to inherit; often the arrangement is explicitly viewed as a service relationship. But younger and elder siblings may vie to place their children in the grandparental home as proof of their aloha and concern.

THE DOMESTIC CYCLE

The statements of elderly informants suggest that even earlier in this century Keanae households included more dependents such as "kept" children and unmarried relatives than at present. Undeniably, households in Keanae are smaller than in former times, and this attrition appears to be a relatively recent phenomenon. The Hawaiian proto-type of the domestic unit is an extended-family household composed of a variety of relatives (Handy and Pukui 1972: 90–91; Howard 1971:37–38). Field studies indicate that such a unit was common among both rural and urban

Hawaiians at least through the 1940s. In Ernest Beaglehole's (1937:48–49) time, household size averaged 6.6 in rural areas and 7.0 in Honolulu. In 1941, Hawaiian households in Hana averaged 7.1 persons, with 5 to 10 a common range; 60 percent of these households housed three generations of the same family (Yamamura 1941:39).

Household size in Keanae today contrasts markedly with these figures. For fifty-one Hawaiian households, the average size is three persons: two adults and one child. The range is from one to eight persons. Nearly a third of the households (27 percent) have only one permanent occupant, in almost every case a retired person living alone. Thirty-three households (65 percent) have no children resident in them. There is a 20 percent incidence of supplemented nuclear families, where a married couple resides with a widowed parent, adult child, or unmarried sibling. But only three Hawaiian households (6 percent) in Keanae include three generations.

With the exception of one polyandrous household, the structural core of the domestic unit is in every case a close consanguineal relationship, either parent/child or brother/brother. The polyandrous family includes a woman, her husband, and her common-law companion, owner of the property and undisputed head of the household; two of the woman's children, now in their twenties, also reside with them. This arrangement is certainly not common among Hawaiians today, but it has a basis in pre-Christian polygamy. The term *punalua* meant cospouse; as a verb, *punalua* meant "to make an equal of one, to come on terms of reciprocity with one" (Andrews 1865:498). *Punalua* "had joint responsibility for the children in the family" (Handy and Pukui 1972:56) and were expected to treat one another like relatives, without jealousy. In this instance, the *punalua* live together amicably in a clearly hierarchical relationship. It is no coincidence that the head of this household is a village big-man; his case is described further in Chapter 8.

Many households in Keanae have undergone a cycle of growth and contraction. Those now housing widowed adults are nearing the end of that cycle. Keanae's location limits the number of teenagers and young adults living in the village. Keanae School goes only to the eighth grade; teenagers must live outside with relatives to attend high school, and many marry after that or go away to college. Once children reach marriageable age, they seldom return to Keanae to live until both parents are dead. Jobs around Keanae are scarce, and individuals usually hold them for years. The limited number of jobs inside is the primary reason for the attrition of the domestic group in Keanae, but there is also a cultural factor: the diminishing permanent population is the result of a modern set of perceptions. As much as they romanticize and openly envy the Keanae lifestyle, most Hawaiians do not choose to live there. The consensus, quite simply, is that the life is too hard. By town standards, the village is isolated; the journey, made often for visiting, would seem a hardship if it were a permanent necessity.

Hawaiians have also perhaps come to value their independence from family more than before. It is still possible for relatives and assorted dependants to live "under" a landowner, but in practice few choose this option. Those who do tend to have some social liability: alcoholism, instability, a reputation for slow-wittedness. Few Hawaiians today seem willing to accept a position of dependency, even under a close relative; the arrangement is all too clearly hierarchical. For most Hawaiians, the option of residing with kin is merely a theoretical possibility. Postmarital residence is neolocal; whether they settle in Keanae or not, young adults expect to establish an independent household after marriage. Parents and their married offspring rarely maintain a joint household, even though they may live in the same village. One man built a small house for his soon-to-be-married son only twenty feet away from the family home.

The pattern of land succession is thus for adult children to disperse until both parents are dead, when one sibling usually takes possession of the land. Tenure-for-life accounts for the large proportion of single-person house-holds in Keanae today. If the past trend continues, one member of the family will return to live on the land—although it may not be the eldest child. When I lived in Keanae, many properties were held by absentee owners, and the large number of single-person households seemed ominous. I feared that young Hawaiians would not return to take up the family lands when these old people died but would sell them to outsiders. When I returned for a visit in 1981, some of my elderly informants were dead. But their houses were occupied by Hawaiians, and their lands were in taro. In 1981 the village seemed younger and more populous than it had in 1975. Hawaiian land succession is thus going on in Keanae. The crisis of a landholder's death is resolved in traditional fashion: even if there are multiple heirs, one relative usually returns to "take care," and many elderly residents are giving parcels to their intended heirs in advance to enable them to stay in the village.

Figure 4.1 illustrates the developmental cycle of Hawaiian households in Keanae. Arbitrarily, I begin with what is really the last stage in the cycle: a single widowed adult living alone. The parent's death is a critical moment in familial land succession. Did the parent bequeath the property to someone, or will the court award fractional interests to all the legal heirs? Will the heir(s) take up residence on the land, leave it unattended, or sell it? Stage 2 in Figure 4.1 represents succession by a nuclear-family household with young children. One older child is shown as a part-time resident while attending high school outside. Stage 3 shows an extended-family household with a married son in residence and a married daughter whose husband works outside and commutes to Keanae on weekends. Obviously, not every family experiences such arrangements; the diagram is meant to show common possibilities. This stage, if it occurs, is short-lived and is seen as a temporary expedient until the young couple is able to establish a home of their own. Although Keanae Hawaiians avoid such extended-family arrangements today, this large *ma* approxi-

Figure 4.1
Hawaiian Household Development in Keanae

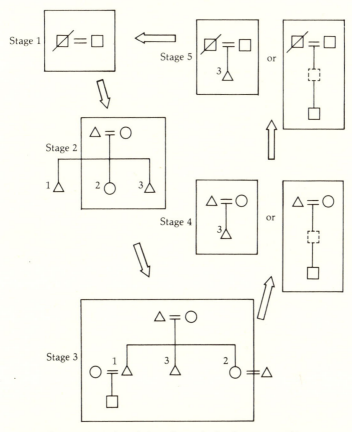

Note: For meanings of symbols in this and other figures, see Abbreviations and Symbols in the beginning of the book.

mates long-term household structure in former times. The large domestic group, with younger couples and dependents living under the middle-aged landholder, was characteristic of rural areas through the early part of this century. Elderly Hawaiians in Keanae describe their childhood homes in substantially these terms. In Stage 4, married children have left the household, and the youngest sibling or a grandchild remains to help the aging parents. After one parent dies (Stage 5), this caretaker may stay on with the widow. Grandchildren generally leave when they reach high school age, but occasionally the *pōki'i* of the family remains with a widowed parent until death, so that either Stage 1 or 5 may be the end of the cycle.

Consideration of some of the unmarried adults in the village illustrates some of the variations in household organization and land succession. Eleven men and one woman in Keanae have never married. Five of these individuals are young adults living at home with their parents. Three of the young men work taro, two with their fathers and one with his mother's brother. The young woman is sometimes referred to locally as "the family pet," or "the baby," as is one of the young men. The status of these two is that of *pōki'i*. One bachelor is a joint owner of his parents' homestead, where they all reside. Another man lives alone on the homestead of his adoptive mother; but he is considered somewhat *lolo* (stupid), and the land is in the name of another sibling. Three other unmarried men own land. One maintains a household together with his younger brother, who owns no property. Another resides and farms taro on the family homestead, in which he has 1/35 interest; none of his siblings live in Keanae, and he is the family caretaker. The third unmarried landowner farms taro with his sister's son, to whom he has already conveyed his homestead, reserving a life interest.

The shift to neolocal postmarital residence seems to have paralleled the transition from farming to wage labor as the primary source of household income in Keanae—a shift that occurred after the opening of the Hana road in the 1920s. The 1890 commercial directory (the equivalent of today's telephone directory) lists twenty-eight Hawaiian taro planters, a storekeeper, a carpenter, and a policeman residing in Keanae. Between 1890 and 1920, Chinese rice planters and storekeepers make their appearance, but most Hawaiians are still engaged in taro farming. In 1920, three Hawaiians are listed as laborers, and there is a haole foreman for E.M.I. living in Keanae. Between 1920 and 1930, the occupations of Hawaiian men in the village change dramatically. In the 1930 directory, taro planters and homesteaders are outnumbered by laborers and truck drivers employed by E.M.I., the road department, and the Keanae Prison Camp.

The opening of the Hana road made it possible for the permanent population of Keanae to become, in part, a transient one. It is now feasible to work and even live outside while spending most of one's leisure time in Keanae. Hawaiians historically have had a penchant for visiting and traveling, "going *holoholo*." Many former residents are regular weekend visitors. Relatives come to fish or hunt pig. Grandchildren come in to stay for variable periods of time, particularly in the summer. Elderly people go out on weekends or for weeks at a time to visit children; several maintain second homes in other communities, a few even on other islands. Luaus too occasion much going back and forth. The tremendous amount of coming and going that characterizes life in Keanae belies the decline in the permanent population and proves the community's viability.

Chapter Five

RELATIVES

A network of relationships links Keanae to other communities. Collateral and affinal ties branch outward, ultimately to encompass all the Hawaiians of Maui in a web of relatedness, although all the details of that relatedness can never be known. Hawaiians constitute a remarkably insular stratum in island society. Villagers conduct necessary transactions of a commercial and impersonal nature outside but then turn to the social sphere of Hawaiians. Even outside, social contacts are restricted largely to people who are known in the village: former residents, relatives, in-laws, and in-laws of relatives. Villagers frequent certain businesses and restaurants and not others. If one goes to a certain supermarket in Kahului, a certain restaurant in Wailuku, a certain laundromat in Paia, one is bound to run into the siblings, children, or grandchildren of Keanae people. This chapter discusses relationships between Keanae Hawaiians and their relatives—those who are said to be linked by blood. As will be seen, although Hawaiians today use primarily English kinship terms, their notions of kinship are not identical to those of Mainland haoles.

HAWAIIAN KINSHIP

I have analyzed the social world of Hawaiians in terms of relatives, affines, and nonrelatives. Although Hawaiians do not explicitly divide society in this fashion, distinctions among those who are related, whether by a known or a stipulated tie, those who are related "only by marriage," and those who are not related are important and correspond to qualitative differences in social relations. The categories denote modes of relationship governed by differing expectations regarding exchange. There is also a genealogical factor in their definition, for Hawaiians distinguish between those who are "really related" and those who are "no blood relation" or "not related, only by marriage."[1] Although Hawaiians recognize these distinctions and consider them important in matters such as land inheritance, the terminology of address and casual reference often ignores them. Relatives, affines, and nonrelatives are classes of persons engaging in specific kinds of reciprocity. Recruitment to a category may accordingly follow from participation in exchange, as the following discussion shows.

The Hawaiian notion of a relative differs from the Mainland meaning (see Schneider 1968) despite the common metaphor of blood for shared substance. For this reason, I avoid using the terms *consanguinity* and *kinship* in favor of *relatedness* to describe the Hawaiian concept. *Consanguinity* and *kinship* carry a considerable burden of past anthropological uses, while *related* is the term most often used by Hawaiians. Genealogies are generally not known above the grandparental generation, and many elderly Hawaiians are unable to supply their mother's maiden name. Yet this very lack of precise genealogical knowledge facilitates the stipulation of relatedness. The Hawaiian concept of a relative includes the idea of sharing a common ancestor, but relatedness in this sense is theoretically unbounded. Although a relationship cannot always be proved, neither can it be disproved; it is always a possibility. If someone fulfills the behavioral expectations of a relative, a relationship may thus be assumed. Allocation to the category of relatives may thus follow from behavior.

The limits of genealogical knowledge thus make possible the potentially unlimited scope of relatedness. Recall the informant's advice: "If you're a stranger in the place, men-

1. This discussion owes an obvious debt to the work of Leach (1958) and Schneider (1965, 1968) for their explorations of the meaning of kinship. I am also indebted to Kelly (1977) for suggesting lines of argument and helping to clarify certain ideas.

tion some family names. You never know, you might be related to somebody in that place. You might have family there, and someone might know you that way. You can explain to them who you are and try to make it all right. Then they may let you go." The Hawaiian theory is that if one could trace descent back far enough, one might discover the most unlikely relationships. It is even conceivable that a Mainland haole might find a relative among the resident spirits of Maui. The point is, as Hawaiians say, "you never know." Mary Pukui (n.d.) has similarly described Hawaiian kinship: "As long as there has been a common ancestor, all collateral descendants are related. It was not necessary for everyone to be able to trace this genealogical descent; it was enough that the family genealogist point out . . . the relationship, and teach the term to be used. . . . A blood relationship was considered close if the common ancestor was no more than four generations back. . . . An acknowledgement of relationship, called *kuhikuhi 'ia*, existed even when a genealogical tracing was not possible but it was known that there had been a common ancestor in the past."

Hawaiians trace known relationships upward to the grandparental or great-grandparental generation rather than down from an apical ancestor. An informant explained the method of pointing out relationships: "If you tell me your name, say, I won't know because there were so many children over there and they got married and had children. I wouldn't know their children's names. But if you tell me your mother's name or father's name or, better, who your grandfather was, then I can tell you who they related to."

Keanae Hawaiians use the metaphor of blood to indicate close relationship. The traditional phraseology invoked images of shared substances to portray relatedness: *he iwi, he 'i'o, he koko*, "bone, flesh, blood" (Handy and Pukui 1972:48). True kinship is being of like kind: *'i'o pono'ī*, "own flesh," the tie that "cannot be untied" (ibid.:48). According to informants, second or third cousin is a close relative, a relative *pili koko*, by blood. In Probate Court cases dating from the 1870s, *pili koko* is applied to such relatives as cross-cousins and one's sibling's children.

Beyond the second or third degree of collaterality, the details of relatedness are unknown. The limits of knowledge thus define genealogical closeness. Where a relationship is said to exist but cannot be specified, the person is "far related." The phrase "fourth or fifth cousin" may be used to refer to stipulated collateral relationships; one long-time resident was said to be "related to everyone around here, but not near-like, cousin-like." Similarly, "all related" describes an unspecifiable collateral link between families. An informant referred to a neighbor as her first cousin, then specified that he was her husband's first cousin but could not say whether the tie was through his father or his mother. "Something like that," she answered; "they're all related." Her limited knowledge also illustrates the fact that Hawaiians are better informed about their own relatives than about those of affines.

Beyond the sphere of known relationships, the deciding factor in whether to call someone a relative is not genealogical. In fact, behavior may so affect categorization that an individual may deny a close kin tie claimed by another. The choice of terms, as between "cousin" and simply "relative," is also not genealogically determined but depends on social distance, on the kind of relationship existing between the parties. Participation in reciprocities is the determining factor, and residential proximity is a significant variable because it facilitates frequent contact. This Hawaiian ethic of relatedness includes the notion of "enduring diffuse solidarity" (Schneider 1968:52), the idea of aloha. In practice, this solidarity is expressed in "generalized reciprocity" (Sahlins 1965:147), the moral necessity to give without stint and without regard to the net balance.

Kinship terms are used to the extent that these expectations are realized in action. Two Keanae householders live on adjacent lots and have the same last name. Yet while one claims that his father was his neighbor's father's brother, the other says that they are not related. The one claiming a relationship is a part-time resident who spends more than half of each year on another island; his social contacts in Keanae are few. Although actual siblingship would probably not be denied in this fashion, a cousin relationship may or may not be acknowledged. Pukui (n.d.) has stated that common ancestry up to four generations back constituted "a relationship known as *wehena 'ole*, one that could not be denied." But as the degree of traceable collaterality has contracted, so has the degree of undeniable relationship, until at present only genealogical siblingship appears to be irrefutable.

At the far reaches of collaterality, friendship grades into relatedness. An informant stated, "That old lady was only a friend of my grandmother, far related." Similarly, "They not related exactly, only far, far back. They were only friends to my grandmother." In the Hawaiian theory, if a friend fulfills the qualities of a relative, some relationship must have existed in the past, even though it cannot be demonstrated. Occasionally such putative relatedness conflicts with the norm of familial inheritance. In this case, descendants of the friends of my informant's grandmother were claiming some relationship and hence a share in her family lands. My informant's point was that these friends were merely assimilated as relatives terminologically; in the Hawaiian view they were accordingly "far" related, "cousin-like" perhaps but "not really related." They were not true descendants of the original owner and thus had no rightful claim to the land.

My informant further clarified the relationship as one of dependency on the landholder: "My grandmother let them live there, and because they lived under her, they claim some land." Hawaiian landholders customarily let others live "under" them and use the land. These dependents might be landless junior collaterals or daughters with their husbands; they might be distant kin or simply "added on" relatives. Pukui (Handy and Pukui 1972:65) describes an engrafted, or added on, relationship, *pili kāmau*: "when one was no relative in actuality [but] was accepted as a member of the family in consequence of his attaching himself to the family."

Since land is passed down through the family, those living in the same locality might logically be assumed to have common ancestry, albeit "far, far back." The Hawaiian model of relatedness stipulates that the people originally "belonging to" a locality, such as Keanae or Kaupo, are of common descent. The long-time residents, the *kama'āina*, are probably related in some way. An informant who had married into Keanae from Kaupo thus explained her relationship to a young Hana woman. Their forebears had lived on adjacent land in Kaupo. The two women referred to each other as "aunty" and "niece" because their families had all "stayed on" the same land: "You know so-and-so? She's from that family. That's why she calls me 'aunty.'"

But because of mobility and exogamy in the past, the residents of a locality are not all related. Keanae informants can point out the families who originated elsewhere: "Those people came from Kailua" or "Wahinepee people" or "long time over here, but from Huelo side." This may be said even of elderly residents whose grandparents acquired land in Keanae. The villagers who married into Keanae from Kaupo in the 1920s are relative newcomers; even after many years of residence they feel somewhat like outsiders, chary of imbalances in exchange and mindful of their status vis-à-vis their neighbors. They claim no knowledge of Keanae genealogies: "My old man knew all that. I don't know who these people are." Two of the Kaupo people, an elderly man and woman, say that they are cousins and have a long-standing relationship of affection and mutual aid.

Since in the Hawaiian theory anyone might be related in the distant past, fulfilling a relative-like relationship is the determining factor in recruitment. Relatedness is predicated on reciprocity and is proven by events. In many tales of the dead and the volcano goddess Pele, the moral of the story is the solidarity of relatives. There is said to be an old

man who lives near the volcano on the Big Island. He gave
Pele a bottle of whiskey, and whenever there has been
an eruption, the lava flows have gone around his house:
"Must be a relative, that. Close, close, very close relative."
Some families are related to Pele; she has told them to put
red flags at the boundaries of their land and the lava will
go around. Many people have saved their houses in this
way, but "only if you're related, like."

The people's link with their ancestors, and hence their
birthright in their ancestral lands, is proven by knowledge
of the family's burial places: "The rule of kings and chiefs
and their land agents might change," wrote Samuel M.
Kamakau (1961:376), "but the burial rights of families survived on their lands." Keanae residents readily point out a
local burial cave accidentally discovered by village boys
and containing a human skull, but when asked whose remains lie there, villagers reply: "Oh, nobody know. Their
relatives all gone, dead." The cave's location would certainly not be disclosed so casually if it were known to be
linked to living residents. Burial caves are family domain,
and their locations are known to only a few close relatives.
The opening of a cave to an individual is proof of relationship, as in the story quoted in Chapter 2, where a cave of
treasures revealed itself to a Keanae man: "Must be he
related," my informant commented, "[or] they won't open
to you." The theme of such stories is that the dead vouchsafe family property to their descendants, who are to be
caretakers in their turn. An informant told how a burial
cave had once opened to herself and her grandmother:
"My grandmother said it was all right for me to take something: that's how they had showed it to us. She showed me
an ivory comb and asked me if I wanted it. She said that
these were my relatives, they wouldn't hurt me. The comb
was for me, not for her, she old already. But I was too
scared. . . . You gotta be related to someone in that cave,
though, before they show to you and say it's all right for
you to take something. They're giving it to you, a relative,
for take care."

Although relatedness is based on solidarity and generalized reciprocity, these qualities may or may not materialize in a specific relationship. Known ties establish a set of possibilities rather than strictures. Given the wide network of persons who may qualify as kin, it is impossible to maintain active reciprocities with more than a fraction of one's relatives. Kinship defines only the potential quality of the relationship, not the content in a particular case. In practice, personal preference and geographic dispersal limit the number of active relationships. The obligation to engage in exchange is a moral one, and certain moral obligations, such as that between parent and child, are more imperative than others. Yet even between close relatives, reciprocity is largely voluntary, to be entered into or not. One mother and daughter living in the village rarely speak, for example, while other mothers and daughters spend most of their time together, work the parents' taro patches together, and grind poi together. "Cousins" living in the village may be much closer than brother and sister. Close genealogical kinship does not guarantee that the ideal qualities of relatedness will be present.

Relatives exchange primarily food and services, but the commodities are generally of higher symbolic value than the items that pass between nonkin. For example, taro-patch labor, poi, and luau foods usually pass between relatives. These are weighty commodities; if they were given to a nonrelative, their high value in the realm of exchange and the necessity for compensation would place a considerable burden on the relationship. Table 5.1 illustrates contrasts in the commodities exchanged by relatives and nonrelatives, both inside and outside the village. The gradient from low to high is intended as a general scheme rather than as a precise ordering of the items listed within one category. This and the following chapter discuss these exchanges in detail.

While "related" denotes common ancestry that may or may not be demonstrable, "family" refers to those whose relationship can be specified, usually the descendants of a

Table 5.1
GIFTS AND SERVICES INVOLVED IN EXCHANGE

	From		
	Insiders		*Outsiders*
	Relatives	*Nonrelatives*	*(Relatives or Nonrelatives)*
To Insiders			
Low	Babysitting	Bamboo	Cigarettes, liquor,
	Transport	Bananas	sweet breads, Chinese
	Luau foods	Avocado	sweets, store-bought
	Poi	Seeds, *huli*	goods
	Taro-patch	Medicines	Transport
	work	Breadfruit	Lawn work
	Luau labor	poi	Home repairs
		Transport	Fresh fish
		Home repairs	Luau foods
		Taro-patch	Taro-patch
		work	work
High		Luau labor	Luau labor
To Outsiders			
Low	Local fruits	Local fruits	
	Watercress	Luau foods	
	Herbal	Hospitality	
	remedies		
	Babysitting		
	Taro corms		
	Fresh fish		
	Dried fish		
	Luau foods		
	Hospitality		
High	Luau labor		

pair of grandparents or great-grandparents. In common reference, a family includes a set of siblings, their children, and their children's children. This meaning is similar to the Handy and Pukui (1972:19) definition of the *'ohana* as a dispersed, extended family occupying separate households within a land section. But the family is not a residential grouping. Adult siblings are likely to be widely dispersed, and few members of the family actually set up households in their natal locality. Keanae Hawaiians seldom use the term *'ohana*, although the nationalist movement has adopted it to evoke family-like solidarity within its organization. As used by informants in the village, *'ohana* includes at least an individual's cousins and siblings and their offspring. "Family" describes a similar degree of relatedness. The family is thus a subset of the larger category of relatives: fourth and fifth cousins are "not the own family."

A family is often referred to by surname, adult siblings grouped together with their offspring, such as the "Kapono family" or "all the Kolouahis." A married woman will be described as "a Hoopii girl," using her maiden name; her daughter would not be called "a Hoopii girl" but would belong to the "Hoopii family" as well as to the family of her father. Association with a locality is also part of the definition: a family is identified with the land that the *kūpuna*—the ancestors, grandparents, or great-grandparents—"belonged to." Informants were often unclear about the surnames of people who married into the family from outside the village. Relationships are not traced down from parents but upward to the *kūpuna*, the grandparental generation associated with the family's natal land.

The family is a category not a bounded group. It has no corporate functions. Once adult children have left home, the family will probably never again be reunited at one time. Even a luau rarely succeeds in assembling all the family members, who may be dispersed from the Mainland to Micronesia. Since "family" describes a category of relationship, it easily encompasses persons who are closely associated with family members. Although Hawaiians distinguish between their own family and that of a spouse, in casual reference "family" also includes affines: in other words, the people who can trace descent to a common *kupuna* as well as those married to them. In this sense, a woman boasted, "There are four sisters in my family," referring to a set of sisters who had married her four brothers. Nonrelatives are even more likely to class together affines and blood relatives: a woman was thus associated with her husband's sister's daughter as "all the same family." The logic of the terminology supports this identification, for the niece of one's spouse is also called "niece." The reciprocal term would be "aunty."

Although Hawaiians' vertical knowledge of relatedness may be limited, the horizontal dimension is extraordinarily detailed. Hawaiians can trace affinal, adoptive, and sibling relationships of dizzying complexity, particularly among peers. The genealogical knowledge of Hawaiians stresses ties between families rather than the lineal depth of a particular family. The term "family" thus denotes the group of people who would attend a luau: a sibling set, their children and grandchildren, and those married to them.

KINSHIP TERMINOLOGY

Although English words have largely supplanted the original Hawaiian, the kinship terms used by Hawaiians today do not have the same content as their Mainland counterparts. To an observer from a society where kinship is assumed to mirror "the facts of nature" (Schneider 1968:33), Hawaiians appear to apply terms of relationship loosely. For most relationships, Hawaiians' use of English kinship terms is not necessarily predicated on the facts of genealogy that a Mainlander might perceive.[2] Terms of address in particular reveal the quality of a social relationship, its expectations and categorical attributes.

The casual transposition of lineal and collateral terms

2. Genealogical information on living Keanae residents derives primarily from informants' statements. For deceased and former residents, I used a variety of documentary sources: Probate Court cases dating from the 1850s to the present, land-claims testimony given by Keanae landholders during the Great Mahele, and deeds in the Bureau of Conveyances, Honolulu. For tutelage in this method of genealogical reconstruction, I thank Marshall Sahlins.

recalls traditional Hawaiian kinship terminology, which grouped relatives together by generation and did not distinguish siblings from collaterals. Within the same generation, kin of the same sex used the reciprocal *kaikua'ana* (elder sibling, same sex)/*kaikaina* (younger sibling, same sex) terms, which embodied ranking by relative age. As long as a relationship was known to exist, the *makua* (parent) and *kaikua'ana*/*kaikaina* terms were used (Handy and Pukui 1972:66–67). The term *hanauna* specifies relatives through a collateral line, descendants of the grandparents' or great-grandparents' siblings (ibid.:68). A more general term for collateral kin is *hoahānau*, which missionaries adopted to mean brethren. Lorrin Andrews (1865:167) defines *hoahānau* as "a kindred; some blood relation, a relative, a brother in an extensive sense." In address and common use, such relatives were not distinguished from lineal kin or first cousins. When tracing relationships, Keanae Hawaiians differentiate between lineal, collateral, and adoptive ties but often ignore these distinctions in everyday usage. The same individual might be called "my son," "my boy," "my nephew," "my sister's son," all in the course of a day. Table 5.2 summarizes the traditional terminology and lists the equivalent terms used by Keanae Hawaiians today.

In nineteenth-century court testimony, the qualifier *pono'ī* is often used to indicate the "own, true" relative as opposed to a more distant or putative relative. Most often this distinction is made to justify claims to land. Whether *pono'ī* describes social or genealogical closeness is difficult to say conclusively. But in testimony of Hawaiians before the Land Commission during the Great Mahele, the term appears only a few times in a sample of three thousand claims, suggesting that the distinction was not significant traditionally. The statements of Keanae informants similarly indicate that *pono'ī* may be used to describe affective quality rather than genealogical closeness. It cannot be said, however, that *pono'ī* has nothing to do with genealogy. *Pono'ī* is usually not applied to unrelated persons who are simply called by terms of relationship, nor is it com-

Table 5.2
HAWAIIAN KINSHIP TERMINOLOGY

English	Traditional Hawaiian	Modern Equivalent
Grandparents, great-grandparents	*Kūpuna*	Grandparents
Grandmother, great-aunt	*Kupuna wahine*	Grandmother, *tutu*
Grandfather, great-uncle	*Kupuna kāne*	Grandfather
Mother, aunt	*Makuahine*	Mother, aunty
Father, uncle	*Makua kāne*	Father, uncle
Elder collateral, same generation, same sex	*Kaikua'ana*	Brother, sister, cousin
Younger collateral, same generation, same sex	*Kaikaina*	Brother, sister, cousin
Brother, female speaker	*Kaikunane*	Brother
Sister, male speaker	*Kaikuahine*	Sister
Son, nephew	*Keiki*	Son, nephew
Daughter, niece	*Kaikamahine*	Daughter, niece
Grandchild, great-grandchild	*Mo'opuna*	Mo'opuna, grandchild
Granddaughter, grandniece	*Mo'opuna wahine*	Mo'opuna, granddaughter, mo'opuna wahine
Grandson, grandnephew	*Mo'opuna kāne*	Mo'opuna, grandson, mo'opuna kāne

SOURCE: Adapted from Handy and Pukui (1972:42).

monly used for distant collaterals. The dispute over family rights to land cited above illustrate this distinction: the friends living on the land were not the "own, true" relatives and hence should have had no claim to the property.

In place of *pono'ī*, modern Hawaiians use the word "own." "Own family" designates the known descendants of a *kupuna*. The "own" relatives are thus distinguished from more distant, "cousin-like" collaterals and those who are merely called relatives. In practice, "own," like *pono'ī*, is most often used within the first degree of collaterality. Hawaiians today speak of "the own first cousin" and "my sister's own son," relatives who are removed from the speaker by no more than one degree of collaterality. The "own aunty" is a parent's sibling, as opposed to many other women, related or not, who may be called "aunty." The Hawaiian equivalent of "own aunty" would be *makuahine pono'ī* (although, without some clarifying evidence, *makuahine pono'ī* could be translated as either mother or aunt).

Yet *pono'ī* may also be used more freely to indicate affective closeness. In an 1867 probate case, *pono'ī* was applied to an affinal relative. Testimony revealed the relationship of Makaole and Kekui to be as shown in Figure 5.1: Makaole was married to the elder brother of Kekui's great-grandfather. In Hawaiian, the reciprocal terms would be *kupuna* and *mo'opuna*. A witness explained that Kekui was the *mo'opuna pono'ī* of Makaole, her *hoahānau pono'ī* (P-400, 2nd c.c.).

In the Hawaiian scheme, however, the line between fictive and putative kinship is indistinct. Since common descent is always a possibility, who can say that those who are called relatives are not in fact related through some unknown tie? As tales of Pele and the spirits indicate, empirical evidence of solidarity is the proof of relatedness. Because those who fulfill reciprocities in the present are called by kinship terms, they might be related; "you never know."

Pono'ī thus can be used to describe any relationship of intense solidarity, affection, mutual help, and sometimes a relationship that involves the right to property inheritance. In keeping with the reflexive quality of Hawaiian kinship, a relative may become *pono'ī* if these qualities are present. In Hawaiian kinship, facts of reciprocity revise the facts of nature. There is some evidence that an adopted child may even be called *pono'ī* if the relationship is as solidary as that between a true parent and child. Inheritance may figure importantly in the designation *pono'ī* and not only for the reason that relatives may claim to be "own, true" kin in

Figure 5.1
Pono'ī Relatives

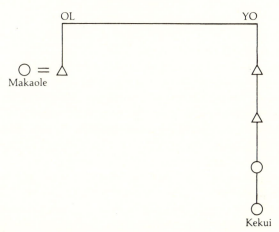

order to justify claims to property. As *pono'ī* kin are those who should inherit the family land, so the heirs may be remembered by succeeding generations as *pono'ī*. Inheriting collaterals can thus be genealogically transformed into lineal relatives over time. The shallow time depth of Hawaiian genealogical knowledge facilitates this kind of assimilation.

Hawaiians use English kinship terms in ways that reflect the classificatory nature of the Hawaiian terminology. "Grandparent" and "grandchild," for example, are used for the traditional *kupuna* and *mo'opuna*. But *mo'opuna* refers not only to the grandchildren and great-grandchildren of oneself but also to the grandchildren and great-grandchildren of one's siblings and one's spouse's siblings. The spouse of a *mo'opuna* may also be called *mo'opuna*, as when a woman referred to her granddaughter's husband as her "haole boy," her "*mo'opuna*." Similarly, the English grandchild terms are applied to grandnieces and grandnephews. An informant speaking of her "grandson" explained: "He's my nephew's son, grandson-like."

The common use of *mo'opuna* is one of the few instances where the Hawaiian term is employed more frequently than its English equivalent. It is perhaps risky to speculate why certain Hawaiian kinship terms and not others have been retained in everyday usage. Yet the use of native terms is exceptional today, and the exceptions deserve some notice. The *mo'opuna*/grandparent relationship is marked by intense solidarity: affection, gift giving, the services of the grandchild, and the doting favors of the grandparent. The grandchild is also the relative most frequently adopted, taking the place of married children who have left home. Not only is this an important service relationship, but, as mentioned previously, the grandchild generation ensures the continuity of family property. The *mo'opuna* replace the *kūpuna* on the land.

Like *mo'opuna*, the grandparent terms ignore the distinction between lineal and collateral relatedness. "Grandma" is used for both grandmother and great-grandmother as well as great-aunt. Speaking of two sisters, the *kūpuna* of a neighbor, an informant said, "They were the grandmothers, that." (In Keanae, "grandma" has for the most part replaced "tutu" in addressing a grandmother.) Just as no distinction is made between one's own niece and nephew and that of one's spouse, so are grandparent terms used for the spouses of classificatory grandparents.

Figure 5.2 illustrates such usage. Fran[3] and her sister call Mele "grandma" and she calls them her "granddaughters." Although Mele's husband is deceased, the relationship between Mele and the young women is active and affectionate. The two sisters and their husbands periodically visit

---

3. Names used in the text and figures are pseudonyms. That some first names are English and some Hawaiian reflects current practice. Hawaiians customarily have both English and Hawaiian names, the Hawaiian name usually being the first or last name of a senior relative or ancestor. Sometimes the Hawaiian name is the equivalent of an individual's English name, such as Kimo for James or Keoni for John. Either name may be used in everyday reference and address, or people may alternate, depending on the social context. The English first name tends to be used more frequently, however. The use of the Hawaiian name then becomes a conscious and deliberate act, done to emphasize someone's Hawaiian identity.

Figure 5.2
Use of Grandparent/Grandchild Terms

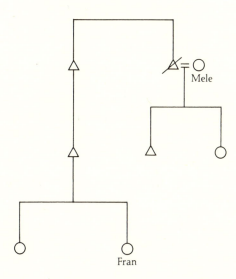

Keanae and stay with Mele. As Fran explained to me, "Actually, she's my grand-aunty, but I've called her 'grandma' for so long." Mele's children call Fran "niece," which is consistent with the generational logic of Hawaiian kinship terminology. Mele's daughter perceived that the Hawaiian usage does not make the distinctions that a Mainlander would expect: "In the family, we don't call each other 'first cousin,' 'second cousin,' or such. We say 'niece,' 'nephew,' 'uncle,' and 'aunty,' like that. That's why I say Fran is like a niece to me. She's my niece." In a similar example, an informant explained why she called someone "nephew": "He's like a nephew to me because my stepfather called his father nephew."

The modern process of pointing out relationships thus resembles *kuhikuhi* as described by Pukui (n.d.): where the precise tie cannot be specified, it is enough to teach younger relatives the term that should be used. Within the "own family," Hawaiians are capable of specifying genealogical details such as the grandma relationship described above. Common reference tends to categorize known relatives by generation, however, much like the traditional terminology. Where relative age and generation appear to conflict, generation takes precedence. An informant adopted her daughter's daughter at birth. A year later, she bore another daughter of her own. The two girls were raised together and were sent to the same schools. Although this fact might have decreed that they call each other 'sister,' they use "aunty" and "niece"; the niece is a year older than her aunty. The young women do parody the situation, however. The elder indulges her younger aunty and calls her "baby," treating her like a younger sibling. She then plays the part of niece and pleads with "uncle," her aunty's husband, for presents.

I do not intend to suggest that Hawaiians use English terms just like the traditional Hawaiian but to warn against assuming that the Mainland and Hawaiian concepts are identical merely because the same words are used. Although situational factors mediate the significance of genealogy, today lineal relatives are generally differentiated from collaterals, a departure from traditional practice. Exceptions are the *moʻopuna* and grandparent terms, which apply generationally to lineal kin, affines, and collaterals alike. For the most part, parents are distinguished from their siblings and other collaterals, and siblings from cousins.

The justification for calling someone by a term of relationship need not be genealogical. Individuals who are "kept" or *hānai*'d by the same parents use sibling terms for one another, as in this example: "Actually she's my cousin, but I call her 'sister' because the same lady who raised her raised me. She's my sister that way." Where the children are known to be unrelated, villagers may say that they are "half sisters" if they were reared together. An empirical rule of modern Hawaiian kinship terminology is that the spouse of a relative is called by a corresponding term: a niece's husband is "nephew"; aunty's husband is "uncle."

A man calls the husband of his wife's sister's granddaughter "*mo'opuna*." In this fashion, the family encompasses affines, but individually: the relatives of these affines are not considered part of the family.

Terms of relationship may be used to describe a degree of solidarity. Outside the "own family," a kinship term conveys the affective quality of a relationship more than its genealogical basis. Actual siblingship and parenthood are undeniable, but, as shown above, even first cousins may dispute their relationship. As a term of address, "mama" usually—but not always—refers to the biological or adoptive mother. "Mama" connotes great affection, a nurturing relationship, and an age disparity appropriate to parent and child. Used by a nonrelative, "mama" indicates greater closeness than "aunty." To call someone "mama" is to say: "I owe you this because of what you have done for me. You don't have to pay me back." In other words, "mama" evokes generalized reciprocity as a corollary of aloha.

Few women are addressed as "mother." Like "mama," "mother" may be used in address and casual reference by individuals who would not say, "She is my mother." One might, however, say, "She is like a mother to me." While "mama" and "aunty" are terms of affection, "mother" connotes primarily respect as well as relative age. The oldest woman in Keanae was called "Mother ———," using her surname. Of the three terms, "mama" is most often used for a specific relative, the biological or adoptive mother. As often as not, "mother" and "aunty" refer to women unrelated to the speaker. "Mother" is a more formal term, implying reserve, whereas "aunty" suggests familiarity and affection. The same person might of course be called "mama," "mother," and "aunty," but by different individuals; the choice depends on the quality of the relationship with the speaker.

The most famous modern Hawaiian kinship term—and the one having the least to do with genealogy—is "aunty." "Aunty" is used for almost any older woman: a friend of a relative, another villager, or an actual parent's sibling.

"Aunty" refers to any older woman with whom the speaker has been associated, regardless of a stipulated relationship. A woman with whom I stayed in the village was pointed out to me as "your aunty" long after I had changed residences. "Aunty" may also be applied to persons in the grandparental generation to whom one is related by distant affinal or collateral ties; the affective content of the relationship would determine the choice of "aunty" or "grandma." Commonly, "aunty" is used for women in the parental generation who are related in some way to the speaker. An informant pointed out an "aunty" of his, then explained that she was actually his "stepaunty." The woman was the daughter of his father's mother's second husband. Thus the use of "aunty" does not depend on an actual collateral relationship.

The reciprocal of "aunty" is not necessarily a kinship term. If the aunty is "not really related," she will call the individual by name. If they are related, the reciprocal may be "niece," "nephew," or "*hūnōna*" (son-in-law)—terms that describe important exchange categories. Aunty/nephew and aunty/*hūnōna* relationships are particularly likely to be active and solidary. But the terms both evoke and depend on the fulfillment of reciprocity. An informant had housed a young girl from Honolulu, but when she wanted to visit in return the girl pleaded sick. The informant refused to answer any more letters and asked indignantly, "Is that real aunty or calabash aunty?" The aunty gives her niece, nephew, and *hūnōna* the kinds of things that relatives give one another, when she has them, and they respond with valued services and gifts such as freshly caught fish. "Nephew" may refer to any related man in the child generation. For example, a woman calls her son-in-law's brother "nephew"; the young man was raised by the woman's daughter. The woman refers to the young man's wife as "niece," and both young people address her as "mama." They visit her often, help her with house repairs, and provide transportation. Less frequently, "nephew" may be used for a grandnephew; a childless woman who was leaving her land to her sister's daughter's son alternately called him "my boy" and "my nephew."

Qualitatively, the obligations of nephew and *hūnōna* are similar. In some cases, either term may be used to describe the same relationship. A niece's husband may be called either "nephew" or "*hūnōna*" (cf. Pukui and Elbert 1971:86). "*Hūnōna*" is usually reserved for the daughter's husband, although it can be used for the *hūnōna*'s brothers as well (Dorothy B. Barrère, personal communication). Besides *moʻopuna*, *hūnōna* is the only native term Keanae Hawaiians consistently use to describe a relationship. A woman's son-in-law may be more helpful to her than her own son; the ethic of the relationship is that he helps her out of affection rather than obligation. In one case a woman had no sons living on Maui, and her *hūnōna* was the mainstay of her yard maintenance.

THE HAWAIIAN MAMA CULTURE

The most active and solidary relationships among Hawaiians are between mothers and their children, aunties and their nieces and nephews, grandmothers and their grandchildren, and mothers-in-law and their *hūnōna*s. In Hawaiian relationships, solidarity is said to be invested in intergenerational and cross-sex ties (Howard 1971:47–72, 89), but the conjunction of these solidarities does not fully explain the Hawaiian mama culture. There is not the same extensive application of the term "uncle" to all older men (although this practice has become obligatory within the Hawaiian nationalist movement). The fathers of the community are not celebrated as are the mothers. The easy, joking reciprocity between niece/nephew and aunty is not as predictable or as frequent in uncle relationships. The quality of relationships between older women and their younger relatives highlights the symbolic focus on women in Hawaiian culture. The oldest woman in the village was introduced to a gathering as "the oldest mother of us all." A white-haired Hawaiian man may weep on the shoulder of his adoptive "mama." A Hawaiian senior citizens' party turns out to be a celebration of "all the mothers." And the guest of honor at a baby's first birthday luau is usually the grandmother of the family. This emphasis is indigenous to Hawaiian culture; it involves emotional ties, solidarities, mythic themes, metaphors, sentiment, and sentimentality.

Tokelau ideology makes explicit several contrasts that are present, but understated, in Hawaiian categories. The premise that women have a special power in spite of ritual subordinacy is common in Polynesia. In Tokelau, women are the "weak side," while men are the "strong side" (Huntsman and Hooper 1975:418). Yet women are also "sacred beings" who have the "power to halt conflicts between men." Women are said to have *mamana*, mystical power, while men have authority and control (ibid.:421). The corresponding Hawaiian contrast is between the concepts of *mana*, efficacy or achieved power, and *kapu*, ritual superiority and privilege. The contrast between male and female in Tokelau ideology is also one of public and domestic domains, another point of similarity with Hawaii. Women in Tokelau are symbolically associated with the land, with stability, and with "the domestic sphere of house and cookhouse, while male activity is at sea, on the outlying plantation islets of the atoll and in the public places of the village" (ibid.:418). As in Hawaii today, Tokelau women fish within the reef, while offshore fishing is restricted to men.

In Hawaii, women are the genealogical authorities, the experts in Hawaiiana. They are the practitioners of the traditional healing arts. The living authority on all things Hawaiian is a woman, Mary Kawena Pukui (cf. Pukui et al. 1972a, 1972b). In Keanae, women exercise leadership in both the Protestant and Catholic churches. Matrilocality is stated as the norm of postmarital residence in Pukui's reconstruction of the indigenous society (Handy and Pukui 1972:44). In Alan Howard's (1971:21–23) studies, matrilaterality in Hawaiian household structure is evident in the high frequency of coresidence for such relatives as mother/daughter, mother's mother/daughter's child, mother's brother/sister's child, and mother's sister/sister's child. As will be seen, the most frequently adopted relative is a daughter's child.

Various rubrics have been proposed to analyze the cultural role of women and, specifically, to explain the fact that while sexual asymmetry appears to be universal, women in many societies play a temporal role that is out of proportion to their inferior jural or ritual position. The most commonly noted contrast is between male de jure and female de facto power: men have authority, women have influence (Lamphere 1974:100; Rosaldo 1974:21). This contrast is often related to a distinction between politico-jural and domestic domains: politics and property are under the control of men, while women dominate household affairs. Polynesian ideology suggests the jural/domestic distinction: in Tokelau, "a man's life is outside and active while a woman's life is inside and largely sedentary" (Huntsman and Hooper 1975:418). There is also Hawaiian cultural precedent for such a contrast: according to Kamakau (1961:238–239), the traditional division of labor was that outside work—planting, fishing, cooking in the underground oven—was men's business, while women were occupied primarily with making mats and tapa cloth. He limits this description to the islands of Kauai, Oahu, and Molokai, however, and writes that on Maui and Hawaii, "the women worked outside as hard as the men."

But the distinction between jural and domestic domains cannot adequately explain the status of women in Hawaii: Hawaiian women, both chiefly and common, did operate traditionally in the politicojural sphere. Two chiefly women orchestrated the abolition of the *kapus* (taboos, prohibitions) and the overthrow of the Hawaiian religion in 1819, before Western missionaries had even arrived. The food restrictions and the prohibition on men and women eating together were the most onerous manifestations of women's ritual inferiority under the *kapu* system (see Dibble 1909; Malo 1951:27–30; Webb 1965). Men and women ate in separate houses, and women were enjoined from eating a variety of choice foods. The penalty for infractions was death. The *kapu*s weighed most heavily on chiefly women, for whom the prerogatives of rank clashed with the low ritual status of their sex. But where the negative implications of femaleness conflicted with the *kapu*s of rank, chiefly status won out. John Ii (1959:35) relates how three men who had eaten coconuts with chiefly women—a double infraction of the *kapu*s since coconuts were prohibited to women—were put to death, while the chiefesses went unpunished. Women were also prohibited from entering temples (*heiau*s) and religious sanctuaries, but Ii (1959:159–160) tells the story of the chiefess Keakealaniwahine, who ruled the island of Hawaii and was of such high rank that she was allowed to enter the *heiau*s but not to eat the offerings with the priests and the men.

Women in Hawaii were paramount rulers less frequently than men, but they did hold high political office. Kaahumanu, the widow of Kamehameha I, shared the rule of the kingdom as premier (*kuhina nui*) during the reign of Kamehameha II and during the early years of the reign of Kamehameha III (see Kuykendall 1938:63–65). *Kuhina* is the Hawaiianization of the English word *queen*; *kuhina nui* means big queen. This office, which conveyed administrative power equal to that of the king (ibid.:64), was held by chiefly women—Kaahumanu, Kinau, and Kekauluohi—until 1845 (ibid.:263). Kamehameha III was only eleven years old when he acceded to the throne in 1825, and the *kuhina nui* effectively ruled the kingdom even after he reached maturity (ibid.:136). At the local level, most land agents were men, but there were also female *konohiki*s who managed affairs for the chiefs. Records from the Great Mahele include cases where men acquired the *konohiki*ship through marriage to a *konohiki*'s daughter.

Land transmission to and through women was always a possibility, even before the Mahele, although transmission through males was more frequent. During the Mahele, female inheritance increased dramatically, but most of this increase resulted from widowhood and constituted temporary placeholding on behalf of the children who were destined to inherit. Women still were a minority of property owners. For the decade 1859–1869, a tally of landowners in five districts shows that women constituted from 8 to 20 percent of all taxpayers, with an erratic but gradual increase through the period (Real Property Tax Books. Originals, AH). In Hawaii, women are considered the stable figures on the land over time. In the late nineteenth century, they were the stable figures, for economic conditions fostered high short-term mobility among Hawaiian men. Among Hawaiians today, although men are still the jural favorites in land inheritance, women symbolize the family's continuity on the land: "My mother has the interest here and we own here. She lived here all her lifetime and we lived here all our lifetime after my mother. And her grandmother lived here all her lifetime" (quoted in Wenkam 1970:76). The role of women as landholders in Keanae today is discussed later in this chapter.

The stability of women on the land and their centrality in Hawaiian kinship suggest a comparison with what other scholars have called matrifocality, or matrifocal family structure. But for all the attempts to modify, revise, and expand the definition of matrifocality (most notably Gonzalez 1969; R. T. Smith 1956, 1974; Tanner 1974), the concept does not offer a complete explanation for the present-day or historical status of women in Hawaii. Most commonly, analyses of matrifocality emphasize the relative economic contributions of husband and wife (cf. Gonzalez 1969; Otterbein 1966; M. G. Smith 1962; R. T. Smith 1956). Also, although matrifocal organization is not synonymous with female-headed household organization (R. T. Smith 1974:126), it does include the aspects of female decision making, control of resources, and domestic authority. R. T. Smith defines matrifocality as a stage where "women *in their role as mothers* . . . come to be the *focus* of relationships" (ibid.:125,

emphasis in original), and he links it to a "discrepancy between ideal and possible performance of male domestic
roles." Nancy Tanner has broadened the concept of matrifocality to refer to "the *cultural elaboration and valuation,*
as well as the *structural centrality, of mother roles within a
kinship system*" (1974:154, emphasis in original).

Tanner's expanded definition is potentially more useful
for the Hawaiian case because it reflects a holistic cultural
perspective where matrifocality is not determined by the
demographic proportion or the economic role of women.
Her notion of structural centrality is also valuable, raising
the important question: who is the figure through whom
most members of the household trace their presence? Certainly Hawaiian kinship and household organization have
some attributes of matrifocality by Tanner's definition. But
even broadened in this way, the matrifocality framework
has an intrinsic limitation when applied to Hawaiian culture in that it focuses inquiry specifically on the mother's
role in society. In Hawaii, women are focal in statuses other
than that of mother. Hawaiian ideology does place a positive valuation on the mother's role, but it also puts a
positive valuation on the roles of sister and aunty. The cultural role of women in Hawaii thus involves more than the
mother's centrality.

The key to the status of Hawaiian women may perhaps
be found in Polynesian ideology: specifically, the distinction between two different kinds of power, *mana* and *kapu.*
Kapu has the dual meaning of "forbidden" and "sacred"
(Barrère 1959:180): a prohibition, but also a privilege accru-
ing to someone of high rank. "In the ancient days there
were many *kapus*," wrote Kamakau (1964:9), "and they
were in the hands of chiefs." *Mana* is efficacious or achieved
power, by which one may overcome the disability of low
rank. A common theme in Hawaiian legends is how a low-
born young man attains great power through his abilities—
and by marrying a high-ranking woman. The male/female
contrast in Hawaii is not one of different domains of influence but of different kinds of efficacy and significance.

Structurally, women in Hawaii were markers of status and points of access to rights: to rank, among the chiefs; to property, among commoners. Women are the rank-differentiating figures in chiefly genealogies, the points of segmentation between superior and subordinate lines (Marshall Sahlins, personal communication). Among the common people, women were the potential means of access to residence options and use rights in land. Settling on the land of one's affines was a traditional recourse for landless junior collaterals. For the disfranchised, it was possible to receive land from the wife's father or to attach oneself to the wife's family as a dependant. Analogous situations can be found in Keanae today, for in practice landholding is still impartible even if ownership is not. Most siblings are expected to marry out, but disfranchised younger brothers may yet gain access to land by marrying locally. In Keanae, women create the interstitial links of society by engendering the family and by serving as agents of alliance between families. In day-to-day village affairs, women are the catalysts in social relations. While the men are dispersed at their several jobs, women and children work together in the taro patches. Women visit, gossip, and carry on most interhousehold exchange. In both kinship and community life, female power is instrumental, as solidarities between men are created by women.

LAND INHERITANCE

Before the Mahele, the norm of land inheritance was that men received land from their fathers. The principle of male primogeniture guided both chiefly succession and land transmission. Ideally, care of the family's land passed to the eldest son's children. Testimony given in support of land claims during the Mahele indicates that transmission was most frequently from father to son; transmission through women was an alternate but less frequent pattern. Since the mid-nineteenth century, however, men have increasingly received land through women, thus realizing a potential inherent in the cultural role of Hawaiian women.

Undeniably, more women hold property in Keanae today than in former times; the available records indicate that land has increasingly come into the hands of women in this century. But it is debatable whether this trend is evidence of a major shift in Hawaiian norms and cultural premises. Since the Mahele, Hawaiian inheritance has been governed by law as well as custom. The inheritance laws complicate the comparison with pre-Mahele land relations because they have worked to equalize ownership between men and women. When an owner dies intestate, the court divides the property equally between the spouse and other relatives. The consistent application of the law has produced such monstrosities as the ownership of an undivided 1/35 share. This is not an isolated example but a frequent occurrence in Keanae, where a single parcel may have many owners.

Many women in the village own land only in such unusable fractional shares. Where this is not the case, the property held by women usually augments that held by men. In 1975, 53 percent of adult Hawaiians in Keanae were listed in tax records as owning or leasing land; 48 percent of the women in the village owned or leased some land. In half of the forty-three landholding households, there was a female landholder. A woman was the sole landholder in twelve, or 28 percent, of these households. But eight of these women were widows; in only four households (9 percent) was a married woman the only property holder. Seven of the nine villagers who lease land (78 percent) are men. Leased land is most often used to increase the area devoted to taro growing. The two women leasing land are married to taro farmers who hold land in their own right.

Besides the inheritance laws, differential widowhood and infrequent remarriage also tend to concentrate land in the hands of women. Nine women and six men in the village have been widowed; of these, one woman and three

Table 5.3
LAND GIVING BY RELATIVES

Donor's Relationship	Sex of Heir		Total
	Male	Female	
Mother	7	2	9
Father	12	1	13
Brother	5	0	5
Husband	—	5	5
Wife	1	—	1
"Uncle" (relationship unknown)	1	0	1
Wife's father	1	—	1
Parents	2	1	3
Wife's mother	1	—	1
Mother's brother	1	0	1
"Grandmother" (mother's mother's sister)	1	0	1
"Grandfather" (mother's mother's sister's husband)	0	1	1
Total	32 (76%)	10 (24%)	42 (100%)

men have remarried, suggesting that women tend to out-
live their husbands and that they remarry less frequently
than men. Five of the nine widows inherited land or an
interest in land from their husbands.

Conveyances between relatives provide a telling comparison with traditional principles of land succession.
Table 5.3 shows land giving by relatives according to the
donor's relationship and the recipient's sex. The totals reflect instances of land giving to current Keanae residents,
including bequests, conveyances, and cases where an individual inherited a spouse's property through joint ownership. The latter is a common legal device for ensuring the
widowed spouse's tenure-for-life; I have counted only
cases where the land originally belonged to one spouse
and a deed was executed to effect joint ownership. The
figures do not include court determinations of heirs-at-law
because these do not reflect the express wishes of Hawaiians. Keanae informants say that the oldest should inherit.

Table 5.4
SUMMARY: LAND GIVING BY RELATIVES

Source of Land	Number	Percent
Matrilateral kin	12	29
Patrilateral kin (including brother-to-brother transmission)	18	43
Parents	3	7
Wife or wife's kin	3	7
Husband	5	12
Indeterminate	1	2
Total	42	100

But instances of land giving to men outnumber bequests to women by more than three to one. Excluding cases of inheritance through survivorship, the ratio is more than six to one.

If we look at who gives the land rather than at who inherits it, we see that the largest single category is from father to son, but the number of conveyances from mother to child is nearly as large; this category includes cases where a widow conveyed land inherited from her husband. As shown in Table 5.4, land giving from matrilateral relatives constitutes 29 percent of the total, with 43 percent from patrilateral kin.

Although women do inherit land more frequently than in the past (and therefore have more land to give than they traditionally did), transmission to women does not have the effect of taking land out of the family. In most cases, the property descends to the child or grandchild who would normally stand to inherit. Figure 5.3 summarizes in rough schematic form the numbers presented in Table 5.3. The cumulative effect of these bequests is to concentrate land in the patriline. Significantly, although there are five cases of brother/brother transmission, there are none from brother to sister. A wholesale transformation of the traditional inheritance pattern has not occurred. The trend toward matrilateral inheritance since the Great

Figure 5.3
Land Giving by Relatives, Summarized

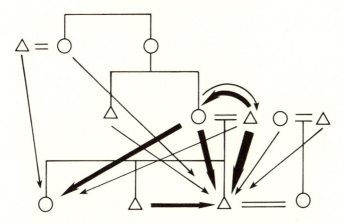

Mahele has not been inexorable. Where women do hold land, they convey it to men and most often to their sons. There is less emphasis on transmission specifically through males than on succession by the *mo'opuna* generation. The jural favorite is still the eldest son, for his son.

In one case, land was earmarked for a sister's daughter's son rather than an adopted son. Figure 5.4 clarifies the relationship of the parties. Flora bequeathed her land, reserving a life interest, to Matt, to the exclusion of her "kept" son Jimmy. This bequest accords with the principle of primogeniture, for the offspring of the first marriage would be senior to the children of subsequent unions. The "oldest" in this case is an older sister, however; land has been given to a male descended in a senior line through women. Male landholding is preserved but through matrilineal ties.

Where the norms of primogeniture and male property holding conflict, bitter disputes between siblings may result. In one family, the parents conveyed their land in Keanae to the oldest child, a daughter. The mother and a younger son continued to occupy the Keanae homestead

Figure 5.4
Land Giving to a "Grandchild"

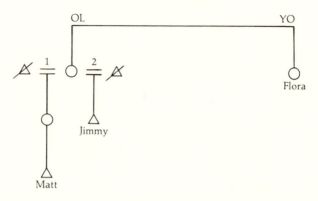

after the father died and other siblings moved outside. Relations between the landowner and her younger brother are hostile; the young man refuses to work the family's taro patches, even though he hires out to another Keanae grower. His grudge is based on the feeling that his sister should divide the land and give him half. Sibling rivalry over property is more traditionally associated with brothers, the historic competitors for land and power. The resentment of a disfranchised junior sibling here taints the relationship of brother and sister, which is usually very solidary among Hawaiians. A contrasting example is that of a Keanae man, heir to the family lands, who partitioned off small parcels and gave equal plots to his two sisters. In the opinion of other villagers, this was a gracious and proper thing to do, although not at all required. In characteristic Hawaiian fashion, the sisters then gave their parcels to their offspring, one to a daughter and the other to a son.

SIBLING BIRTH ORDER

Within the same generation, relatives of the same sex were traditionally ranked by relative age as reflected in the terms *kaikua'ana* and *kaikaina*, which referred to older and younger siblings or collaterals of the same sex. Interestingly, cross-sex sibling terms do not embody ranking by relative age; *kaikunane* means brother, female speaking, and *kaikuahine* means sister, male speaking (see Table 5.2); the brother/sister tie has been historically an active and affectionate relationship among Hawaiians. The Hawaiian sibling terms are rarely heard in Keanae today, but there is still a sensitivity to the relative age of same-sex siblings if not of cousins. In common reference, "the oldest" often means the oldest of one sex, as in "She's the oldest . . . oldest of the girls" and "He's the oldest of the boys." Informants disagree about whether an older sibling of the same sex should be addressed with reserve. One said that she jokingly called her older sister "old lady." Another said that in her family the younger siblings never joked in such fashion but addressed an elder sibling only as "sister."

The behavioral expectations of older and younger siblings were well defined among Hawaiians and are much in evidence today (Howard et al. 1970:37). Older siblings are expected to care for the younger, who are obliged to work for their seniors when requested. Among the Hawaiians of Nanakuli, as Howard (1971:91–95) has noted, junior relatives of the same sex are particularly likely to be recruited to assist at a luau, with younger brothers "especially targeted." In Keanae too, younger siblings, and particularly younger brothers, form the mainstay of luau labor, although not always willingly. Within the sibling set, the statuses of oldest and youngest are unique and have distinctive attributes. The oldest's descendants will inherit the family property; the youngest is the last to leave the parental home and is likely to become the "pet," the sentimental favorite of the family. The Hawaiian terms for these categories are *kua'ana* and *pōki'i*.

As is characteristic of Hawaiian kinship categories, however, the appellation may be given without regard to actual birth order. Categorization may follow from fulfilling the role of *kua'ana* or *pōki'i*: "Sometimes the actual older brother or sister is considered later as a 'younger' if the younger exceeds him in adult life" (Pukui n.d.). Although acknowledged as the genealogical younger, such an individual may be called the *kua'ana* in the family. A nineteenth-century Hawaiian story (Kanepuu 1867:14–15) tells how a younger brother became the "older brother and master (*kaikua'ana haku*)" through the prophecy of his grandmother, a seer, and by virtue of his achievements:

> We have just seen earlier that Niheu was the older brother and Kana was the younger (*he mua kaikua'ana o* Niheu . . . *he muli hope o* Kana) and how through Uli (their grandmother, a reader of omens), Kana herewith becomes the older brother and master from that time on until now. For the people who seek and obtain great wealth, they are the older brothers (*kaikua'ana*), and those who get nothing are the younger ones (*pōki'i*). Meanwhile Uli knew that Kana would be the worthy one later on.

Mary Pukui, although not a descendant of the senior line, had "a *kaikua'ana* status in actual practice" because she was her grandmother's chosen favorite, or *punahele*; she was, however, older in years than her genealogical seniors and was an adopted sister in their family (Pukui n.d.). As her grandmother's favorite, she had a privileged position in the family that belied her genealogical status as junior collateral.

Hawaiians feel that the youngest child should stay at home and care for the aging parents, while older siblings leave and set up their own households. Traditionally the "baby" in the family is indulged and is not expected to shoulder any responsibilities. The youngest may be treated like a child well into adulthood. *Pōki'i* are represented in two Keanae households, but neither is actually the youngest. Both individuals are in their twenties and are next-to-youngest in actual birth order; each has a younger sibling who has married and left home. Both are *pōki'i*, however, by virtue of their social immaturity. The young adults who have remained with their parents in Keanae have social handicaps of one sort or another and are not considered marriageable. One young man living with his aged mother is known locally as a liar and a thief, but he is "the baby" in his mother's eyes. Although favored in sentiment, the *pōki'i* is the jural inferior and does not usually stand to inherit property through the family.

THE LUAU

The attributes of Hawaiian relationships, hitherto described in abstract terms, find concrete expression in the luau. Categorical expectations materialize in exchanges of luau work and food. Long-established forms of mutual aid come into play as the household giving the luau depends on normative reciprocities and enlists relatives to provide raw materials and workers. From the village, friends of the family may also be recruited as workers in the knowledge that they will be well rewarded afterward with high foods. The etymology of the word luau supports the event's fundamental association with food. The gloss of "feast" is a recent use of the word, which literally means the leaves of the taro plant. Andrews (1865:351) also gives a figurative meaning: "a parent; one to whom a child can resort for food." The focus of a luau is indeed the accumulation, preparation, and distribution of large quantities of food. The luau is made possible by the assistance and cooperation of a network of kin and friends. Several days in advance, relatives arrive from other islands and even from the Mainland to assist in the preparations. Friends come from other parts of the island to work for one or two days during the week before the feast.

The family is the center of the luau: a sibling set, their children and grandchildren, and those married to them come from far and wide to make and attend the luau. If grandma is alive, she will be the most honored guest. The luau has tremendous social and symbolic importance for Hawaiians. No other event brings together the dispersed members of a Hawaiian family. By reuniting relatives, the luau reaffirms the family's solidarity and awakens long-dormant relationships.

The luau celebrates relatedness and the ideal of aloha. Luaus are held to mark weddings, anniversaries, and birthdays. Often the occasion is a milestone for a woman in the family. Hawaiians sometimes marry on the bride's birthday; now and in the future the luau will celebrate both occasions. In one case, the wedding coincided with the first birthday of the bride's daughter. When a luau celebrates a birthday, it is grandma's birthday or baby's first birthday, and baby is usually a daughter's daughter. Again one sees the Hawaiian emphasis on relationships through women and on solidarities created by women. Although men participate in the preparations as actively as women, the pretext for calling together the entire family is frequently a celebration of mothers and daughters.

Luaus vary in emphasis and magnitude, however. A son's wedding is a luau occasion as well as a daughter's and is less of a tribute to mom and grandmom. Wedding luaus are likely to be elaborate and well publicized and to draw guests from a wider area than a small family luau; workers are also recruited from a broader network of relatives. Birthday luaus are more private affairs and do not require as many workers. Often they can be recruited from within the family, without calling on nonrelatives for assistance.

Work at a luau is exchanged for food. The workers are well fed during the preparations and are given the leftover food and liquor after the event. The most popular food used to compensate workers is *laulau*s, steamed bundles of greens and either pork or beef, wrapped in *ti* leaves. At one Keanae luau, the host planned to make two thousand *laulau*s for a feast at which perhaps 400 guests were expected (and which about 125 actually attended). The *laulau*s were quite generous, each containing a few large chunks of beef; a relative had donated three cows for the occasion. Given the rest of the food that would be served, a hungry guest might be able to finish two *laulau*s. With an ethnographer's ignorance, I asked why they were making such a vast number. The answer was "Well, they have to feed the workers too." *Laulau*s are ideal for compensating workers because they are prepackaged. It is simple to measure quantity; the host counts out a specific number for each person. The hardest worker receives the most *laulaus*.

Luau foods and work are the highest commodities exchanged among Hawaiians, for historically the luau can be traced to feasts dedicated to the gods. With minor variations, the standard fare at a luau consists of the foods listed in Table 5.5. Most of these derive from traditional ceremonial items and are descended from the ritual goods of the native Hawaiian religion. In descriptions of rituals (Kamakau 1964, Malo 1951), pork is the highest ceremonial food and is second in value only to human sacrifice as an offering to the gods. Chicken, fish, and dog were secondary flesh offerings. Bananas, coconuts, and *'awa* also figured prominently as ceremonial offerings. Red was the high color: the color of the *kūmū*, the fish most often used in sacrifice; the color of the *'i'iwi* bird, whose feathers adorned the chiefs' cloaks and helmets. Before the abolition of the Hawaiian religion, pork, bananas, coconuts, the *kūmū* fish, and "certain dark and pink pois" were among the *kapu* foods forbidden to women (Kamakau 1964:64).

Table 5.6 lists some of the occasions on which sacrifices were presented to the gods. Not all rites are represented here, but a sampling of major and minor ceremonies illustrates the set of high goods from which offerings were drawn. The point is simply that the high foods that weight today's luau tables are drawn from the same set of ritually high commodities. The pork, sweet potatoes, and *kūlolo* are *kālua'*d, baked in an underground oven that is constructed by men. The lomi-lomi salmon is bright red, both from the flesh of the fish and from the tomatoes with which it is mixed, a substitute, perhaps, for the red *kūmū* fish. The value of these high foods derives from their former ritual status. Even though in many rites the prestations were *mōhai 'ai*, to be eaten by the celebrants (Kamakau 1964:77), presenting food constituted a gift to the gods. Consumption was itself an offering.

Hawaiians fed the chiefs as they fed their gods. Malo

Table 5.5
THE STANDARD LUAU MENU

Item	Description
Kālua pig	Whole pig baked in the *imu*
Laulaus	Steamed bundles of greens with pork or beef, wrapped in *ti* leaves
Chicken luau	Chicken cooked in coconut milk with taro leaves
or	
Chicken long rice	Chicken with gelatinous noodles
Lomi-lomi salmon	Salted salmon rubbed between the fingers with green onions, ice, and tomatoes
Kūlolo	Taro-coconut cream pudding, baked in the *imu*
'Opihi	Sea limpets, served raw, sometimes with seaweed
Haupia	Jelled coconut pudding, served cold
Poi	Taro paste
Sweet potatoes	
Rice	

(1951:189) writes that if a large fish should be washed ashore, it was "to be offered to the gods (i.e., it was to be given to the priests for the use of the king)." In the annual Makahiki rites, each land section provided tribute to the chiefs. The local *konohiki* presented the taxes as offerings to the god when the Makahiki idol made its circuit around the island. Foods prepared for the coming of the god included *kūlolo*, breadfruit pudding, poi, bananas, fish, and *'awa* (ibid.:143). A Hawaiian proverb states that "a chief is a shark that travels on land." Kamakau (1964:76–77) describes a rite of transfiguration where the shark is fed the same goods that Hawaiians offered to the chiefs. For protection at sea, Hawaiians sometimes changed a dead relative into a shark guardian god, or *'aumakua*. A pig, tapa cloth, and *'awa* were brought to the *kahu manō*, keeper of the shark, as sacrifices to the god for changing the body into a shark. The ceremony involved pouring the *'awa*, pig, bananas, and other offerings into the shark's mouth. The

Table 5.6
CEREMONIAL OFFERINGS IN ANCIENT
HAWAIIAN RITES

Occasion	Offerings (mōhai)
A child's weaning	Kālua pig, bananas, coconuts, 'awa (Malo 1951:87–88)
Rites of vengeance for a death by sorcery	Chickens, dogs (ibid.:103)
Cutting of koa wood for a canoe	Kālua pig, coconuts, kūmū fish, 'awa (ibid.:127)
Atonement ceremony	Pigs, 'awa, tapa, kūmū fish (Kamakau 1964:13)
Propitiating the 'aumākua (guardian gods)	Bananas, pigs, coconuts, red fishes, tapa, 'awa (ibid.:97)
Propitiating the fishing gods	Pigs, white chickens, coconuts, potatoes, bananas, poi (Malo 1951:157–158, 209)
Tribute for the Makahiki god	Yellow and red feathers from the 'o'o, mamo, and 'i'iwi birds, pigs, tapa, hard poi (ibid.:145)
Feeding the Makahiki god	Kūlolo, arrowroot, bananas, breadfruit pudding, coconuts, fish, 'awa (ibid.:143, 145)
End of Makahiki	Kālua pig, kūlolo (ibid.:150)
Dismantling of Makahiki idols	Taro, potatoes, bananas, pork, breadfruit, coconuts (ibid.:151)

celebrants also prepared 'awa and kālua pig for themselves to eat, and, after the offering, they threw the remainder into the sea. The luau descends from ceremonial feasts such as these; luau foods are high in the Hawaiian symbolic scheme because they were once offered to gods and chiefs.

MAKING A LUAU

The necessity for luau labor cannot be projected from the activities alone without considering the Hawaiian style of making a luau. Doing things in the most efficient manner from a haole point of view is not the goal when making a luau. Certain tasks must be accomplished, and they almost always are, albeit with some last-minute scurrying in the kitchen or banquet hall. Luau preparations resemble orchestrated chaos. To amend a saying for the Hawaiian context, there are too many Indians and no chiefs. Characteristically, no individual stands out as the director of operations. Responsibilities are allocated by consensus rather than command. Since luau fare is more or less standardized, all the workers know what must be done. The host household establishes the exact menu and sees to the raw materials, and the activities follow. Major jobs such as making *laulau*s and *kūlolo* are communal, with many workers participating. Individuals volunteer for smaller tasks such as making *haupia*, a gelatinous coconut pudding.

Preparing for the feast is only part of the effort; a major job is keeping the workers well fed during their labors. Tying *laulau*s, for example, begins before dawn to avoid the flies; work and the partying afterward may continue until the early morning hours. Full meals are usually served at lunch and dinner, with poi, rice, vegetables, and hot dishes. All this food must be prepared, tables cleared and set, and everything cleaned up afterward. Ample stores of soft drinks and beer must also be kept on hand. In addition, on the day of the luau, workers and family pick flowers, clean and decorate the hall, and set the banquet tables. (Birthday luaus are often held in a garage, larger and more formal events such as wedding and anniversary luaus in a church hall or rented facility.) Young nieces, nephews, and grandchildren are recruited to serve and clear tables. The aunties who have helped to prepare the food stand guard over it during the feast and dole out portions.

Although most workers are from the family, all is not peace and aloha during the preparations. Along with the jokes, there are disputes and bickering. Parents and children, older and younger siblings may argue over the coordination of tasks. Recriminations fly when a job is not done or food is allowed to spoil. Panic sets in when there are not enough cracker tins to hold the *kūlolo* during baking. An argument begins over the best way to construct the underground oven. Although eager to offer advice, workers have their individual *kuleana*s and take no responsibility for the mistakes of others: "That's not my *kuleana*. The chicken is my *kuleana*, and as long as that's done, okay."[4] Because Hawaiians say that it is a bad thing for people to argue when they are working together, good-natured patter and bawdy jests help to preserve a spirit of fun and sociability during the activities. In general, amity prevails as long as everyone participates freely in the work. No one is more roundly criticized than someone who hangs back and does not do his or her share of the labor. A few detailed examples of luaus will substantiate the Hawaiian ideas of aloha, family, and relatives as they have been presented here. In the luau, abstract obligations are realized as work; solidarity is translated into the offer of service and the distribution of food. Younger siblings are frequently enlisted as workers; nieces and nephews further enlarge the pool of potential helpers.

A Keanae man and his sisters made the luau for his niece's wedding, which coincided with her baby's first birthday. Figure 5.5. diagrams the relationships of the important parties. The girl (Kiele) was marrying a boy in Hilo. "The bride's folks" were supplying the pig and the *kūlolo*, as well as other delicacies from the country. The bride's mother, Akuna, and her siblings, Billy and Vickie, coordinated preparations for the luau. The relationship between Billy and his sister Akuna is especially close. Her children often visit their cousins in Keanae, and the young people in Billy's household spend much time at their

---

4. *Kuleana* has come to mean a land claim, but other glosses are "portion, responsibility, jurisdiction, authority, interest, claim, ownership" (Pukui and Elbert 1971:165). Hawaiians use *kuleana* to denote a particular task for which they are responsible.

aunty's home in Wailuku. Billy supplied the taro for the *kūlolo*. Vickie and her three daughters grated the coconut, and the pudding was *kālua*'d at her house. Akuna's "niece," Lizzie, spent most of the week before the luau at Akuna's house to assist in the preparations there. In all, the households of Billy and Vickie contributed *kūlolo*, *'ōpae* (freshwater shrimp), *'opihi*, watercress, two bags of taro, poi, and the pig, which was taken on the plane and *kālua*'d in Hilo. Although twenty-six cans of *kūlolo* were baked, only four went to Hilo. One can went to Billy's household and one to Vickie's. Six were saved for another upcoming luau: the wedding anniversary of an elderly Keanae couple, the parents of Vickie's son-in-law, Naida's husband. The remaining fourteen cans were distributed to the workers.

Akuna, her siblings, and the bride's siblings flew to Hilo for the event, along with Pearl and Lizzie. Some stayed with one of Pearl's sons, who lived in Hilo and knew the groom. Interestingly, Leo and his father did not attend the luau. Although Pearl is an affine to Akuna's family because of her relationship with Billy, her legal husband, Henry, is not part of this family and had no place in the festivities. Even though Lizzie went readily, her brother Leo was said to be "too proud" to attend, perhaps out of loyalty to his father.

On the way back from Hilo, Billy's nephew and namesake, Young Bill, stopped in Keanae with his mother and sister Kahale. In the course of the visit, he helped pull taro for his uncle. Billy's household was again mobilized as Akuna prepared a hundred *laulau*s to send home with her son. Once again there were the tasks of gathering *ti* leaves and cleaning taro greens. When Aunty Akuna and the cousins left Keanae, they took several taros, a bag of frozen fish, breadfruit, and a stalk of cooking bananas, as well as "nephew" Leo.

The most striking theme in this description is the relationship of brother and sister: not only of Billy and Akuna but also of Kahale and Young Bill. This bond is often more solidary than that between husband and wife. Between

Figure 5.5
"The Bride's Folks," Showing Places of Residence

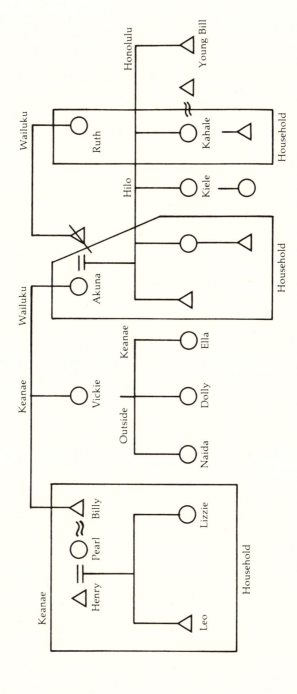

Billy and Akuna, there is unrestrained giving and open affection, more so than between the sisters Vickie and Akuna. In this case, the youngest sibling, Akuna, was the person to solicit her family's help. Unquestionably, the sibling set of Billy, Akuna, and Vickie was the center of the luau, at least from the viewpoint of "the bride's folks." The bride's siblings were also important guests, and the brother and sister, Kahale and Young Bill, were constant companions until the latter returned to Honolulu.

Relationships of and through women are also notable here. With the exception of Billy, who provided materials more than work, the people who made the luau were women: mothers and daughters, aunties and nieces. The bride's other aunty, Ruth, is closer to Akuna than a sister; as affines they escape the possible tension between senior and junior siblings. Her "niece" Kahale and classificatory *mo'opuna* reside with her. As sister-in-law and "family to" Akuna, Ruth has been assimilated into this family; she visits Billy's household freely as Akuna's "partner."

An obvious advantage of having a big family is that one can make a luau without recruiting nonrelatives as workers and without becoming indebted to neighbors. The personnel represented in Figure 5.5 would be adequate to prepare a small, family luau. In this example, the bride's family was not responsible for the entire wedding; hence the work force was sufficient.

The most elaborate luau I attended was for the wedding of a young Keanae man. His father predicted four hundred guests, and since "the worst thing is to give a luau and not have enough," a great quantity of food had to be prepared. The mother's side was responsible for making this luau. As shown in Figure 5.6, this meant primarily the mother's sisters and persons recruited through them. Here again, the stress is on solidarities among women. Hawaiians tend to associate daughters with their mother's family. Through her identification with the mother's side, the groom's sister was said to be "doing" the luau; she herself did little work, but her husband was the hardest worker of all. Figure 5.6

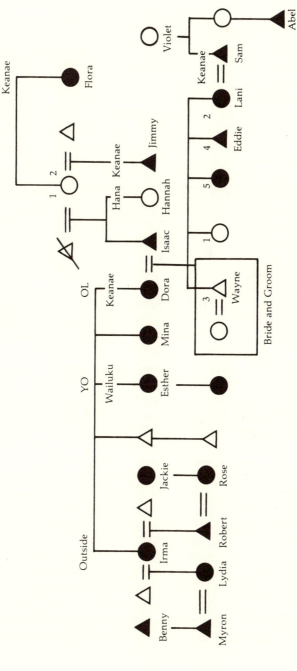

Figure 5.6
Workers and Family in a Wedding Luau

Note: Shaded figures denote luau workers.

diagrams the relationships of the groom's family and the luau workers. Unrelated workers included a few college friends of the groom's younger brother and three women neighbors.

The mother's side was represented by the mother's sisters, nephews, and nieces. Several workers were recruited through Irma: her son-in-law (Myron), his father (Benny), her daughter-in-law (Rose), and her daughter-in-law's mother (Jackie). Relations between Irma, Rose, and Jackie were affectionate; Irma fondly called Rose "my girl," and Jackie had flown in from Denver to help make the luau. As stated earlier, a nephew's spouse is referred to as "niece." Although a niece's husband may be either "nephew" or "*hūnōna*," Keanae Hawaiians commonly use "nephew," reserving "*hūnōna*" for a daughter's husband. Accordingly, Myron was the "nephew" of "aunty" Dora, and Rose was her "niece." Logically, Benny and Jackie thus stand in a sibling-like relationship to Irma and her sisters. The marriage of children does not guarantee that their parents will henceforth behave like brothers and sisters, but it does create the potential for a solid and close relationship, like that between Irma and Jackie. These women were closer to one another than most genealogical sisters because their relationship was free of the potential strain between older and younger same-sex siblings.

In general, the senior men in the family—here the groom's father and mother's brother—provide raw materials for the luau, while nieces, nephew, *hūnōna*s, younger brothers, and women supply the work. The groom's mother's brother did not work for the luau, but he did donate the pigs and *aku* (tuna) for sashimi (the Japanese word has been adopted for raw fish dishes). His son, a minister, presided at the marriage ceremony. The groom's brother-in-law (Sam), younger brother (Eddie), and father's younger brother (Jimmy) were the most energetic male workers, Sam most of all, Eddie less so and somewhat reluctantly. The groom's father, Isaac, had three cattle slaughtered for the *laulau*s and bore most of the financial burden of feeding the workers. One daughter's father-in-law, manager of a supermarket, donated vegetables. Another relative gave the salted salmon for lomi-lomi salmon. The taro for the *kūlolo* and the poi came from Isaac's patches.

The following description of this luau exemplifies the qualities of Hawaiian relationships and illustrates the exchanges of food and work at a luau. The narrative describes activities during the three days prior to the luau and on the day of the event.

THREE DAYS BEFORE

In the morning, Eddie and his friends husked coconut for the *kūlolo*. Sam and a female neighbor grated taro, she with a hand grater, he on a grinding machine. When the taro was done, the groom's Aunty Flora, Esther, Sam, and the neighbor switched to grating coconut, the women using hand graters, he using the machine. While Sam prepared the *imu*, Eddie and his friends stripped and washed *ti* leaves. Esther, Dora, and the neighbor mixed the *kūlolo*. Raw taro can cause a skin irritation, and the women complained that it made their arms itchy. Reluctantly, Eddie was enlisted to help mix. Informants said that men formerly made the *kūlolo*, except for the coconut grating. Aunty Flora used *ti* leaves to line the cracker tins for the *kūlolo*. The women argued over the sweetness of the mixture. Finally, Eddie and his friends placed several tins of *kūlolo* in the underground oven, then went to gather banana leaves for burning. The groom had constructed the *imu*. Sam criticized him for doing a bad job. There was a further mix-up over a delivery of beer, and the groom was scolded again by his father.

After lunch, Flora, Esther, and Irma continued washing *ti* leaves for the *laulaus*. The groom's father and younger brother went to catch *'opihi*; Dora made bags for them out of rice sacks. Later Aunty Flora, Eddie, Sam, and Eddie's friends went to Flora's house to collect more *ti* leaves. With two leaves each, the planned two thousand *laulaus* required four thousand *ti* leaves, stripped and washed. The groom's mother and one of her sisters were in charge of meals; Flora complained of the "same old stew" and told Isaac that his "in-laws only good for cook." A close bond seemed to exist betwen Eddie and Sam, the groom's younger brother and the groom's sister's husband; they went off alone to an upland stream after dark to catch *'ōpae*, which Flora, Dora, and Mina cleaned. After dinner, the women stayed up to sing bawdy songs, play the ukulele, and dance the hula.

TWO DAYS BEFORE

Flora and two female neighbors went to Sam's house to peel and clean the taro for poi. Isaac had sent four bags because his own machine was broken. Sam boiled the corms while the ladies washed. Flora and the neighbors adjourned to Dora's house to wash taro there with Mina and Esther. Eddie and his friends pulled taro for Isaac's market order. The *kūlolo* was ready by afternoon, after baking overnight, and the *imu* was opened. There was much discussion over the number of cans and whether the pudding was overdone. Esther, Flora, Myron, Lydia, Benny, and the neighbors cut the vegetables and fish for lomi-lomi salmon.

ONE DAY BEFORE

Most of the workers rose before dawn for the biggest job of the luau: making two thousand *laulaus*. The groom's father ferried two loads of meat from the slaughterhouse. The work party included the mother's side in full force, with Aunty Flora and a neighbor. There were many jokes about suitable marriage partners and the suggestion of a double wedding with Benny and Flora. While the *laulaus* were boiling, Robert, Jimmy, and Sam butchered the pigs. Flora and Robert took the entrails upstream to be washed for *loko*, a dish favored by older Hawaiians but shunned by most of the young people.

THE DAY OF THE LUAU

A neighbor and the groom's sister Lani made breadfruit salad, while Flora and another sister picked flowers for leis from a neighbor's yard. Esther made the *haupia*. There was much discussion about the hall decorations and some criticism of the bride's party by the Keanae people for setting the tables "haole style, not Hawaiian style." Lani and the groom's aunties rearranged the settings and decorated the hall with flowers and miniature *kahilis*, models of the red and yellow feather standards carried before Hawaiian chiefs. The banquet tables were set with paper dishes in a tapa-cloth pattern—standard luau table service; one reason for using paper is that it is easier for the guests to take away leftovers, as they are expected to. A special dish made of *kukui* nut and whitefish was not put out for the general feast but saved for the family. Aunty Flora carried off salmon, raw fish, *'opihi*, and taro leaves for her freezer even before the luau began.

THE EVENT

Isaac came to church bearing a *"mo'opuna"* on his shoulders; the child was actually his wife's grandnephew. The groom and his men wore "traditional" Hawaiian wedding garb: white open-necked shirt, white slacks, red cummerbund, leis of fragrant maile and the orange ilima flower. Despite their close relationship to the groom, Sam and Flora did not go to church for the wedding; they were too busy working in the kitchen.

At the time, I was surprised that many Keanae people did not attend. Those who worked to make the luau did, of course; yet most of the colorfully dressed guests were outsiders—people I never saw again and was never able to identify. Even late in the day, motorists from Hana and from communities outside were stopping and asking local people on the road for directions to the luau, although not all of them were sure of the host's name. Long afterward, I began to understand why it is sometimes easier to attend a stranger's luau than a neighbor's, and why Keanae Hawaiians may be loath to attend a village luau unless they helped to prepare it. The reasons for this reluctance will be discussed further in the following chapter.

After the wedding ceremony, the guests drifted into the banquet hall and the liquor tent, which was kept separate out of deference to the church. The patrons at the liquor tent were for the most part men, with some women guests from outside. Most Keanae women refrain from drinking alcoholic beverages in public, although there is no such reluctance on the part of their menfolk. The groom's aunties manned the serving table and Lani the guest table. Sam seemed to feel personally responsible for keeping everything running smoothly; he and his nephew Abel kept the food table stocked and cleared place settings as people finished eating. The other workers frequently commented on his diligence. At a buffet-style luau, the lowest-status guests eat first; people hang back waiting for someone to be first through the line. At this event, children were pressed forward to head the queue. One of the last to go through the line was one of the oldest residents in Keanae, the elderly Mother Violet. A place of honor was reserved for her, but she ate only a little poi at the feast.

Isaac, a master of the Hawaiian slack-key guitar, and his sister Hannah sang while Esther acted as mistress of ceremonies. The bride's father and one of her aunties also sang, prompting derisive comments from the groom's relatives who were working in the kitchen. When most of the guests had eaten, Sam was the first to move the benches and clear the floor for dancing. He complained that the people from Hana had come late, when the food was almost gone. The guests at a luau are expected to carry off "the balance," and many left with paper plates filled with cake, *haupia*, and *laulau*s. The bride and groom danced, and some guests put money in the bride's mouth. The Keanae people commented that this was a "Filipino custom, not a Hawaiian custom," and noted that Esther's husband was Filipino. The guests continued socializing in the churchyard, and by sundown the liquor tent was drawing a large crowd. Cars were still leaving at ten that night—not a late luau, the Keanae people commented.

According to Isaac, the groom's family had planned for a thousand guests. At the event, Aunty Flora estimated that perhaps 400 had come; Isaac later acknowledged that about 125 had attended.

AFTERMATH

Immediately after the event, the luau workers took away some of each dish. The greatest number of *laulau*s, one hundred, went to the groom's brother-in-law Sam; the next day Sam gave thirty to his sister, also a Keanae resident, who had not assisted at the luau. All the other workers received fifteen *laulau*s each. The bride's guests were given ten each, boxed, to take home with them on the plane. Aunty Flora carried away several loads of food and stored them in her freezer—this in addition to what she had taken on the morning of the event. The father's younger brother Jimmy received cake and *laulau*s for his wife and children but soon after gave most of the *laulau*s to his taro agent during a drinking bout. *Laulau*s were also given to Mother Violet, spiritual leader of the church, who had given her permission for the use of the hall and grounds.

THE STRUCTURE OF SENTIMENT

As is evident from this description of a luau, it is difficult to discuss relatives without also speaking of affines. Relations between in-laws sometimes prove to be more solidary than those between blood relatives. Yet this is not a paradox because the degree of relatedness does not necessarily determine the affective quality of the tie. Some affines maintain more active reciprocities than "own, true" relatives. The difference between relatives and in-laws thus does not lie in the content of particular relationships. Rather, these categories differ in their initial expectations, in the starting premises of exchange, and in how persons are recruited to the categories. A known tie of relatedness defines an ideal: the potential for aloha, mutual aid, and solidarity. A kinship category is in part a set of expectations: the affection of brother and sister, the obligations of a child to a parent. The potential may or may not be realized in any particular case.

Among Hawaiians, genealogical facts are relative; they depend on the prevailing state of reciprocities. Individuals may deny a relationship when the tie has no substance in practice, thus emphasizing that communication and the exchange of commodities have ceased. In the Hawaiian scheme of relationships, persons may be recruited to kinship categories if they fulfill the expectations of a relative. Neighbors are called relatives if they participate unstintingly in exchange, without regard to the net balance and without using the gift to create indebtedness. In similar fashion, putative ties are transformed into collaterality. Long-time friends are called cousins; since they came from the same place, the possibility of the relationship is enough evidence, without specific genealogical links. For Hawaiians, the distinction between true and classificatory, fictive, or "called" relatives becomes significant primarily in the contexts of marriageability and land inheritance.

Certain Hawaiian cultural premises about kinship roles have not changed significantly since pre-Mahele times. Elder sons are still favored in property inheritance, although the number of male and female landowners in Keanae today is nearly equal. Some women do acquire land in their own right, and the proportion of female heirs has increased since the Mahele through widowhood, the legal division of estates, and placeholding on behalf of one's children. But in most cases women hold the land for a time and eventually convey it to men. Men still receive land from their fathers, but often they do so through their mothers. A woman is expected to reside on her husband's land, and this norm is realized to a high degree in practice.

But there is also a significant alternate pattern of relationships, which runs counter to this patrilineal bias in matters of property and authority. Among Hawaiians, normatively weighty relationships tend to have a formal and strained quality, while ties that are based on voluntary contacts and spontaneous affection are more solidary. Same-sex ties are the traditional inheritance relationships: property from father to son, esoteric knowledge and family lore from mother to daughter. These ties may become clouded by disagreements over property and authority. Frequently, parents' relations with their younger children are more affectionate than with their older children. The relationship between aunty and her nephew or *hūnōna* is often more active and openly affectionate than that between mother and son or father and daughter. The aunty/nephew and aunty/*hūnōna* relationships illustrate the solidarity of intergenerational and cross-sex ties among Hawaiians.

Ideally, a one-way flow of goods and services is expected between parent and child; it merely reverses over time, first from parent to child and later from child to aging parent. The metaphor of feeding symbolizes the quality of the relationship. Andrews (1865:351) cites an early figurative meaning for luau: "a parent; one to whom a child can resort for food; probably so called because a parent is one to whom a child can resort for his food." In practice, relations between parents and adult children are more variable than the ideal suggests (cf. Handy and Pukui 1972:174–175). Figures on coresidence support the relative solidarity of the cross-sex tie. In four households, mother/son and father/daughter reside together. In three other cases, parents live together with an adult son. There are no instances of mother/daughter coresidence, however, and no cases where father and son live together without the mother.

Adult children are expected to provide for their parents (Howard 1971:90). In Keanae, taro-growing sons supply their widowed mothers with poi and maintain their houses but not always without complaint. Underlying the ethic of aloha is a felt obligation that sometimes provokes resentment, the sense that one has to provide food and services for a parent. Although the parent/child tie is one that "cannot be denied," there are many cases of strained relationships. Solidarity is more predictable between grandparent and grandchild than between parent and adult child. An informant admitted that he rarely visited his mother except to bring her high foods: "I don't go to see my mother much except when I have *kālua* pig, *laulaus*, or something like that. They know I'm coming when they smell food." Therein lies the qualitative difference between the parent and aunty relationships. In a world of potential aunties, the nephew/*hūnōna* role is more freely entered into and thus is likely to be more affectionate.

The affection between aunty and nephew and between mother-in-law and *hūnōna* is the complement to patriliny in land transmission. These cross-sex, nonlineal ties are the inverse of the normative property relationships. Where land giving does not follow patrilineal succession or where it violates impartible inheritance, the justification lies in just such emotional attachments. The structural alternatives are the sentimental favorites. A mother-in-law's affection for her daughter's husband and his reciprocal attentions provide the pretext for uxorilocality and giving land to a son-in-law—an option described in Hawaiian legends and substantiated by commoners testifying in the Mahele. Similarly, the *pōki'i* may live with doting parents well into adulthood. A "kept" child may receive a small parcel of land from an adoptive parent, either out of aloha or in appreciation for services rendered. Jural norms provide for elder brothers; younger brothers are provided for in sentiment: as *pōki'i*, *hūnōna*, and the adopted children of other families. These sentimental favorites are alternative roles for the disfranchised siblings in the Hawaiian family.

The role of sentimental favorites in Hawaiian social organization is intrinsically linked to the cultural role of Hawaiian women. Against the jural—and, in former times, ritual—inferiority of women stands an opposing emphasis: a symbolic and emotional complex that accords to women a far greater say in events than might be predicted from their formal status. Many Hawaiian women dominate their households by force of personality. Relationships to and through women are sentimentally focal among Hawaiians, and this affective preference is the basis of alternative jural patterns. Women are points of attachment by which men claim *kuleana*s in other families. Relationships through men are the normative lines of property transmission, but often the descent is to men via women. Certain close blood relationships carry a considerable burden of normative expectations. Property relations can divide the family and create tension between siblings because the land descends to only one child. It is affection for mom and grandmom that calls together the entire family; it is the mothers who are celebrated at a family luau, for they symbolize the unity of the family rather than its division.

Chapter Six

EXCHANGE BETWEEN NEIGHBORS

Two forms of reciprocity operate among Hawaiians. One involves short-term cycles of gift giving, where the gifts are hospitality, favors, perishables, and portables. The other is a long-term, less apparent cycle that links families over time, primarily through marriage and adoption. This chapter considers reciprocity—and the lack of it—between unrelated persons in Keanae. I use the term *neighbors* for a category of people who lie in the same community but do not share common descent and are not linked by marriage. Exchange relationships between neighbors of the same generation should be balanced and symmetrical. Residents on the land are a stable population, and their association is long-lasting, whether or not it is amicable. Contact with unrelated Hawaiians living outside Keanae is a matter of choice; if the ethic of reciprocity is violated, it is easier to break off contact with an outsider than with a neighbor whom one sees every day. People whom a Mainlander might call "close friends" tend to be assimilated as cousins, aunties, and uncles among Hawaiians. Outside the sphere of putative relatedness, neighbors are village exchange partners whose relationships cycle between amity—talk story—and animosity—talk stink.

EQUIVALENCE IN
EXCHANGE AND STATUS

The Hawaiian social ethic demands that individuals deny their achievements, repudiate special status, and avoid differences in social position (Gallimore and Howard 1968: 12–13). Between kin, gifts and services pass relatively freely under the mantle of aloha. Gifts may go in one direction for a long time and, among close kin, may not be repaid at all. But between unrelated persons, a one-way flow is not only inappropriate but intolerable to the recipient because it creates a "shadow of indebtedness" (Sahlins 1965:147). To be indebted to another is to be lower until the debt is repaid. Between neighbors, the return on a gift is expected and is usually provided in the near future, within weeks if not days.

Between young and old, asymmetry in exchange is not only proper but expected. Relative age overrides the potential status ambiguity between nonrelatives by defining the terms of reciprocity. Age is the only ascribed basis for prestige among Keanae Hawaiians; an age disparity defines a relationship as hierarchical. It is a long-standing Hawaiian cultural precedent that the young have a diffuse obligation to respect and give service to their elders. In return, the old lavish affection and attention on the young. In effect, a wide age disparity creates a kind of relatedness, for all older women in the village may be called "aunty," regardless of actual relationship to the speaker; the expectations are then unequivocal.

Neither kinship nor affinity defines the mutual obligations of neighbors of the same generation, however; their relative status is ambiguous before entering into exchange. The ethic of equivalence should guide transactions between these neighbors, for it is between such persons that "the shadow of indebtedness" is most threatening. The most enduring and amicable interpersonal relationships in Keanae resemble a continuous give-and-take, where neither party attempts to introduce a major disparity; at any one time, the material imbalance is minor and easily corrected. Symmetry is maintained by mutual consent, as the participants tacitly allow each other to equalize the relationship over time.

The interplay of exchange and status is not a conscious model in the sense that Hawaiians articulate the rules, but Keanae Hawaiians do use the terms "higher" and "lower" to describe the relative status of individuals, which depends on the current balance in reciprocities. After one woman had unsuccessfully tried to establish a lien on my services, an astute informant explained that I was now "more high than her." Hawaiians recognize and disapprove of acting high, a kind of behavior akin to our status seeking. E. S. Craighill Handy and Mary Kawena Pukui (1972:195) cite many proverbs and injunctions warning against self-aggrandizement. Hawaiian children were taught to "not put on airs; remain peaceful, quiet and unassuming." Hawaiians felt "contempt for those who made unwarranted pretensions." A Hawaiian proverb advises, "Stay among the clumps of grasses and do not elevate yourself."

Keanae Hawaiians do not perceive exchange as a set of prescriptions or specific obligations but as proper behavior in certain situations. As opposed to relationships with strangers, relationships with neighbors as well as relatives are based on generalized reciprocity: the nonspecific expectation of some future return (Sahlins 1965:147). Even when a direct return is desired, Hawaiians phrase all prestations as spontaneous gift giving. As Pukui (n.d.) has said, "It is *hilahila* ('shameful') to say, 'I will give you this for that.' Instead, 'I have come to see you and brought some *'uala* (sweet potato).'"

Hawaiians say that monetary transactions have no place within the village. As one informant explained, "Keanae is a small place. The minute you sell, you going to get into trouble. You *give*, don't sell. When you give, something tastes good; but when you sell, it not going to taste so good." Pukui (n.d.) describes a similar ethic for her home district of Kau, on the island of Hawaii: "Never *kū'ai* ('buy, barter') amongst family, and in Ka'u, it was all family. But at the boundary of Kona and Ka'u there would be *Kū'ai*: even exchange." The norm of exchange within the village thus operates as if all neighbors were relatives. The sometimes stressful character of exchange in Keanae results because not all villagers are in fact related. Solidarity, measured by the strength of the ethic of generalized reciprocity, decreases with collateral distance and must be demonstrated between affines, who are not "really related."

Although the expectation of a return is never made explicit, it is nonetheless an imperative between neighbors of similar age. In its realization as opposed to its altruistic ethic, exchange between nonrelatives thus approaches "balanced reciprocity," the class of transactions "which stipulate returns of commensurate worth or utility within a finite and narrow period" (Sahlins 1965:148). The norm of exchange stipulates spontaneity, at least in theory, but it is precisely the necessity of making a return that empowers the gift to create status differences. Hawaiians frequently profess their distaste for owing anything to anyone and admittedly try to repay a favor as soon as possible. To acknowledge a debt is to admit one's lower status vis-à-vis another and to accept the constraints that the unrequited gift entails.

Immoderate gifts or favors violate the premise of equivalence between neighbors. If exchanges between neighbors do not balance, either the relationship becomes hierarchical, a state most Hawaiians will not tolerate, or it will be terminated. Perceiving the threat of subordination, the recipient has recourse to desertion before the disparity becomes too great. Ultimately, hierarchy within the village is thwarted by excluding from sociability those who covet superior status. The person who is obviously calculating, who overtly aspires to be high, is eventually cut off from the network of social relations. "Simple" generosity between neighbors is suspect precisely because it is assumed not to be simple but to be motivated by the desire to create indebtedness. The deviate in village society is the recognizable status seeker, the individual who attempts to be above his or her peers. The sanctions against this ambition are rigorous; the result of acting high is a leveling of status, expedited by a goodly round of talk stink within the community. Overly generous or inappropriate gifts and favors ultimately result in avoidance of the giver, whose pretensions to superiority are effectively ignored and defused by popular denial. The everyday give-and-take of food, aid, and visiting ceases, for the person who becomes high is, by definition, a stranger.

In this enforced egalitarianism, local-level Hawaiian society resembles some Melanesian communities. The pressure on Keanae Hawaiians to maintain symmetry in relationships is analogous to the mechanism of *br'ngun'guni* described by Burridge (1969:129ff.) for the Tangu. Social relations in Tangu are characterized by "competitive egalitarianism." Mutuality and equivalence are publicly enforced through *br'ngun'guni*, a ritualized debating where the Tangu form of acting high is opposed to equivalence in exchange. The resolution of *br'ngun'guni* is the return of "overt amity" and the restoration of equivalent reciprocities. Both here and in Keanae, the gift can be an instrument of status differentiation: "in an egalitarian society such as Tangu the only way to influence another is to give him something—lands, specie, resources." And, in another point of similarity, "the breach of equivalence places a wrongdoer outside the complex of reciprocities which in his act he has already denied or ignored" (ibid.:14).

In effect, the ambitious Hawaiian tries to act like a chief, but there are no more chiefs. As Samuel M. Kamakau (1961:376) wrote, all we have left now are "the teachings of the common people." The chiefs' open invitation to outsiders proved the downfall of the native hierarchy, which historically was imposed on the local level from outside. The system of hereditary ranks that defined inborn status has long since ceased to operate, and in any case the chiefs were wanderers who did not reside among the commoners and whose relationship to the people was putative. The shallow genealogies of the *maka'āinana* and the severing of the kinship bond with the chiefs meant that no commoner was intrinsically higher than another. Commoner egalitarianism was the complement to chiefly rank. Economic superiority too was reserved for the chiefs. Through their *konohiki*s (headmen or land agents), the chiefs prevented the development of economic centricity at the local level. As many early sources attest, the threat of expropriation deterred commoners from appearing prosperous or accumulating material goods. This is the historical backdrop to Hawaiians' sensitivity about appearing more prosperous than their neighbors.

Generosity was expected of a chief, but there is no justification for largesse from a neighbor, nor is there any basis for one neighbor to command the assistance of another. Before the Mahele, the chiefs owned the land and could apportion it at will, but they appointed *konohikis* to administer their holdings locally. These lower-level *konohikis*, who usually lived in the *ahupua'a*, collected tribute and, later, taxes. They oversaw the maintenance of the irrigation ditches and could appropriate and reallocate the commoners' lands if they were neglected. The Mahele eliminated this stratum of local *konohikis* and with it the only recognized authority within the community. According to the nineteenth-century court testimony of Hawaiians, internal dissension intensified after the Mahele. Since there was no one to direct the repairs of the irrigation ditches, villagers quarreled among themselves while the water system deteriorated. "The common people are *konohikis* now," a witness in a nineteenth-century water-rights case (E-305, 1st c.c.) complained; "everybody that has a *kuleana* of his own is a konohiki."

Despite the absence of recognized local authorities, Keanae Hawaiians prefer to solve problems within the village and seldom resort to outside agencies of social control. When a haole woman in the area wanted to open a photo gallery in her home, the residents petitioned against starting a business in Keanae. The petition drive, however, was not instigated by a Hawaiian but by another haole who owned a weekend home there. During fieldwork, the police were summoned only once, to investigate the use of firearms, which turned out to be firecrackers. Predictably, a "hippy lady" had called in the complaint. When a local boy stole my camera, I was praised for going to his relatives for help in recovering it. His aunty, cousins, and friends united in finding the camera without revealing the theft to his aged mother. It was said that he had committed other thefts, but villagers hesitated to call in the police "for the family's sake."

Keanae villagers' reluctance to call on outsiders does not mean that neighborly relationships are particularly harmonious, however. Social relations in Keanae evidence solidarity toward the outside and dissension within, a combination that has often been noted in small rural communities (cf. Redfield 1956:28–33). In spite of the village's apparent integrity toward the outside, large-scale cooperation within the community is rare. The irrigation system is still the subject of much bickering and talk stink. Residents blame the erratic water supply for the abandonment of Keanae lands by Hawaiians; before, one informant complained, there was plenty of water, but now there is not enough to open more patches. As villagers note, the natural watercourses in Keanae tend to be either overabundant or dry, depending on the amount of rainfall in the uplands. In dry spells, the taro patches can suffer from lack of water. Some Hawaiians blame the Koolau Ditch, which siphons off water far up the mountain for the canefields of central Maui. I have no evidence to support this claim, but the diversion of water for large plantations has recently become a heated political issue in other parts of the islands. In 1975, patches seemed to be uncultivated because there were not enough able-bodied residents to work them. On a return visit in 1981, the area planted in taro was much greater, and the patches seemed to be thriving. Nevertheless, disputes betwen taro-patch neighbors may intensify in dry periods because many growers depend on the overflow of water from the patches above them. Taro farmers sometimes accuse each other of "fooling with" the irrigation outlets and taking too much water.

Taro-patch neighbors also depend on each other for keeping the irrigation ditches free of grass, which impedes the flow of fresh water so necessary for healthy taro. The rule is that every grower is supposed to clean that part of the ditch adjacent to his or her patches, and the lapse of this responsibility provokes talk stink and finger pointing: "It's only hard when the fellow above you doesn't take care. If so-and-so would just take care of his side, we wouldn't have so much grass growing down here. He isn't taking care by his patches, that's the trouble. I told them, when they were grumbling before, if four you guys only get together and make a good job, do it once, then you won't have so much trouble." The "trouble" is, of course, that no one will undertake to organize communal acitivity. Cooperation is tenuous outside the bounds of relatedness. There is no recognized village leader, and Hawaiians are likely to desert anyone with pretensions to authority.

The lack of solidarity between neighbors, as opposed to relatives, correlates with at least one account of the early society. In 1824, a missionary at Lahaina wrote, "For a man . . . to receive any assistance from his neighbors, is a thing unknown in the Sandwich Islands, unless the neighbor is a relation" (William Richards, 13 August 1824. Missionary Journal. HMCS). In Keanae, interpersonal divisions within the village seem to stem from fluctuating balances in exchange between neighbors, the "competitive egalitarianism" described above. The same observer also noted the gift's instrumental power among Hawaiians: "It is indeed universally true here, that those who give do it hoping to receive as much again."

EQUIVALENCE IN LIFESTYLE
AND SOCIAL POSITION

As stated earlier, the social ethic among Hawaiians demands that individuals try to minimize apparent differences in material lifestyle—this despite the fact that very real income disparities exist in Keanae. One of the local big-men lives in a household of five adults, three of whom hold wage-earning jobs, and markets a large taro order each week. In contrast, a widow in the village receives a monthly

income of $186 from Social Security. Nevertheless, the pro-
tocol of reciprocity does not depend on the material under-
pinnings of the exchange relations. In the Hawaiian view,
the impoverished widow is as good as the man with an
annual salary of twelve thousand dollars. In fact, she is
likely to be regarded with greater esteem than he by virtue
of her age and experience. The point here is not that economic differences do not exist, but that they are not per se
the determinants of social standing.

Overt evidences of economic inequality are few in Keanae, as the result of a more or less conscious attempt not to
appear more prosperous than one's neighbor. The material
circumstances of life appear much the same for all the Hawaiian households. Obvious symbols of wealth, such as
expensive clothing and luxury automobiles, are notably ab-
sent. Nearly every house is a wooden A-frame with an iron
roof and assorted outbuildings in back. Roofing material is
a barometer of relative social status and, by implication,
social distance. Excluding the haole homes, the only house
in Keanae with a shingle roof, as opposed to corrugated
iron, belongs to a land-wealthy Japanese widow, formerly
married to a Hawaiian. She maintains a home in Wailuku,
returning to Keanae on alternate weekends and holidays,
and has little social contact with Keanae Hawaiians. Her
neighbors recognize the finery of her house and regard her
as essentially an outsider, more because of her apparent
wealth than her ancestry. Her sister, who is also married to
a Keanae man, lives in the Hawaiian style and is accepted
as any Hawaiian would be.

Another widow in the village, of Chinese-Hawaiian parentage, has a large, impressive home, albeit with an iron
roof. She has a modern indoor bathroom, which is reserved for the use of guests; for her own toilet and bathing,
she uses the wash house behind the main building. An
older, ramshackle house, composed of one large room,
also stands on the lot. Although the owner denied to me
that she had ever lived in it, informants said that this was
the family's dwelling until her husband built the new

home. To other residents, that "big, beautiful house" is symptomatic of social climbing; as one of her neighbors commented, "That's why she come so high." Other evidence of her desire to be high is the fact that she likes to entertain haoles from outside and brag about it afterward. It is not coincidental that this woman is widely disliked for offering gratuitous favors. Other residents suspect that her eagerness to help is based on a calculating desire to indebt them to her.

With these exceptions, no Hawaiian household is visibly higher than the others. Every house has at least cold running water, and about half have indoor plumbing. It is common for families to have two automobiles, a "good" car and one for work, or an automobile and a truck or jeep. Most residents have telephones, and no house is without a radio. Other entertainment items such as stereo phonographs, tape decks, and cassette recorders are popular but usually fall quickly into disrepair. Several households also have televisions, in spite of Keanae's poor reception; under optimal conditions, one channel is available and poorly at that.

The Hawaiian avoidance of overt economic disparities has its roots in the political relationship of the common people to the chiefs in pre-Mahele times. The chiefs enforced egalitarianism at the local level with the threat of expropriation, effectively thwarting any accumulation of goods by commoners. Through their *konohiki*s, the chiefs confiscated commodities that were qualitatively or quantitatively inappropriate to the commoners' status (Ellis [1827] 1917:322; Mathison 1825:385). In the ongoing definition of their relationship to the *maka'āinana* after contact, the chiefs monopolized European goods (Sahlins 1981:28–31, 44). At a time when the chiefs had garnered such a surfeit of iron that they no longer valued it, commoner Hawaiians were still without metal tools (ibid.). In the modern Hawaiian community, social sanctions against acting high have replaced political ones, but the premise of equivalence between neighbors remains. To derive modern

Hawaiian egalitarianism from this historical relationship does not seem far-fetched to one who has witnessed an elderly Hawaiian in Keanae hoarding rusty iron nails as if they were gold.

The leveling of aspirations among Hawaiians also extends to the workplace. Ronald Gallimore and Alan Howard (1968:10–13) have characterized Hawaiians as "affiliation-oriented" in contrast to the islands' other, "achievement-oriented" ethnic groups. In Keanae as in Nanakuli, Hawaiians seek to avoid differences in social position. The foreman of the state road garage in Keanae was an outsider, a Portuguese. He could not understand why his Hawaiian workers seemed to resent his efforts to offer them chances for advancement. One had been a common laborer for four years without a promotion; another worked four years without a raise. The foreman was perplexed by the men's evasiveness and jealousy. They attacked him with anonymous telephone calls to the head office and committed petty meannesses against any co-worker who was being considered for promotion. The foreman summed up the situation quite accurately: "They cannot stand the minute you little bit higher than them." I once witnessed three young Hawaiian men playing a game of water tag in an upland pond. One tagged the other, who then had to catch the third. The third always had to tag the first player. The tagging order was unchanging, and no one was "it" more often than another by virtue of being slower. The game was played out in a circle, with no winner, until one of the swimmers tired and gave up. The game seemed to me to be a parable of Hawaiian peer relationships, for its resolution was equivalence rather than hierarchy.

TALK STORY, TALK STINK: CYCLES OF EXCHANGE

In Keanae, exchanges between neighbors may vary widely over time in frequency and intensity. There may be a lull as a cycle is closed and relative balance is achieved. More frequently, a cycle is interrupted by disagreement when one party is suspected of trying to tip the balance of reciprocities. The recipient begins to avoid the donor, who complains of being uncompensated for gifts or services rendered; one party is overheard talking stink about the other, and a breach ensues. The interruption may last weeks, months, even years, depending on the severity of the inequity that precipitated it. The parties turn to other neighbors for solace and initiate new exchange cycles. Sometimes only when these relationships also break down are the original parties reconciled, and another cycle begins.

Interpersonal allegiances within the village thus fluctuate over time. This is not to say that there are no lasting friendships between neighbors. As stated earlier, neighbors become long-time friends when neither party tries to be higher than the other. More frequently, however, relationships between neighbors pass through a cycle from amicability to critical gossip. Often, this gossip concerns violations of reciprocity: alleged obligations, unpaid debts, or anything that might create an imbalance in the relationship. A rule of social etiquette cited by Pukui, whose material reflects the early twentieth century, suggests that maintaining equivalence is a long-standing source of dissension among Hawaiians: "Past favors should never be recalled and told, such as, 'I was the one who helped her by doing this, that or the next thing.' This is called *helu* or counting. Sometimes the person so offended would return every gift given to her and would replace others she had used" (Handy and Pukui 1972:186).

This cycle of personal relations is implicit in the semantic opposition of talk story and talk stink. "Come talk story" is the invitation to engage in casual, friendly conversation. If one goes uninvited to talk story in someone's home, it is proper to bring a small gift, such as an avocado or a bunch of bananas. Talking story with a friend or a relative may or may not include talking stink about a third party. While talking story is communication between allies, talking stink is communication about someone with whom one is not friendly, at least for the moment. Thus talking stink evidences a breach in both verbal and material exchange.

AVOIDING SHAME

Hawaiians' concern for symmetry in interpersonal relationships is understandable in light of the public nature of exchange in Keanae. Gifts and favors are usually common knowledge and are the stuff of everyday gossip. A loss of status does not remain a private matter but quickly becomes common knowledge in the community. The minor prestations and interactions of village life are highly visible. House lots are close together along the road, with the taro lands behind. There are few trees around the houses to block one's view, and in both Lower Keanae and Wailua Valley, there is only one road in and out. Villagers spend much time gardening and working outside and invariably notice the social contacts of other residents. The Hana Highway also provides spectacular overlooks of both Keanae and Wailua. The activities of neighbors are frequently the subject of casual mention in conversations. It is a matter of public knowledge when one drives outside and with whom; even what one does outside is often carried back to Keanae since villagers and their relatives tend to frequent the same businesses in town. Informants often reported that other villagers had seen me outside with relatives of Keanae people and were able to relate my activities with a startling degree of accuracy.

Keanae Hawaiians exhibit flawless deductive reasoning where social events are concerned, a talent that I could only admire. Most residents are well aware of current alliances and feuds in the village, and it is common for a Hawaiian to draw accurate conclusions about interactions from minimal data. A single glance at someone's homestead from a moving car may be enough to reconstruct a whole series of events: "So-and-so stopped by so-and-so's house this morning. Now I see bananas on her porch. Must be she brought those bananas. Must be from the nephew's place."

The distribution of poi illustrates some of the imperatives of exchange in Keanae. The commodities that pass between nonrelatives are rarely basic subsistence items but are specialty foods such as bananas and avocados. Fish and poi, the traditional staples, circulate primarily between close relatives and frequently between parents and children. To Hawaiians, poi symbolizes Keanae's special and enviable position, for not only is fresh poi available, but the locally grown taro selected for home use is of much higher quality than the market variety. The taro growers admittedly send the poorer taro to be sold outside, while keeping the finest corms for their own tables. One reason local luaus are popular is "that fine, white poi of Keanae." Yet even in Keanae, not everyone is able to get poi. Those who do not grow taro are loath to ask it of those who do, and it would be shameful to try to buy poi from a neighbor. A household with no patches "open" must rely on a taro-growing relative who is obligated by kinship to provide poi, else go without. Those who are too old or ill or disinclined must rely on the gift that is freely offered but is in some sense due them because of an established obligation. Without such a source, older Keanae villagers can no more easily eat in the Hawaiian style than can a resident of Honolulu. For some Hawaiians, avoiding indebtedness thus creates the paradox of living in "the taro place" and having to buy poi outside at the supermarket.

The protocol and etiquette of gift giving are all the more important because of the injunction against sale within the village. Knowing how to get something without paying for it is an art; there is a proper way to elicit a gift without overtly asking. One way is to offer to pay, with the knowledge that a villager will almost never sell to a neighbor. I once asked an informant to recommend someone who would sell me a single taro. After considerable thought, she proposed a strategy for approaching her taro-patch neighbor: "He hardly ever sells, but you do this: you go down when he's pulling, and he'll give you some. Two or three is nothing to them."

This sort of connivance would not be proper between peers, but two factors in the situation made it an appropriate thing to do in this case. My informant's taro-patch neighbor was much older than I. To most villagers, I was "that haole girl." I was as a child to this man, and children often "beg" their elders for treats without incurring shame. The other important variable was the nature of the item being requested. One or two taro corms are indeed insignificant to a taro farmer on pulling day; as my informant explained, "He just throws them up on the bank." In other words, giving me a couple of corms from the patch would occasion no extra effort on his part. When freshly pulled, the taro is wet, muddy, unaltered, and raw. It would have been much less possible for me to go to this man's home in pursuit of taro, for by then he would have carried the heavy bags of corms out of the patches. By going down as he was pulling, I eliminated even this effort. In general, growing things that one picks oneself are low in the hierarchy of exchange commodities.

Under other circumstances, this transparent begging for a gift can provoke resentment. An elderly informant spent much of her time growing sweet potatoes in her yard. A neighbor's relative came and asked to buy two bags for a luau. This neighbor had recently treated the woman's son to a trip to Hilo. Although the old woman felt that she worked hard for the potatoes and should be paid, she had no choice but to give the produce. The quantity requested was not small in this case, either as a proportion of the total crop or in terms of the woman's effort. Here the offer of payment was an obvious ruse; the neighbor was cashing in on an obligation and taking advantage of an existing imbalance in the relationship. The old woman felt shame because the transaction reminded her that she was lower than her neighbor. When she later related the story to her daughter outside, she described a fictitious scene in which she reminded the visitor how much she had to work for the potatoes. With much invented dialogue, she insisted that she had indeed been paid.

Hawaiians use the word "shame" to denote embarrassment, disgrace, or a feeling of being lower than another. Shame is thus both an emotion and a description of one's standing in a relationship. A passage by Kamakau (1868) suggests that this is not a new concept among Hawaiians: "My people were . . . ashamed to be where they were unwanted, to go constantly to the homes of others, to look around to see what can be seen, to behave in a boisterous manner, jumping around from place to place, to speak out of turn, to start a quarrel, to gossip, to act the vagrant and to be sour tempered." Many of the causes of shame among modern Hawaiians resemble those cited by Kamakau. Shame accrues to an individual in social situations—for example, when guests are invited and the poi is lumpy; when a young man curses at an older woman in public; when a brother lies to his sister; when someone displays eagerness and eats too much. Hawaiians usually eat before going to a party so as not to appear greedy. If a guest holds back, the good host will insist, "Eat, eat! Don't be ashamed!" (Handy and Pukui 1972:193). The host thereby reassures the guest that taking food in this situation implies no subordination.

The shame that results from being reminded of lower status should not occur between relatives. An informant hesitated to attend her niece's birthday luau because she had no gift to bring: "I some shame. I too ashamed to go." Her sister coaxed her with words that reminded her of the solidarity in relatedness: "It's only all the own family. No need be ashamed." Because of the fear of shame, long-time neighbors will often not attend another villager's luau, while hordes of Hawaiians from outside feel no compunction about attending although they barely know the host. More accurately, they do not hesitate *because* they barely know the host. Paradoxically, it is possible to be eager among strangers because, without future contact, shame has no enduring consequences. The potential for shame is thus greatest between neighbors, the people whom one sees every day. One way of avoiding shame is to maintain equivalence in a relationship. Avoiding indebtedness to one's peers is a quite conscious and clearly stated concern: "I don't like someone to give me something unless I pay it back." "I no like bother anybody, that's all. So long as I no bother anybody, all right." "She's not feeding me. I don't owe her nothing. As long as they're not feeding me, I don't give a damn what they say. I don't have to depend on them. I don't see them giving me *kaukau*."[1]

EXCHANGE COMMODITIES

Rarely does an occasion, whether stopping by or staying overnight, demand a particular kind of gift, but certain commodities are appropriate to certain situations. In Keanae, food is the gift most frequently given between neighbors and relatives. As in Tangu, food is "the heart of the complex of reciprocities" (Burridge 1969:149) and is the focus of Hawaiian exchange, both symbolically and materially. Food is not an undifferentiated category, however. Some foods are appropriate for everyday visits with neighbors, while others pass only between relatives. The commodities involved in exchange differ in symbolic value; some are higher than others, both in their compensatory power and in the sense that they more imperatively obligate the recipient to make a return gift. The vitality of the established exchange categories was impressed on me when I faced the difficulty of compensating informants in a way that would not create an unbreachable distance be-

1. Unless speaking in Hawaiian, villagers commonly use *kaukau* to mean food. This has supplanted the Hawaiian word *'ai*. According to Andrews (1865:238), "*Kaukau* is said to be a corruption of a Chinese word, and signifies to eat, to drink. It is used by foreigners in conversing with natives and by natives conversing with foreigners."

tween us. I would have been more intelligible to the people of Keanae if I had been dealing in bananas or dried fish, but I tried to introduce an alien commodity: information.

On any visit longer than a brief talk story, it is customary to bring food when one goes to a Hawaiian home. The stated rationale is "Bring your own food, bring what you like to eat," but the reality is closer to "Eat my food, I'll eat yours." The kind of gift depends on several variables: the nature of the occasion, the giver's motives, and the current state of reciprocities between donor and recipient. In general, villagers take local foods, the specialties of the country, when they go outside to visit. Outsiders bring store-bought goods and fancy delicacies when they visit Keanae. The principle is that different things should travel in different directions. One should give a commodity to someone who cannot easily get it. The villager with a bunch of ripe bananas will break it up and give hands to neighbors who do not have bananas. An informant explained that it was foolish to take fish to people in Hana because "they always get fish. . . . Give them to somebody who doesn't get fish, or keep them yourself."

Coconuts and breadfruit, which grow wild along the roads and on public lands in Keanae, are never given in their uncooked state to other villagers; they are too common—anyone can have them for the taking. Most Hawaiians also consider breadfruit "an inferior food" (Handy 1940:189). Keanae people rarely eat breadfruit, giving the explanation that few know how to cook it well. Even breadfruit poi, although cooked and prepared, is not a high food; it is too watery and sweet compared with taro poi and represents merely a novel use of a secondary food.

In general, raw plant foods are most often given between neighbors (see Table 5.1). Often, specialty items of this kind have come to the donor as a gift. Friends may bring mangoes or squash from Hana, or an absentee landowner may instruct a neighbor to harvest his bananas. The produce will then be divided and distributed to neighbors and relatives, both within and without the village.

Villagers frequently exchange plants, vegetable seeds, and the *huli* (tops, used for planting) of unusual taro and sweet potato varieties. Most women in the village are avid gardeners, always eager to obtain an interesting new plant to augment their colorful displays of dracaenas, crotons, and coleuses. The taro shoots exchanged in house-to-house visits are those of dry-land, decorative varieties, destined to adorn the garden rather than to provide food.

The wet-land taro farmer usually has plenty of shoots available in his or her own patches, but taro-patch neighbors may request *huli* of one another if they are on good terms. Most of the *huli* are not needed for replanting and are simply discarded when the taro is harvested. Seeds and cuttings are capable of reproduction, but they are incomplete and unfinished and have a lower value than the mature product. Although it is a small thing to give taro *huli* to a neighbor, it would be unseemly to give a taro corm, unless the person had worked in the patches. Taro-patch neighbors will help each other when their own work is done, but they are concerned that this mutual aid should balance out. As one informant explained: "I'll go over if I'm *pau*, but I don't want him to help me too much. I do my own work. I don't have the time to help him in return, then, later, so I'd rather do my own. Besides, when he helps us, it's clean. When we help him, it's grass."

To a Hawaiian, taro evokes associations comparable to "mother's milk" and "our daily bread." The large corm at the center of the plant is called "the mother taro," and the smaller tubers that grow from it are the "*keikis*" (children). Symbolically, if no longer in reality, taro is the staff of life, the staple food. Supplying someone with taro signifies a nurturing, feeding relationship such as that between parent and child; the custom of informal adoption was called *hānai* (feeding). Between neighbors, the feeding relationship is untenable because it would imply subordination. As mentioned, the stated principle of gift giving among Hawaiians is that one gives a commodity to someone who does not have it. Thus the gift of taro implies that the recipient cannot get her or his own taro, that there are no relatives inside to provide it. The effect would be similar to that of presenting a neighbor with a quart of milk. The implication is that the recipient cannot secure her or his own staples. For this reason, "not everybody get" taro in Keanae, the taro place. Taro can be more freely given to outsiders, such as the Portuguese road foreman or the Japanese *akule* (mackerel) fishermen, than to neighbors.

The casual gift of mangoes or bananas does not carry the connotation of feeding for subsistence in the sense suggested by an informant's indignant statement, "She's not feeding me." Providing taro is symbolically a life-sustaining relationship and is a more weighty gift. Supplying a relative with taro is appropriate as an expression of aloha, as from brother to sister, or as the fulfillment of an obligation to an elder, as from child to parent. Between unrelated villagers, however, such feeding implies a hierarchical relationship. Either the giver is obligated by previous indebtedness to provide taro and the gift is in the nature of a tithe to a superior, or the donor is presenting taro to a dependent, a person of lower status. Taro is associated with the family, with the domain of relatives. Yet it is also unusual, in casual visiting, to give a neighbor something that has been prepared, cooked, or labored over. Describing the staple crops of precontact Hawaii, David Malo (1951:206) wrote: "food was a child to be cared for, and it required great care." In general, things that have been cultivated have greater weight in exchange than things growing wild; items that have been prepared, cooked, or altered are higher in exchange value than raw commodities. Some examples of exchanges between neighbors will illustrate the interplay between situation and the intrinsic value of commodities.

Bamboo and plumeria, the fragrant flower most often used in leis, grow on many lots in Keanae. These may be gathered with relative freedom, as long as one has obtained the owner's permission sometime in the past. Hawaiian bamboo grows wild in thick stands in Keanae, but the less common Chinese bamboo is preferable for fishing poles because it is more flexible. One resident had a jungle of Chinese bamboo behind her house and let it be known that "anybody can go get." A neighboring couple stopped by one day and asked to cut bamboo and plumeria for a school affair. While the two women picked flowers, the man took the householder's lawn mower and finished mowing most of her yard—a task usually done by the elderly woman's daughter and son-in-law. The woman went to considerable lengths to repay this couple for mowing her lawn, even though they had initially taken bamboo and plumeria from her yard. She had her daughter bring in a case of beer and sent for the man and his wife several times. When they finally came again, she insisted that they take the beer, with the words: "I don't drink beer, and if you don't take it why should I give it to my other neighbor, who doesn't help me?"

The son of another neighbor fixed this woman's lawn mower and helped her with yard work—again, jobs that the woman's daughter and son-in-law usually do. She tried to lure him close to slip a ten-dollar bill into his pocket, but he refused. Her initial plan for repayment was to send beer to the house, but she reasoned that only the young man's father would drink it. Instead, the woman had Hasegawa's General Store in Hana deliver a cake to the family as a Father's Day gift; this would be a present they could not refuse.

These examples illustrate the value of labor in the Hawaiian scheme of reciprocities. As was apparent in the description of the luau, working for someone is a high and powerful gift. The amount of work invested imparts greater value to a commodity; this is why luau foods are high in the hierarchy of items exchanged. Most herbal medicines fall into the category of raw plant items. Villagers readily provide or point out wild-growing herbs, such as *māmaki*[2]

---

2. *Pipturus albidus*, a plant similar to the paper mulberry, from which tapa cloth was made (Neal 1965:318). A medicinal tea is made from it.

and *popolo*,[3] for neighbors who need them. These are less valued, and require less immediate repayment, than *lēkō*,[4] a medicine for respiratory problems, made from whiskey, honey, and watercress juice. Not everyone knows how to make *lēkō*, and those who do will not divulge the recipe. The local expert, an elderly woman, will make a batch if one supplies the raw materials. On one occasion when she was making some for a neighbor, she had to add some of her husband's whiskey; the neighbor responded by buying a quart of whiskey to repay her.

These examples also illustrate the dynamic of overcompensation in exchange. When one is dealing in bananas, *huli*, and other such things, one can never be sure when equivalence has been attained. By paying back excessively, one can be sure there is no lingering imbalance. But this overcompensation merely reverses the debt instead of canceling it. The protagonist in the examples involving yard work is a woman who married into Keanae from Kaupo, on the dry side of Maui. After almost thirty years of residence in Keanae, she still feels herself to be somewhat of a stranger since she has no relatives among the villagers. Her anxiety about receiving unsolicited favors stems from the feeling that her children should provide these services, not her neighbors, who might thereby become more high than she. In exchange for wild-growing bamboo and plumeria growing with little care, the couple provided work; in effect, they performed a highly valued service in return for a gift of little significance to the elderly householder. Their overcompensation prompted an anxious overcompensation in return.

In fact, the woman's panicky desire to repay was unwarranted in the instances cited; the couple and the young man felt that they were helping a village aunty, someone to

3. Black nightshade, *Solanum nigrum* or *S. nodiflorum* (Neal 1965:744). The plant is ground, and the juice is taken for asthma and other respiratory difficulties.
4. The word means simply watercress.

whom such favors are due by right of advanced age, without implication of subordinate status. The recipient of their kindness, however, perceived the danger of nonequivalence, the danger of being lower than her neighbors. Her return gift of beer did have the effect of closing the cycle; thereafter her relationship with the couple was limited to an infrequent talk story.

The delay between a gift and its repayment is inversely related to social distance, which is simply another way of saying that relations between neighbors approach the norm of balanced reciprocity (Sahlins 1965:148). Between nonrelatives, a gift must be compensated for within a finite period of time: the more distant the parties, the shorter the time.

As an outsider within the village, I found in my own exchange cycles that repayment for an unsolicited gift was indeed prompt, perhaps within a day or two. Where I was able to establish a niece/uncle or niece/aunty relationship, I could offer my services relatively freely under the ethic of generalized reciprocity. But with other adults in the village, my relationship was tenuous and potentially hostile. I once succeeded in presenting a particularly unfriendly neighbor with a jar of mango sauce that I had made. Although dismay registered on his face, he could not refuse the gift; he did return the following day with a bag of vegetables. In this case, the return gift closed a cycle of exchange, both social and material. My antagonist avoided further contact with me because, I suggest, he was afraid I might give him something and thus initiate a communication in which he would have to participate, however reluctantly. Another man in the village initiated an exchange cycle with me. In an ostensibly casual visit, he described some vegetable seeds that might grow in my garden. I picked some lettuce and gave it to him, and he responded, "Well, I guess I'll bring those seeds tomorrow." Again, the return gift closed a cycle, and much time elapsed before any further overtures.

In both these transactions, an equivalent return for a gift was soon forthcoming. The two instances closely approximate direct, symmetrical exchange and thus exemplify the quality of relations with a stranger. The commodities involved here also represent categorical equivalents in exchange. A jar of mango sauce—a wild-growing fruit cooked and prepared—is not, perhaps, the kind of gift a Hawaiian would have chosen, but the compensation was a large bag of raw vegetables from the family garden—an uncooked commodity that also represented some labor. In the second example, the exchange of seeds for lettuce was more in the Hawaiian style and is in keeping with the general scheme outlined earlier in Table 5.1.

Commodities possess a value in exchange that derives from their intrinsic qualities. In the course of this discussion, I have proposed a ranking of values for these qualities: cooked is higher than raw, for example. The high valuation of work and service lends value to items that are cultivated, prepared, and cooked, as opposed to those that are wild, unaltered, and raw. Figure 6.1 summarizes this hierarchy of qualities, and Table 6.1 categorizes some of the specific items that Hawaiians give to one another. The rank order outlined in Figure 6.1 is not only deduced from exchange transactions and informants' statements but also takes cues from the ritual hierarchy of goods in early Hawaiian society. I did not make an a priori assumption that cooked was higher than raw merely because Claude Lévi-Strauss (1969b:142) has written that "cooking brings about the cultural transformation of the raw." Hawaiians also make this categorical distinction. An informant criticized a neighbor for serving "just cold drinks" as opposed to "real *kaukau*, hot food." The main course at a luau is always *kālua* pork, pig cooked in an underground oven; in the Hawaiian religion this was the preeminent ritual offering to both gods and chiefs, second in value only to the sacrifice of a man.

The preference for ocean fish over reef fish accords with the symbolic precedence of sea over land in Polynesia. In Fiji, the "sea people" are higher than the "land people," for the chiefly stock is said to have come from the sea (Sahlins

Figure 6.1
Valuation of Qualities of Exchange Items

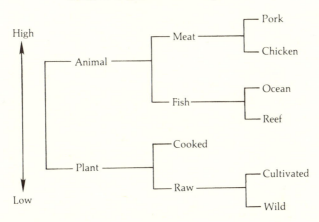

1962:299). In Hawaii too, the chiefs were said to have come from over the sea, from Kahiki. In their relation to the common people, the chiefs were "divine sharks" (Sahlins 1981:28ff.), propitiated with high foods. Symbolically, the sea is the realm of gods, chiefs, and men. Under the *kapus*, women were prohibited from the sea while priests were officiating at religious rites. Certain products of the ocean, such as shark, sea turtle, porpoise, and certain deep-sea fishes, were also forbidden to women (Malo 1951:27–29). Even today, Hawaiian women do not normally go out in a boat to fish. An informant related an occasion when a young woman in the village went out in the boat with the men: they didn't have enough men that day, and, besides, he explained with a snigger, "she's a tomboy." It is the men who participate in deep-sea fishing, whether in a boat or from shore with spinning equipment. Women customarily dip from the rocks for reef fish with long bamboo poles.

The most coveted eating fish are those that must be caught away from shore. *Akule* are netted by the school fishermen from outside and distributed to villagers who offer assistance. *Akule* are preferred for drying and salting

Table 6.1
VALUATION OF EXCHANGE COMMODITIES

High

Food	Cooked	Altered	Raw
Animal	*Kālua* pig *Laulaus* Chicken luau	Dried fish Lomi-lomi salmon	*'Opihi* Fish Crabs
Vegetable	*Kūlolo* Poi *Haupia*	*Lēkō* medicine	Taro corms Bananas, fruit Vegetables *Huli*, seeds

Low

and are given away both raw and dried. Hawaiians like oily fish such as *akule* and the *enenue*, which may be taken occasionally from a few precarious spots overlooking deep water. Other desirable food fish, such as *moi* and *pāpio*, may sometimes be caught from the peninsula with spinning equipment.

Certain shore fishes are considered more appetizing than others by virtue of what they eat. The *hīnālea* are a colorful class of small fishes that are often caught but are not desirable, both because they have soft scales and are difficult to clean and because "they eat any kine thing." One informant refused to eat *hīnālea*; others would not categorically reject them but nevertheless avoided eating them. The *manini*, in contrast, is much desired for pan frying, and some Hawaiians even eat the *'opu* (belly, stomach) of the *manini*—that is, without cleaning the innards. As an informant explained it, the rationale for this custom is "you are what you eat": "That fish guaranteed no eat other fish, not a cannibal. Only eat all the kinds of *limu* [seaweed]. Some Hawaiians like the taste of all that *limu*. It's medicine, good for you. They take it for medicine. The *manini* don't eat rubbish."

As animal food, fish are not usually given to nonrelatives. Dried fish particularly require much preparation and are parceled out carefully, often to children living outside. In one instance, however, a woman drove her elderly neighbor outside and in return received fresh crabs and fish from the neighbor's sister. Chauffeuring is a highly valued service for elderly Keanae residents who cannot drive. The sister expressly stated that she was giving the fish and crabs in return for the favor of transportation. Some villagers are expert at manipulating the protocol of exchange in order to obtain a high gift from a neighbor. A villager may perform a valued service for another, or make a series of small presentations, with the deliberate intent of provoking a higher return gift than would ordinarily pass between neighbors. In this case, during the next week the benefactor offered several times to drive the neighbor outside again or to her sister's house, at one point waiting a half hour on the chance that the woman might like to visit her sister. Finally, the unwilling recipient of her favors angrily refused, cut off communication, and began to talk stink about the woman, whose calculating motives were too obvious to be tolerated: "She only hoped to get more crabs and fish, see."

The significance of a gift thus depends not only on its intrinsic value as a commodity or a service but also on motives and situation. Context is another dimension of the customary grammar of exchange. The example just cited demonstrates that the categories and the rules can be manipulated; a high service was provided in order to obligate the recipient. The donor's motive—compensation for a prior imbalance or the initiation of a new cycle—affects the choice of a gift. The above anecdote also illustrates the result of trying to extract high gifts from nonrelatives.

MANIPULATION

Incidents such as the one just described and the statements of informants suggest that the status manipulator—

the person who uses the gift to create indebtedness and expects much in return—is a recognized character type among Hawaiians. The Hawaiian word used sometimes to describe such an individual is *maha'oi*, meaning "bold, impertinent . . . presumptuous" (Pukui and Elbert 1971:202). *Maha'oi* is also used in the sense of meddlesome or busybody. As Keanae Hawaiians use the phrase, to go *maha'oi* is similar to the meaning given in Lorrin Andrews's (1865:365) dictionary: "to be forward in asking questions." Andrews's other definitions suggest that *maha'oi* is similar to acting high: "to treat a superior as an equal or with great familiarity . . . to be asking or begging of a chief frequently . . . impertinence in addressing a superior." Since there are no recognized superiors among Hawaiians today, the only way to be *maha'oi* is to act higher than one's neighbors, to elevate oneself, to behave as a creditor in a village of debtors.

One of the most active status manipulators in Keanae is the elderly woman described earlier as living in the "big, beautiful house" and having haole friends. During the course of fieldwork, several of her friendships deteriorated from close companionship to bitter talk stink. Often, she precipitated their breakdown because she could not resist the sin of *helu*, counting the favors one has done for another. This is the woman who coveted her neighbor's crabs and fish. Her prestations highlight the gift's power in Keanae and illustrate the felt imperative of avoiding indebtedness. As another resident observed, "Whenever she gets food, she always takes a little bit to someone else." More accurately, when this woman receives food, she takes a little to as many of her friends as possible. She always volunteers to serve on work parties for local luaus and is in the front ranks of helpers when the *akule* fishers are opening their nets. The *akule* and the luau food she receives as a worker go into her freezer for later, discretionary giving. As her nephew confided to me, "Don't ever let her give you anything. Let her work for you one day, and you work for her one year."

Ultimately, however, the aspirations of such an individual are doomed by their own transparency. To be *maha'oi* is to be an obvious status seeker and inevitably unsuccessful in the village context. Neighbors are too sensitive to the net balance in a relationship to tolerate a one-way flow for long. A neighbor always has the option of withdrawing from a relationship when it threatens to become asymmetrical. Some individuals in Keanae successfully establish others' long-term indebtedness to them, but they do so by denying any special personal status; Chapter 8 develops this point further.

LUAUS

The luau appears to violate the premise that largesse is not permissible between neighbors. This most Hawaiian of events is nothing if not the display of generosity; most of all the luau centers around the consumption and distribution of vast quantities of food. As one informant remarked, "The worst thing is to give a luau and not have enough." Usually the only invitation is word-of-mouth, for knowledge of the luau is the only invitation required. Persons related and unrelated to the host flock to the luau from far and wide. The guests are encouraged to consume much and to carry off "the balance" when they depart.

The ethic of giving food freely to guests is long established among Hawaiians; in 1825, a missionary described "the peculiar manner of Hawaiian hospitality": "Whatever is brought forward for his entertainment is given him as his own. He eats when he likes and what he likes, and is at liberty to give away as much of his food as he chooses, and carry away the remainder with him" (A. Bishop, 1825. Notes taken on a tour of Hilo. Missionary Letters II:614. HMCS). The observer also noted the power of the gift of food: "this custom puts it in my power to confer favors on such as have put me under any obligations, by distributing my superfluous food to my host and others, which tends greatly to conciliate the good will of those on whom these favors are conferred."

The luau is an exceptional event in several regards, primarily in that it is the only redistributive event among Hawaiians. Generosity is not suspect but is proper and expected behavior from the family that makes the luau. In part, largesse is permitted here because it is ritualized. The luau does not belong to the realm of everyday social relations; from the point of view of the host household, it is a special and infrequent event. The luau also involves a large number of people, both as workers and as guests, and it is partly this relative anonymity that allows people to accept the generosity. Such largesse would be intolerable in day-to-day transactions between individuals, but on this occasion a household distributes publicly and indiscriminately to friend and stranger alike.

Although, as previously described, no shame accrues to people from outside for accepting food at a luau, villagers are reluctant to attend a neighbor's luau if they have not helped to prepare it. It may be easier on one's pride to attend a luau outside than within one's own community; a neighbor of many years may demur for fear of shame tainting the relationship with the giver, with whom there is an ongoing association. It is unseemly to display eagerness about a neighbor's luau, at least for an adult; for young people into their early twenties, looking forward to a luau need not be concealed.

For the host's neighbors who have not worked for the luau, the typical answer to "Are you going?" is "I might go later." No one wants to appear greedy by going early. Even at the feast, guests hold back for some time before eating; it would be shameful to display eagerness by eating first. At a luau, the highest-status person eats last. Children are herded toward the tables first, then outsiders and young adults. Members of the household giving the luau may not eat at all during the event or may at least wait until all the guests have been served. At a buffet-style luau, the last person through the line is likely to be the oldest and most respected individual in attendance. At a sit-down luau, young relatives and friends of the host household act as servers, bringing small paper dishes of food to each guest. Here social status is reflected in the order not of eating but of seating: older persons and close relatives of the host household sit closer to the guests of honor.

Neighbors are often recruited as luau workers, a role that places the host in their debt. The luau menu is so standardized that preparations for every feast require more or less the same sequence of tasks and a predictable labor force. Workers are definitively not guests; anything they receive is seen as their just due for helping to make the luau. Not requesting assistance can be interpreted as an affront to a close neighbor, to the extent that she not only will refuse to attend but may arrange to spend the weekend of the luau outside. Not compensating luau workers adequately would be a disgrace and would make it almost impossible to recruit workers in the future. One informant swore that she would never give any more help to a family that had not repaid her with a share of luau foods. In repaying unrelated workers, the host is especially concerned that the compensation be more than adequate. In the case of the wedding luau described in Chapter 5, the host evidently did not feel that *laulau*s alone were sufficient repayment, for in subsequent weeks he took every individual who had worked for the luau to dinner at a restaurant outside: another instance of paying back more than enough in order to ensure that the debt is canceled and equivalence restored.

The luau is descended from rites of sacrifice and propitiation. The ceremony is all the more socially meaningful because the family giving the feast does not profit materially from it; all is given away. The ethic of unstinting generosity calls for the host to give away "the balance" to guests and workers after all have partaken of the meal. Of course, the modern luau is not a religious rite; the old gods and chiefs are long dead. Nonetheless, the luau draws meaning and weightiness from its historical precedents, and this link with the past lends credence to the idea that the meaning of *Hawaiian*—what may remain of Hawaiian tradition—lies in the categories, values, and rules that guide exchange.

It is characteristic of Hawaiian egalitarianism that the luau, unlike redistributive feasts such as the potlatch, does not directly make the giver "great" vis-à-vis his or her fellows. The pretext for a luau is always the observance of a family milestone: a wedding, a birthday, or an anniversary. A gathering of relatives from far and wide, the luau is the preeminent statement of familial solidarity and is said to be for the family above all. Those who would feel threatened by accepting the host's largesse simply stay away. Guests from outside may have infrequent contact with the host household, and their status is not at risk. Neighbors who are recruited as workers are performing a favor for the host and will receive their due afterward. The luau is an offering to family and friends and a celebration of relatedness. It is also a propitiation to the spirit of social amity, for the public divestiture of accumulated goods symbolically lowers pretensions by means of redistribution. It is in keeping with the ethic of Hawaiian social relations that this highest of occasions should effect the restoration of equivalence rather than the creation of hierarchy.

THE DYNAMIC OF EXCHANGE

Exchange in Keanae shares characteristics of gift giving in non-Western societies. The Trukese category of *niffag* (Goodenough 1951:37–38) makes explicit the driving principles of Hawaiian exchange. *Niffag* is the gift that embodies its own return, for when a gift is repaid, "the obligations are presumed to be reversed, not simply canceled." *Niffag* must not be compensated for on the same day since any suggestion of a direct return "in Trukese opinion robs the *niffag* of its quality as a gift." Although in theory freely offered, *niffag* is often made expressly to obligate another and to provoke a return gift. The rules of giving *niffag* are implicit in the protocol of Hawaiian gift giving and illustrate the paradigm of non-Western exchange: gifts are powerful and productive of further transactions.

Because exchange-in-kind usually implies an exchange of different things, the net balance is always potentially ambiguous. In Tangu, such ambiguity is often the subject of *br'ngun'guni*: "Critical assertions of equivalence occur in food exchanges. . . . But food stuffs . . . are difficult to measure, weigh, or evaluate against each other; and unless and until those who are making exchanges are prepared to decide that enough is equivalent . . . the equivalence of particular exchanges can always be made subject to doubt" (Burridge 1969:126).

Exchange in Keanae, and in many other, simpler societies, is self-driving; it is kept going by its own rules, which stipulate that (1) a gift must be repaid (2) but not immediately, and (3) different things must be given in exchange. It is this last principle, that different things go in different directions, that above all constitutes the dynamic of exchange-in-kind, for it makes an unequivocal balance impossible to achieve. Ambiguity about equivalence keeps people exchanging. When one traffics in foodstuffs and favors, how can one be sure that a debt has been canceled? This uncertainty and the fear of indebtedness impel people to overcompensate, to give more than enough in order to ensure that, at least, they are not the ones who will be lower in the end. But overcompensation has the effect of merely reversing the debt rather than restoring equivalence. Thus Keanae villagers are inevitably drawn into cycles of reciprocity with their neighbors, and they are just as surely led to overcompensate in these transactions. A felt imbalance on either side ensures future exchanges, until a phase of talk stink interrupts the social commerce between the parties. In the absence of some other mechanism for restoring symmetry (such as the Tangu *br'ngun'guni*), the talk story/talk stink progression is inevitable.

Chapter Seven

MARRIAGE
AND ADOPTION
AS EXCHANGE

Marriage has both structural and economic significance in Keanae. Previously, I described how marriage establishes the household as a productive and landholding unit. The present chapter considers marriage as
a form of exchange that conjoins families, and examines
how marriage and adoption operate in long-term cycles of
exchange among Hawaiians. David Schneider (1965:58)
has said that in a society without a prescriptive marriage
rule, marriage is "the innovative, inaugurative relationship
which 'creates.'" Marriage creates alliance. Unlike the
plane of day-to-day reciprocities between neighbors, marriage engenders new relationships and has the unique
property of creating long-term ties. Once entered into,
marriage is a lasting tie among Keanae Hawaiians, so that
the relationship between families is an enduring one.

According to Samuel M. Kamakau (1964:26), the arrangement of *ho'āo pa'a* marriage was marked by an exchange of valuables called *lou*, hooks. These gifts "testified
to the betrothal of the two parties to a binding marriage."
Such a marriage was celebrated with a feast and gifts of
land. The imagery of hooks becomes intelligible in light
of another meaning for the word *kuleana*, as "the relatives
through whom a person lays a claim to relationship by
marriage" (Handy and Pukui 1972:70). A man's wife is his
kuleana in her family, his claim on their resources, and
"anyone in his family claiming relationship with anyone in
hers" would refer to her as such. The hooks symbolize each
family's claim on the other, their enduring connection established with a binding marriage. Marriage is still marked

by a luau; cohabitation is not. As will also be described in this chapter, the practice of adoption completes this exchange between Hawaiian families.

"FAMILY TO US"

Describing the custom of *ho'āo* marriage, Kamakau (1964:26) wrote: "The children born to them sealed the relationship between the two families." The offspring of a marriage are *mo'opuna*, grandchildren, of both parents' families. Since a family includes those tracing descent cognatically from a pair of grandparents or great-grandparents, every married couple is potentially the beginning of a new family made up of their descendants. Children thus embody the conjunction of two families, as illustrated in Figure 7.1. Affines are incorporated into the Hawaiian scheme of relatedness as "family to us." The phrase evokes an image of two families brought together through marriage. Although affines are acknowledged to be "not really related," not blood relatives, an inmarrying spouse is casually called one of the family. Outsiders are thus transformed into quasi relatives, and their relatives are "family to us." A Hawaiian woman, describing the frequency of intermarriage between Keanae families, noted, "They're all related." Her companion commented with a smile, "Not good to have too many families, eh?" Marriage transforms nonrelatives into persons with whom exchange is possible under the ethic of generalized reciprocity.

The assimilation of sons-in-law and daughters-in-law as quasi relatives helps to explain the apparent incongruity between Hawaiians' historic willingness to marry outsiders and their unconcealed resentment of strangers who intrude into village life. An outsider who marries a villager is no longer an outsider. A Hawaiian father issued an imaginary warning to his new in-laws, the relatives of his son's Portuguese bride: "Step lightly when you walk in the valley. You leave her here; she's one of us now."

Several facts lend credence to the view that marriage cre-

Figure 7.1
The Conjunction of Families

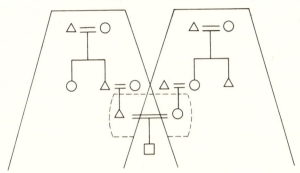

ates an alliance between families. Hawaiians recognize the family as an important category, identified by surname and associated with a particular locality, and they distinguish between family and in-laws, the relatives of someone married to a family member. Neighbors may not make this distinction but will classify affines on the basis of where they reside. A woman who marries into the village is henceforth associated with her husband's family in the eyes of other villagers. Neighbors may specify relatives belonging to "the husband's side of the family," where the woman would say "my husband's family." The difference illustrates structural relativity; husband and wife look to their own families, while other villagers see them as one, the start of a new family.

Affines are quasi relatives but they are categorically differentiated from those who share common ancestry, so that, from the perspective of the parental generation, marriage establishes a tie between previously unrelated families. Hawaiians consider marriage to be a matter of individual choice as long as there is no known kin relationship between the parties. Although Mary Pukui (n.d.) has said that marriage between first cousins was permissible, my informants felt it was somewhat scandalous. Marriage between relatives does occur rarely, but the families prefer to conceal the relationship. This aversion to consanguineal unions is probably not indigenous to Hawaiian society but evolved through missionary influence and the encounter with Western notions of incest. The Hawaiian Laws of 1842 prohibited marriage with a variety of relatives, including full and half siblings, stepchildren, parents' siblings, and siblings' children, but did not forbid unions between first cousins or more distant collaterals (Thurston 1904:46–47). Cousin marriages did occur in the past and can be documented even among Hawaiians now in their forties. If two individuals call each other by a kinship term but are known to be unrelated, they are still marriageable. A woman wed her adoptive "brother" because they were not "really related." The stricture against marrying relatives does not severely restrict marriage choices since genealogical knowledge is broad rather than deep.

Since nonrelatives are distinguished from relatives by the absence of common descent, repeated marriages in the same generation are possible between families. Indeed, the number of such parallel marriages among Hawaiians is striking. The marriage of two sisters to two brothers appears relatively frequently in genealogies and not only in the distant past. Even among today's young adults, there are occasional marriages between sets of siblings; in one case, a woman's four brothers married four sisters. There are isolated instances of the levirate and of a man serially marrying two sisters. There is no stated preference for parallel marriage, but Hawaiians approve of repeated ties between families within the same generation. "Family to us" remain marriageable, and the bond is strengthened with further unions.

AFFINAL TERMINOLOGY

Hawaiian kinship terminology categorically distinguished affines from consanguines. The spouse's parents were *makua hūnōwai*. The parents of the married couple addressed each other as *pūluna*, a collective term applying equally to the parents and parents' siblings in each family (Handy and Pukui 1972:69). According to Pukui, *pūluna* was used reciprocally between the parental generations of the two families. *Pūluna* were "nominally" related, which was "almost equivalent to 'blood' relationship." The birth of the first child "sealed" the relationship between the families (ibid.:70). Keanae Hawaiians no longer use a term corresponding to *pūluna*; parents-in-law refer to one another descriptively, as for example "my daughter-in-law's father" or "my *hūnōna's* mother." Yet the prior term *pūluna* suggests that this was a recognized category of relationship: the parental generation in a family related to one another through marriage.

The term *kaiko'eke* was used reciprocally between affines of the same sex in the marital generation. For a man, *kaiko'eke* referred to his wife's brother, his sister's husband, or the husband of a classificatory sister; a woman applied *kaiko'eke* to her husband's sister, her brother's wife, or the wife of a classificatory brother (Morgan 1909:428–432). Spouses called each other man and woman, *kāne* and *wahine*. A husband's brother was similarly *kāne* and a wife's sister *wahine*. *Hūnōna* referred to both son-in-law and daughter-in-law; *hūnōna* is the only Hawaiian affinal term commonly used today in Keanae, and it is reserved for son-in-law. The English terms "brother-in-law" and "sister-in-law" have replaced *kaiko'eke*.

The terms for affines share most of the distinctive features of the kinship terms described in Chapter 5. Affines are grouped by generation, and, in the speaker's generation, cross-sex ties are differentiated from same-sex. Later in this chapter, I consider the expectations and affective qualities of these relationships. For the present, the most significant feature of the affinal terminology is the absence of ranking by relative age within the same generation. Although same-sex siblings are always senior/junior to one another, same-sex affines are unranked, or, at least, that is the logic of the terminology.

RECIPROCITY

Marriage creates reciprocal obligations and the expectation of symmetry; each family receives a *kuleana* in the other, a claim of relationship and a right to expect mutual assistance. (In practice, however, residence affects the exercise of this claim. When a child of the family marries into a different locality, this *kuleana* is effectively lost. As will be shown below, marriage between localities is more frequent than local endogamy, and most marriages are virilocal.) The premises of exchange suggest that there should be a return on the transaction. Since the Hawaiian ethic stipulates that equivalence should prevail, the "gift" of a sister or daughter to another family should be reciprocated in some way. The chant for the consecration of a *punahele* (favorite) child asks that the child's chiefly mate safeguard the family from harm: "devote her to the man that will rule the land . . . to preserve us the parents, and your offspring" (Kekoa 1865:41). Here protection is expected in return for the gift of a daughter in marriage. But as a quasikin relationship, affinity defuses the anxiety that would otherwise result from the unrequited gift. The "indebtedness" is felt as a general expectation of some unspecified future return.

Marriage creates a structural basis for reciprocity where none existed before and the expectation of a symmetrical relationship. Hooks connect the two families. Each now has a claim on the other. Between unrelated persons, exchange may be competitive; their relative status is undefined because their status as relatives is not established. Unrelated families either remain strangers, who may try to assert high status over one another, or become affines through the marriage of their children. Before marriage, there is no affinity between them, no normative pretext for exchange without concern for repayment. Marriage resolves status ambiguity by encompassing previously unrelated persons within the sphere of, ideally, generalized reciprocity. The alliance thus engendered is an agreement of symmetry. It would be disgraceful to act high over a relative by marriage; the families may exchange services and favors without regard to the net balance. Marriage declares a truce in contests of exchange.

Yet there is an ethical difference between generalized reciprocity between relatives and generalized reciprocity between affines. The aloha between blood relatives stipulates that no accounts are kept; concern for equivalence is simply irrelevant. Between affines, the expectation is that symmetry will be fulfilled. The type and the timing of the return are unspecified, as would be appropriate between relatives. Marriage creates the expectation of mutual aid. In-laws are expected to offer assistance when needed, without concern for repayment. Where kin may be counted on to supply material help, affines primarily exchange services: taro-patch work, babysitting, and many small but significant favors. In this spirit, and out of affection for her *hūnōna*, a Keanae woman made the luau for his parents' anniversary; they would have been called her *pūluna* in former times. In practice, affines who maintain active contact ensure that reciprocities balance out over time. Generosity is not suspect between affines, but generosity that is too frequent and too lavish would be inappropriate and ultimately would cause a breach in the relationship. Personal disputes do occur between in-laws, but usually the result is mutual avoidance rather than overt hostility. The affinal tie prevents talk stink from becoming too acrimonious.

Like kinship, affinity defines a potential solidarity that is variable in experience. In general, affinal ties are neither as active nor as close as blood relationships. Since most marriages are locally exogamous, the two families are unlikely to have frequent contact. There are exceptions in relationships between *kaiko'eke* (brothers-in-law, sisters-in-law) and between mothers-in-law and *hūnōna*s. In some cases *kaiko'eke* are closer than "own" siblings, for their relationship is not colored by senior/junior ranking. Within the village, affinal relations range from affection to avoidance; but even where social contacts are minimal, they are at least not competitive. Day-to-day reciprocities with affines are possible but not mandatory. Marriage is, after all, a way of relating people who would ordinarily be mutually opposed, and at times the truce is an uneasy one.

In the earlier example of a wedding luau the groom's relatives directed much hostility at their new in-laws from Honolulu. Partly, their criticism reflected the villagers' distrust of outsiders, but the in-laws had also violated the ethic of the new relationship. By refusing to participate in luau work, they appeared to reject the association with their affines-to-be. In effect, they were acting high. Yet part of the wedding luau's purpose is to bring together both families and to celebrate their new relationship. The feast is one of the gifts, or hooks, connecting the families. In this instance, the affines did not behave as "family to us," hence the appellation "in-laws," which Hawaiians sometimes use to refer to their affines pejoratively. "Daughter-in-law" and "son-in-law" do not carry the same negative connotations, however.

Marriage is a way of assimilating strangers into the village. An inmarrying *hūnōna* or daughter-in-law is incorporated into the spouse's family. Outsiders are acceptable as "family to" other villagers. I might add that they are also intelligible as affines. They are knowable. Their presence in the village can be understood; they become persons with whom communication is possible since their motive for being in Keanae is proper and traditional. Under any other pretext, a stranger in the village is the object of mistrust, suspicion, and resentment.

RESIDENCE AND SOLIDARITY

Most Keanae Hawaiians were born in the locale of Keanae-Wailua; 67 percent of adult residents are from this area. As shown in Table 7.1, the disproportionate number of local-born men in the village, as opposed to local-born women, accords with the male bias in landholding and in-

Table 7.1
ORIGINS OF MARRIED HOUSEHOLDERS

	Local Man	Nonlocal Man
Local woman	15 (32%)	10 (21%)
Nonlocal woman	20 (43%)	2 (4%)
Total = 47 households (100%)		

NOTE: The tabulation excludes four households where the origin of both spouses could not be determined.

heritance. Men and women do not leave the village with equal frequency. Women are more likely to marry out; men remain if they are able to secure land. Accordingly, one would expect virilocal marriages to predominate, and the data support this inference. The figures are drawn from forty-seven marital histories where the origin of both spouses could be ascertained. It must be noted, however, that these histories are only of persons who stayed in Keanae, a small proportion of the offspring of Keanae families. Several of the Hawaiian households were quite large in former times, when the children were young and living at home. Keanae Hawaiians were extraordinarily prolific, one family having thirteen children, another seventeen. Since employment and landholding prospects in Keanae are limited, most siblings leave by the time they reach adulthood. Nevertheless, many former residents marry people from Keanae. About half of the local-born adults whom I encountered living outside were married to the offspring of other villagers; although not a random sample or a precise statistic, this observation suggests that the frequency of intermarriage between Keanae people may be comparable both inside and outside the village.

Among those who have remained in Keanae, taking a spouse from outside is twice as common as village endogamy, by 64 to 32 percent. In locally exogamous marriages, virilocality predominates within the choice of postmarital residence, although within the village a couple nearly always sets up a new household. As a woman from Kaupo

explained with some regret, she had come to live in Keanae
because she married a Keanae boy, and "you have to go
live with him, no can help." Table 7.1 indicates that virilocality is twice as frequent as uxorilocality in marriages
where one spouse came from outside, virilocal here meaning that a woman married into her husband's natal locality.
In 43 percent of exogamous marriages, a woman married
into Keanae; in 21 percent of these unions, a man came to
reside with his wife. In marriages between local people,
most couples obtained land for their homes from the husband's family. Overall, residential affiliation is with the
husband's family in 67 percent of Keanae marriages. Uxorilocality, 33 percent, is a significant alternative, but my find-
ings do not support Pukui's claim that the husband always
went to live with the wife (Handy and Pukui 1972:44). This
may be her reconstruction of the aboriginal situation, or
it may have been a regional norm in her home district
of Kau.

I have said that, ideally, the eldest son returns to Keanae
as heir to the family lands. Younger brothers may remain if
they are able to secure land, either through the family, by
buying it, or from the father-in-law. Parents may give a
small parcel to a younger sibling after the primary heir has
been accommodated; the eldest son may inherit the homestead, a younger brother a *kuleana*. Out of a sibling set, one
brother and one sister frequently remain in Keanae, the
brother as landowner, the sister as the wife of another resident. Brother/sister coresidence in Keanae is high, but
women who remain are more likely than men to have a
cross-sex sibling in Keanae because men are more likely to
secure land and stay in the village. If village coresidence
simply reflected solidarity in relationships, one would expect to find a low incidence of same-sex siblings living in
the village. But residential choice depends more on where
one can find a job and a house site. Two-thirds of the men
in Keanae have a brother also living in the village; 44 percent of women with a living sister have a sister in Keanae.
These figures are another indication that women are more

Figure 7.2
Relationships Among Keanae Landowners, c. 1854

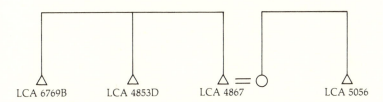

LCA 6769B   LCA 4853D   LCA 4867   LCA 5056

likely to marry outside the village. Men stay in Keanae because of property. Women who stay are likely to have a
brother (and sister-in-law) residing there as well.

Since most siblings leave the village, householders are
likely to be related to one another as *kaiko'eke* and *pūluna*.
Within the same generation, the pattern of sibling and affinal ties among current residents is strikingly similar to
that of nineteenth-century Keanae, when landowners were
related as brothers and brothers-in-law. Figure 7.2 diagrams as example of such ties between Land Commission
Awardees. In this case, three brothers all obtained awards
during the Mahele. Similar examples could be cited from
other land districts.

An example from present-day Keanae, diagramed in
Figure 7.3, nicely illustrates the range of inter- and intra-
generational ties between residents and also shows repeated affinal links between families. Jimmy and Roslyn
are Ben's *pūluna*; the two families have exchanged children.
By the logic of the Hawaiian terminology, the cousins
Walter and Dolly would be classificatory brother and sister.
A "sister" exchange has taken place between the two families. As wife of another householder, Becky has remained
in Keanae. Her brother's wife, Dolly, drives in from outside
to work Ben's taro patches; Ben is elderly, and Dolly and
her husband will probably live in the Keanae homestead
after his death. Related through a brother/sister tie, Walter
and Ella are extremely close. "Uncle" Walter dotes on Ella's
children far more than on his own. This cousin relation-

Figure 7.3
Relationships Among Keanae Residents, 1975

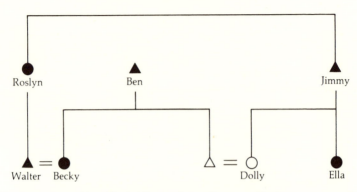

Note: Shaded figures denote Keanae residents.

ship is more solidary than that of husband and wife; at the time of fieldwork, Ben's wife had recently died, and Becky was living in her father's house with her children, while Walter continued to reside with his parents. Cultural precedent suggests that the basis for Walter and Dolly's relationship is the affective solidarity between "brother" and "sister."

In the marital generation, brother/sister, brother-in-law, and sister-in-law ties are channels of exchange between households. *Pūluna*, the parents of *kaiko'eke*, also have the option of participating in reciprocities, and strong affective ties may develop between those who choose to activate the relationship. But *pūluna* in the village have less frequent contact than siblings-in-law, who are related through a brother/sister tie. Parents-in-law are more likely to interact with the daughter-in-law or son-in-law individually; although their child is associated with the spouse's family, the parents-in-law are not. Relations between *pūluna* are voluntary and variable, ranging from extreme solidarity to marked distance. In contrast, reciprocity and affection between brother and sister bring *kaiko'eke* into close and frequent contact. The Hawaiian terminology reveals an es-

sential feature of affinal relationships: these ties are terminologically unranked, suggesting that marriage establishes
equivalence between persons who would otherwise be potential status rivals.

While high foods pass between relatives, mutual assistance is the most frequent article of exchange between
affines and particularly between *kaiko'eke*. Brothers-in-law
may help one another in the taro patches and in home repairs. When a man receives luau food, he takes a share to
his sister's household. Although phrased as a gift from
brother to sister, the food ends up in the *kaiko'eke*'s household. Brothers-in-law are often good friends, unless one is
economically superior to the other. The successful village
big-man is related by marriage to several other landholders.
But the brother-in-law relationship is one of symmetrical
obligations. When one party fears that he will be unable to
repay a favor, equivalence is threatened, and he will begin
to avoid contact with the other. I return to the subject of
big-men and their affines in the following chapter.

A brother-in-law is a person who can be counted on for
luau work and emergency assistance. At the wedding luau
described in detail earlier, the hardest worker was the
groom's sister's husband; other villagers even credited him
with the success of the event. Once when I was driving an
elderly woman home, we stopped to help a Keanae man
whose car had broken down on the Hana road. As we
made arrangements to get help, the man's wife's brother
also drove up. To my companion, this was the signal for us
to leave, for we were no longer needed: "It's all right now.
That's the brother-in-law."

Assistance freely offered by a brother-in-law contrasts
strikingly with the help normatively expected of a younger
sibling. This was evident at the luau preparations when
a brother-in-law's selfless labor was a foil to a younger
brother's erratic and rather grudging contributions. The
younger brother's contributions are structurally defined;
his aid is a matter of duty, a requirement of his status. The
brother-in-law is subject to a more general and less im-

perative set of expectations; his status is initially defined through an exchange relationship. Brothers-in-law are expected to help one another but out of friendship and mutual regard. The word *mutual* is the key here. *Kaiko'eke* are often closer than same-sex siblings, for their relationship is symmetrical, while that of older and young siblings is inherently asymmetrical. The significance of the *kaiko'eke* bond is sentimental rather than jural; the relationship stresses affection rather than obligation.

Although precipitated by a brother/sister tie, the bond of both male and female *kaiko'eke* attains a solidarity in its own right, independent of relations between brother and sister. Sisters-in-law are often extremely close. They may see each other daily and exchange small but important favors, such as driving, babysitting, and grocery shopping. Frequently, the brother/husband enters little into their relationship and even appears to be extraneous to the bond between the women. Female *kaiko'eke* and their daughters may form a core of intense and active relationships. In one example, a woman's daughter and grandchild lived with her deceased husband's sister; the child would be a classificatory *mo'opuna* to this woman, the mother's father's sister. The two older women were constant companions, although the brother/husband had been dead for several years. Again, solidarities between women are much in evidence. The Hawaiian child's affectionate relationship to the father's sister, which is a structurally important tie in other Polynesian societies, stems as much from the affection of sisters-in-law as from the solidarity of brother and sister. Female *pūluna*, the mothers-in- law, often have a relationship similar to that of sisters-in-law. In the luau described in detail, a woman flew from Denver to help her son-in-law's mother prepare a luau. While the sisters in the family making the luau bickered among themselves, these two women and their children worked together without strife.

A pattern of sentimental ties running counter to jural relations again emerges in Hawaiian kinship and affinity. The solidarity of *kaiko'eke* and mothers-in-law is not predictable

from the concepts of family and relatedness. The friendship that often develops between siblings-in-law com-
plements the potential strain between same-sex siblings;
brothers-in-law are effectively unranked brothers whose
relationship is not strained by competition for family resources. Female affines such as *pūluna* and sisters-in-law
may be closer than actual sisters because their relationship
is not defined as hierarchical. Normative obligations can
impede easy affection and undermine the aloha that should
exist between relatives. Questions of authority and inheritance create tension between older and younger siblings
and between parent and child. The counterpart of these
relationships, which are normatively solidary but tense in
practice, is a set of ties that are normatively unstressed but
solidary in practice. The roles of *pōki'i, hūnōna, kaiko'eke*,
and parent-in-law fall into this category. These relationships tend to be sentimentally favored perhaps because
they are jurally unmarked. The intensity of such ties is a
matter of choice rather than duty.

ADOPTION

Ties between Hawaiians and their adopted children
often exemplify the ideals of aloha and solidarity embodied in the metaphor of feeding, although *"hānai"* is now
reserved for legal adoption; the more common term is
"keeping." In contrast to the tense relationship adult offspring sometimes have with their parents, adopted children are often lavished with affection, particularly when
they are grandchildren. Hawaiian women are eager to keep
their *mo'opuna*s because solidarity between grandparent
and grandchild is more predictable than that between parent and adult child. One couple legally adopted their
daughter's daughter; neighbors implied that the only thing
they wanted from their daughter was her child to adopt:
"They never cared for that girl much. Now that they've got
the baby, they don't care. They're happy." It is not only the

childless household that seeks children to keep; if there is only one child or if the children are all of one sex, the parents will try to take in another. An informant said that her grandmother adopted a girl "to be like a sister for my father," then took in another boy because she had only one son.

The apparent casualness with which parents give and take children in adoption is a distinctive characteristic of Polynesian societies (cf. Carroll 1970). Hawaiians' love for children is well known. A childless woman in the village was said to have "never known love." People with children are expected to share them with childless households. In the remainder of this chapter I argue, however, that the Hawaiian custom of adoption cannot be explained simply by reference to aloha but is part of a long-term exchange relationship between affinally related families.

Hawaiian grandmothers readily adopt their daughters' illegitimate offspring, for the Hawaiian attitude toward illegitimacy is the inverse of the Mainland explanation: "Well, sometime you can't help. The girl may want the baby and not want to marry the man." Even when the adopted grandchild grows up and leaves home, the grandmother/grandchild relationship is often much closer than the tie between the grandmother and her daughter. *Hānai* children are supposed to be "just like your own in feeling," but Hawaiians distinguish between those who are related and those who are not. The *hānai* child usually takes the name of the adoptive parents, although Hawaiians recognize that this is not the "real" name. The adoptive mother is usually addressed as "mama," but the *hānai* child may refer to her as "the mother who raised me" to distinguish her from the biological mother. Nonetheless, the enduring aloha is between adoptive parent and child.

But not all adoptions are characterized by mutual affection. In 1868, Kamakau wrote, "There are some adoptions and some taking care of others now but most are for the purpose of personal gain. . . . It was not so in olden times." Pukui (Handy and Pukui 1972:168) has also hinted that there is another side to Hawaiian adoption: "it is a mistake . . . to think that the desire to adopt children was always motivated by pure altruism." She quotes a Hawaiian proverb: "feed human beings for they can be sent on errands." The moral of the proverb is that "an adopted child, well cared for, will be a help later on." The underside of the *hānai* relationship is service. In Keanae, *mo'opuna*s work side by side with their grandparents in the taro patches. Pukui (n.d.) describes the *hānai* child's lifelong debt to his adoptive family: "In later years he was expected to not only accord respect, but active support to all those who had had a share in taking care of him. This obligation towards themselves was felt so strongly that great resentment was held against anyone else who put the youngster or young adult to work. . . . A boy, who moved in with his wife's people upon marriage, presumably had a more difficult time and perhaps had more than once to neglect his own wife and children in returning to his former home to help some relative in need."

An example from Keanae mirrors this description. A woman and her sister's son were both raised by the same couple; when these parents died, she and her husband kept the boy. Other villagers say that *hānai* refers only to taking a child as an infant. A neighbor insists that the woman and her husband had "not really adopted him, just took him because they needed someone to work, another hand for the cattle. He was old already." The boy was put to work in the couple's poi factory and made to water their watercress patch at night. The man's wife claims that when they were first married, he left their bed at two in the morning every night to tend the watercress. The adoptive "mother" still calls him "her boy" and expects him to supply her with poi every week; she calls him to fix her car and repair her plumbing. The man describes his life as a kept child with great bitterness: "Jack of all trades, master of none, that's what I learned from my uncle and aunty. She likes to say she reared me, brought me up, but I worked for them. She still comes to me because she needs me. And after all the years of service I gave them, they gave me nothing to take away when I left them, only one hundred dollars when I got married."

Other villagers feel that this was a perversion of the *hānai* relationship, but the treatment of kept children may vary widely even within the same household. In one case, a woman was keeping her husband's sister's daughter and her own daughter's daughter. The granddaughter was obviously the family "pet," doted upon, fed treats, made much of. The adoptive mother spoke gruffly to the other child, who was continually given chores and in general fulfilled a servant's role in the household. No one seemed to notice the favoritism, however, and the adoptive mother professed great love for both her kept children.

In both these instances where the *hānai* relationship appeared to violate the ethic of aloha, the adopted children were the offspring of collaterals rather than grandchildren. Although intergenerational ties are generally solidary among Hawaiians, open affection is more predictable between alternate than between adjacent generations; that is, ties between persons in the grandparent and grandchild generations are more consistently close and free from tension than are relationships between those in the parent and child generations.

Grandparent/*mo'opuna* is the most common adoptive relationship, and the overwhelming preponderance of adoptions by relatives are by the mother's parents. In my tally of adoptions involving Keanae residents and their offspring, eleven of seventeen (65 percent) were by the mother's parents. Since these adoptions involved six boys and five girls, the sex of the child does not appear to determine the adopting relative. I uncovered no instance of adoption by the father's parents. Most adoptions (seventeen out of twenty-one cases) involve relatives, and adoptions by matrilateral kin account for fifteen (88 percent) of these. *Mo'opuna* adoptions, by actual or classificatory grandparents, constitute 76 percent of adoptions involving relatives. These results are comparable to Alan Howard's data on

Hawaiian adoption (Howard et al. 1970:36–38). The only two instances of patrilateral adoption in my sample do involve boys, one "raised by" an older brother and his wife and the other legally adopted by his father's brother to become his heir. The prevalence of matrilateral adoption suggests that "gifts" of children figure in long-term exchange between families.

Although *hānai* can be a service relationship, there is a long-established Hawaiian custom of singling out an adopted grandchild to be indulged as the "family pet": "Sometimes boys thus taken as foster children (*hānai*) were not allowed to do any work, or to carry anything in the hand, or to plant, or to carry anything on the shoulders, or to fish. This was in accordance with a vow taken by the foster parents never to see the child perform any kind of labor as long as they were alive. It was the same with some girls; the grandparents or foster parents made great pets of them, and they were not allowed to carry anything in their hands. . . . Such children would be . . . fed poi by dropping it into their mouths . . . lest they choke and the precious ones come to harm" (Kamakau 1964:26–27). Mary Pukui was such a *punahele* child. The *punahele* was called a *kapu* child and was treated like a high-ranking visitor in the family. According to Pukui, the status of a *punahele* child in the household was in some ways more privileged than that of the eldest. These "precious" children "had the best of everything, choice foods, the best mats" (Handy and Pukui 1972:101). Although not the genealogical senior, the *punahele* was accorded a unique respect by her siblings. Pukui was her mother's first-born, adopted by her grandmother to inherit the family's intangible property: the genealogies, chants, and esoteric knowledge. A Hawaiian manuscript dating from 1865 describes a ceremony for consecrating a *punahele* child to the goddess Lilinoe, with phrases suggesting that the *punahele* was a child destined for chiefly marriage (Sahlins 1981:40). For a boy: "But join your body with a chiefess daughter, beloved (*punahele*) that the lives of your parents be preserved, also to preserve your offspring to give birth to chiefs to dwell as lords." For a girl: "Devote her to the man that will rule the land, a husband with an *ahupua'a*, a chief, to preserve us the parents, and your offspring" (Kekoa 1865:41). If the parents were "honorable, and distinguished, or related to chiefs" (ibid.:40),[1] they might consecrate their child in this fashion. Presumably, these "parents of distinction" were lower-ranking relatives of chiefs, perhaps the descendants of junior collaterals. Pukui was herself descended from a priestly family (Handy and Pukui 1972:82), and priests were customarily recruited from younger-brother lines. A child who married up would join the ranks of chiefly retainers. The connection with a high chief would safeguard the family from tyranny and expropriation. With the demise of the chiefs, the traditional function of the *punahele* custom was lost, even though the privileged, high-ranking quality of the favorite child's status remained.

Pukui's description of the *punahele* custom stresses the handing down of family knowledge; the favorite was "one chosen by a *kupuna* for strict rearing and special training in traditional arts and lore" (Handy and Pukui 1972:46). She also states that, in adoption, the father's parents always took the eldest son, and the mother's parents the eldest daughter. The Keanae data do not bear out these claims, nor does Howard's work on modern Hawaiian adoption (Howard et al. 1970:39). Rather than dismiss Pukui's claim as a temporal or regional difference, I propose an underlying logic: she is describing inheritance relationships. Pukui's own experience suggests that although land was customarily transmitted through the line of senior males, the family lore and traditions were passed down through women, from a grandmother to the granddaughter chosen to be her successor. This would explain why the *punahele* child is said to be a kind of *kaikua'ana*, or eldest in the

1. I am grateful to Marshall Sahlins for drawing this text to my attention and for sharing his interpretation of the *punahele* custom with me. The Hawaiian for this quotation is: "*inā he mau makua hanohano, a ko'iko'i ho'i, a pilipili ali'i pa'a, a me na mea like.*"

household, for she has been designated as heir of the family's spiritual property. The preponderance of adoptions by the maternal grandparents also supports this hypothesis. While the eldest son's family remained on the land, a daughter normally went to live with her husband. If her child did not return to the mother's parents, the family's intangible property could not be passed on to her.

Keanae Hawaiians today do not explicitly recognize the custom of *punahele*, although a few residents resemble "family pets" in their favored status within the household. Villagers do not formally pass down family traditions as they did in Pukui's childhood in Kau, and informants acknowledge that much family knowledge has been lost. Today medicinal lore and religious leadership are passed on to a daughter-in-law as often as to a daughter.

The destiny of kept children is variable. Most grow up, marry, and leave the locality where they were raised. As adults, they may or may not maintain contact with their adoptive families; the quality of this contact effectively depends on whether the child was treated as a servant or a "pet." A much-loved adopted child may be accommodated with land after the other children in the family have been provided for, and when a couple has no children, one may be adopted specifically to be designated as heir. This custom partly accounts for the sense of betrayal in the kept child's remarks quoted above; although his adoptive mother was childless, she had bequeathed her land to a classificatory grandchild, a sister's daughter's son, while the *hānai* son, with no property or legacy of his own, lived on a house lot given by his wife's father.

AN EXCHANGE MODEL

Both marriage and adoption occasion the movement of persons between different lands. Most marriages are exogamous; most siblings leave their natal locality and settle elsewhere. Marriage and adoption have historically connected families of different localities and figure in past patterns of migration. Affines are the mediating term between relatives and nonrelatives. Marriage brings strangers into the realm of relatedness. Whether locally exogamous or endogamous, marriage creates a kin-like relationship and a basis for exchange where none existed before. There is evidence that in the past affinal relationships were channels of exchange between localities; certain lands were linked by repeated ties of trade, intermarriage, and adoption. Hawaiians traded with places where their affines lived, and even today informants can identify localities that were once closely linked with Keanae.

The one-sidedness of the adoption data supports the inference that adoption is also part of an exchange between families. As stated earlier, 88 percent of the adoptions that I recorded were to matrilateral relatives, with 65 percent by the maternal grandparents. As mentioned, inheritance relationships could at least partly account for this pattern. One reason for adopting a daughter's daughter was to pass on the family lore and genealogies. While land was inherited by sons and sons' sons, intangible property was handed down through women. A granddaughter became heir to the family's spiritual legacy and returned to her mother's natal household to receive this oral knowledge. But adoption also fulfills the reciprocal exchange of persons between families and between different lands. In every case of adoption by the maternal grandparents, the daughter had married outside and no longer lived in Keanae. When a woman marries outside her natal land, the family effectively loses its *kuleana*, its right or claim, on the other family's immediate services, for daughter, son-in-law, and grandchildren will not be in their locality to offer assistance. Grandchild adoption is the return on the exchange and accomplishes symmetry between affines. "Sister" exchange between families has the same effect.

In practical terms, a daughter's child is her replacement in the parental home. The daughter who marries out becomes a member of another family, and her parents have the right to expect a return. A child's spouse is the family's claim, *kuleana*, in another family. Significantly, Kamakau (1964:26) also uses the word *kuleana* to describe the imperative quality of the grandparents' claim on their grandchildren: "The claim (*kuleana*) of the grandparents upon their children's children took precedence over that of the parents who bore them; the parents could not keep the child without the consent of the grandparents."

In suggesting these long-term exchange relationships, I am describing a model that is never perfectly realized in practice. Although most adoptions are by the maternal grandparents, only one or two daughters of the family ever give back a child. The grandparents never take a *mo'opuna* from every daughter who has married outside Keanae. And the ethos of *hānai* is variable, as I have described; when their children have grown and left home, an aging couple may adopt a grandson or some distantly related "stray" primarily to provide service at home and in the taro patches. There are seldom more than two adopted children in a home at any one time. The elderly parents may take one grandchild and then another when the first is nearly high school age, the time when the child must leave the village.

Nevertheless, outmarrying daughters are expected to give a child if the parents request it; conversely, a daughter knows her parents will always take her child if she does not want to rear it. Marriage sets up a general expectation of a future return, but the return may take the form of a son-in-law's service or some later personal favor. If the daughter does not move away, she and her children will continue to assist her parents. As will be detailed in the following chapter, a local big-man, a taro agent, recruited his growers primarily from the family into which both his sister and his daughters had married. This relationship was justified by the ethic of aloha between *kaiko'eke* and *pūluna*, but if in some unstated structural sense they owed him something, their allegiance was at least a partial fulfillment of exchange.

Matrilateral adoption predominates in Howard's figures, but there is about a 16 percent incidence of adoption by the father's mother (Howard et al. 1970:34–38). Significantly, he notes that adoption by patrilateral kin tends to be formalized by legal adoption. I uncovered no instances of adoption by the father's parents in Keanae families. One Keanae landowner who had no sons of his own legally adopted a brother's son and designated him as his heir. I suggest that adopting a patrilateral relative is done for purposes of property transmission since it is consistent with the norm of patrilineal inheritance. Adopting a son's child accords with the premise that grandchildren replace their grandparents on the land. Legally adopting the *mo'opuna* effectively bypasses the child generation in inheritance and ensures the bequest to the grandchild. Most grandchild adoptions are of a daughter's child, however, and are not landed property relationships. Howard notes that only about 12 percent of adopted grandchildren were legally adopted.

There are two reasons to want a grandchild in the home. One is that Hawaiians love children and feel that a home is incomplete without them. Those who are fortunate enough to have children should share the wealth with those who do not. The other, more practical reason is that children can be a great help, particularly to the elderly. Their usefulness in this regard is suggested by Hawaiian proverbs and by the fact that some adopted children assume service roles in the household. In the recent past, many Keanae families have been quite large, and there is often a wide age spread between the oldest and youngest, even in families with only five children. The youngest child is often born after the first grandchildren. This pattern of child spacing ensures that there will always be a child in the house. Women usually adopt after they have passed child-bearing age. Kept grandchildren are not necessarily loved the less for providing service, but they usually do their share of chores around the grandparental home. Normatively, *mo'opuna* are expected to offer service to their grandparents. From the age of eight or nine, they can work in the taro patches, where a twelve-year-old boy can accomplish as much as most adults. There is usually great affection between grandparent and grandchild, expressed as indulgence on one side and as deference on the other. But the adopted *mo'opuna* does not usually inherit land. The child lives with the grandparents until called away by schooling or marriage. The fondness between them continues through the life of the grandparents, however, and the grandchild will still do things for them whenever possible. The reunion of a grandparent and an adopted *mo'opuna* who has settled far away is a joyous occasion, where the parties may try to outdo each other in lavish gift giving.

Case histories compiled from informants' statements and documentary sources reveal long-term patterns of intermarriage and adoption between certain localities. Some of the evidence is tantalizingly incomplete, but these gaps are unavoidable because of limitations in archival material and in Hawaiians' genealogical knowledge. There have been repeated ties between Keanae and Kailua, about halfway outside on the Hana road, and Kaupo, on the dry side of Maui. Several Keanae families are also related by marriage to Hana families. Adopted children have been taken from Kailua and nearby Huelo, and the siblings and offspring of Keanae families have married into these localities.

The relationship with Kaupo is particularly interesting because it reveals past patterns of exchange between the wet and dry sides of the island. Like Keanae, Kaupo has suffered the attrition of its Hawaiian population. The loss in Kaupo has been even more severe because it is far less accessible from the towns than Keanae and because ranches have systematically swallowed up Hawaiian lands. With scant rainfall and few natural water sources, Kaupo is marginal land for agriculture. Most of the area is now used for cattle pasturage. The state highway becomes a jeep track a few miles beyond Hana, and Kaupo can be reached only with a four-wheel-drive vehicle. Keanae prospers partly because it is relatively accessible from the outside. There are even fewer job opportunities in Kaupo, and residents must accept being cut off from town society. Hawaiians who have left Kaupo find it impractical to return, even to check on the status of their property, so that it is relatively easy for pretenders to sell Hawaiian lands to the ranches. Elderly Keanae villagers who came from Kaupo frequently express anxiety about this possibility. With no knowledge of the legal process involved, they feel helpless to protect their family lands. Tax-office functionaries have little time for the inquiries of old Hawaiians who are hazy about tax-map references and grantees' names.

Kaupo residents formerly carried on internal trade, both within the valley and with Keanae. According to informants from Kaupo, the upland dwellers relied on sweet potatoes and breadfruit as staple foods. There was some dry-land taro in the vicinity of the springs, but the Kaupo people "got their poi from Keanae." A mule train brought the bags of poi from Kipahulu, just below Hana. Early in this century, when much of Keanae was planted in rice, the Kaupo people got rice from Keanae. These were monetary transactions; Kaupo residents ordered one-dollar, five-dollar, or ten-dollar bags of poi, specified which poi shop they wanted, and paid in cash. Within the valley, exchange-in-kind prevailed. This system accords with Pukui's statement that exchange within a land district was always phrased as gift giving, while between lands transactions could take the form of buying and selling. An old-time resident who lived "far up the mountain" in Kaupo described exchange and ecological specialization within the valley: "We knew everything about the mountain, how to get meat, all the animals. But fishing no. I can't fish with a rod for nothing. I don't know how. We never knew how to fish. We used to get fish by exchange with the people who lived down at the beach: give them wild pig, meat from the mountain, and they would give us fish. Or if we wanted fish, we used powder and blasted them."

A Keanae man explained that the relationship of Keanae and Kaupo was an ancient one. Long before the Mahele, he said, several families came from Kohala, on the island of Hawaii: "They came because too many wars, bloody, people losing their land. The chiefs made all the money from the land and the people got nothing. Some came here, others went to Kaupo. That's why so many Kaupo families related to families here, lots of families." And he cited names of Keanae families and of Kaupo families whose children had married into Keanae. It is in keeping with the Hawaiian theory of relatedness that putative distant kinship is associated with long-term exchange relationships. But this description of past migrations is also consistent with early writers' accounts of precontact Hawaiian politics. The Kamehameha dynasty, which came to rule the kingdom, originated on the island of Hawaii, and Kohala has been cited as Kamehameha's birthplace. Kohala has also been described as a politically important area in precontact times, with bitter dynastic disputes and endemic warfare. Here legend and history may be indistinguishable; I doubt that my informant had ever read Kamakau (1961).

With Kaupo's depopulation during this century, the movement of persons from the leeward side of Maui seems less of an exchange than an emigration. A similar fate befell Kahikinui, a barren land of lava west of Kaupo, now wholly deserted. Informants say that because of the dearth of water, the Kahikinui people long ago came to live in Kaupo. Kaupo people have since moved to Hana and Keanae, as well as to the towns and other islands. Yet nineteenth-century evidence indicates that in the past there was more of a two-way flow of persons between these lands. Figure 7.4 illustrates relationships among several Keanae Land Commission Awardees who received parcels during the Great Mahele. The brother and brother-in-law ties at the local level are not unusual. What is unusual is that this family held land in both Keanae and Kaupo; Wahapuu, Ohule, Naha, Pali, and Charlotte Harbottle were also corecipients of a Royal Patent Grant in Kaupo. Charlotte lived outside with her haole husband, but Wahapuu's daughter Leiau married a Kaupo man. This Royal

Figure 7.4
Relationships Between Keanae and Kaupo, c. 1850

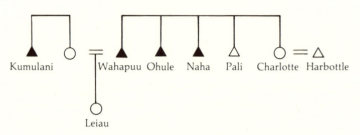

Note: Shaded figures denote Keanae Land Commission Awardees.

Patent Grant is one of the family lands of a present-day Keanae resident who married into the village from Kaupo. This family's affinal ties and landholdings in two localities are indicative of the close historical relationships between the two places.

Five settlers, one man and four women, came to Keanae from Kaupo during the 1920s. Two of the women were sisters; the man was said to be their cousin. The other two women were unrelated, but all the families knew each other well. The sisters' grandmother "stayed with" the third woman's relatives in Kaupo, and their mother was midwife to the other woman's family. The older sister stated that she first came to Keanae because her family "had relatives" there. The sisters' Kaupo grandmother had adopted a Hana girl "to be like a sister" for their father, but she only stayed a few years and then returned to Hana. This woman later married into Keanae, and the older sister met her husband, Albert, while visiting her "father's sister" there. After they were married, the husband's younger brother, Joseph, lived with them. The woman's sister met him during visits and married him; the two sisters married two brothers. Figure 7.5 diagrams the relationships. Their husbands' sister Maggie married into Hana. Their "niece" Julia, who married into the family and resides in Keanae, was from a Kaupo family that had lived on land adjacent to

Figure 7.5
Adoption and Intermarriage: Keanae, Kaupo, and Hana

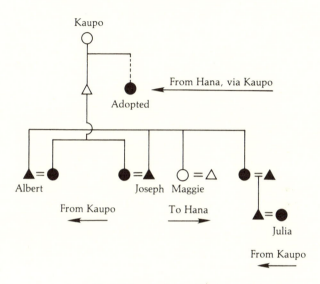

Note: Shaded figures denote Keanae residents.

theirs. Thus women from Kaupo families married into Keanae and particularly into the family of Joseph and Albert.

Figure 7.6 shows relationships between two families of Kailua/Huelo and Keanae. In the eyes of other villagers, Violet represents her family in Keanae. Although she was born in the village, her family is said to be "from Huelo side, not from 'round here." Her mother married a Chinese rice planter in Keanae. The progenitor of this family, Ben T., owned land in Huelo, Kailua, and Keanae; the family has a reputation for acquiring land and holding on to it. Although Violet inherited parcels that her parents had purchased in Keanae and bought a homestead there in her own name, most of her family's lands were in the vicinity of Huelo and Kailua. I found no evidence that Ben T. or his son David ever lived in Keanae. Ben's grandchild and namesake, Ben Junior, inherited the Keanae land, but his

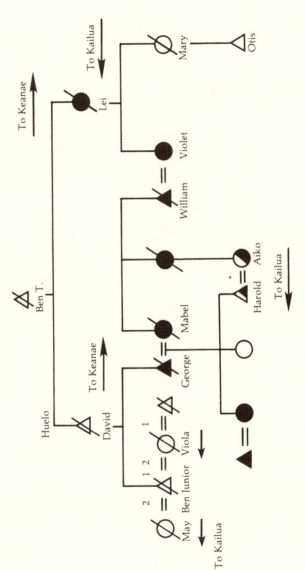

Figure 7.6
Relationships Between Keanae and Kailua

Note: Shaded figures denote Keanae residents.
* Previously lived in Keanae.

primary residence was near Huelo. Both of Ben Junior's wives were from Keanae; Viola first married a man from Peahi, a community west of Huelo where Ben Junior's family also had land, then married Ben Junior. In Probate Court after the death of his second wife, May, Ben Junior testified that "we had two places but her real place is Keanae." His younger brother, George, was born in Huelo but married a Keanae woman.

The relationship between the two families resembles that diagramed in Figure 7.3: a classificatory sister exchange has taken place between George and William. Informants referred to William's family as the "in-laws of T." Again, two families are linked by repeated affinal ties, accomplishing a symmetrical exchange. The brother-in-law relationship between George and William is created in two ways: through George's marriage to William's "own" sister and through William's union with George's classificatory sister Violet. It should be noted that in the 1920s, when these marriages took place, Hawaiian was still spoken in Keanae, and Hawaiian kinship terminology was used. Thus it is not artificial to call this a sister exchange, for at the time it was precisely that. The same pattern of affinal exchange between families can be found in the marriage of persons now in their thirties who barely know Hawaiian and use English kinship terms (see Figure 7.3). The cultural categories have survived the loss of the original terms for them.

George leased and then purchased a homestead in Keanae. Three of his children married Keanae offspring. The first-cousin marriage of Harold and Aiko is unusual among modern Hawaiians, but there is a logic of repeated affinal alliance to the union. As pointed out in Chapter 5, Hawaiians tend to associate women with their mothers' families, and sons with their fathers'. In the wedding luau preparations described in that chapter, the groom's sister had primary responsibility for the event, but villagers said that the mother's side was doing the luau. In this first-cousin marriage, George's family has again taken a spouse from its affines, Mabel's family. The couple later returned to Kailua, the home locality of Harold's family, and in so doing completed a reciprocal movement of persons between the two lands.

Similarly, Lei's Keanae marriage was reciprocated by Mary's return to Kailua in the next generation. I do not know whether May was kept by her mother's parents or whether she returned to marry a Kailua man. Her son Otis was legally adopted by and designated the heir of a man in Kailua. Although I was unable to discover a genealogical relationship between the two families, they resided on neighboring lands. George's son, Harold, is a close friend of Otis's children, several of whom live in Keanae.

As shown in Figure 7.7, Otis serially wed two Kailua women; the sororate and levirate occasionally appear in Keanae genealogies and are consistent with parallel affinal ties between families. The daughter of a Keanae woman from Kaupo married into this family. There is great aloha between Helen and her son-in-law Harvey, and a friendly relationship with her *pūluna* Otis; Helen was an honored guest at a family luau given in Kailua for her daughter's wedding anniversary. Irene's grandmother was also from Kaupo and was known to Helen's family. Although villagers may be linked in a chain of *kaiko'eke* relationships, Hawaiians do not recognize any special tie to the in-laws of in-laws. The *pūluna* relationship is dyadic and does not extend to other *pūluna* of the son-in-law's daughter-in-law's family. Similarly, the affinal relationship does not include the wife's sister's husband. Affines of the same family may see one another at their spouses' family luaus but are considered to be unrelated.

Hawaiians have a historic penchant for traveling and visiting friends and relatives in other places, often staying for extended periods. Parallel marriages often result when a young sibling visits an older living in another place and meets other members of the affinally related family. Parallel unions create an outpost of the inmarrying spouse's family in a strange place. Two sisters who marry two brothers are not forced to live in a village where they have

Figure 7.7
Adoption and Intermarriage: Keanae, Kailua, and Kaupo

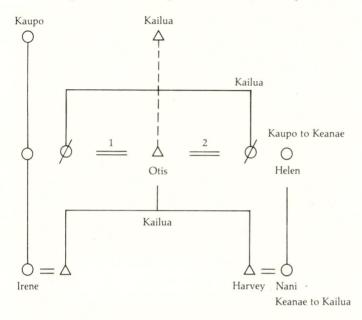

no kin. The position of an inmarrying stranger in the village can otherwise be difficult, for most neighbors will be neither kin nor affines, and everyday relations with such persons are likely to be stressful. Since most women marry out of their natal locality, sisters are particularly likely to be separated in adulthood. In the case of the two Kaupo women who married brothers in Keanae, the older met her husband while visiting an "aunty" in Keanae. Since the brothers lived together, the younger sister met her future husband while visiting the elder in Keanae. In the early 1940s, both brothers secured Homestead Lease Awards, one in Keanae and one in Wailua. By 1975, both sisters were widowed and still felt themselves to be outsiders, often referring to other villagers as "these people." Although their personal relationship was not always smooth, the sisters relied on each other more than on their neighbors. When the younger wanted fish, she would go to "the old lady's" house, where she knew she had a claim and would not have to worry about appearing greedy.

While parallel marriages reinforce the tie between families, it is advantageous to have multiple alliances and *kuleana*s in more than one family. Marriage also creates relatives who are unmarriageable in the next generation and thereby forces the dispersal of affinal ties. A family is likely to have affinal relationships with several others. In Figure 7.6, George's offspring are cousins to the children of Mabel's siblings and are not considered marriageable by today's standards. As shown in Figure 7.8, the *pūluna* ties linking George and Ben Junior to another Keanae family replicate the pattern represented in Figure 7.6, but in the next generation. The family of George and Ben Junior gives daughters to the family of Charles and Ah Hu. A possible objection to this interpretation is that Sarah did not belong to Ben Junior's family because he was not her biological father. Hawaiians can of course distinguish between stepchildren and "own" offspring and between full and half siblings and will do so when pointing out family relationships to someone unfamiliar with the parties. But in casual reference, they ignore such distinctions. Ideally, a spouse's child is treated just like one's own. A child comes into frequent contact with his parent's current spouse, and the affective bond is likely to be quite close if the child actually lives with the stepparent. As with adoption, it is expected and proper that a child's emotional allegiance is to the parent who raised him or her. Ben Junior had no children of his own; he legally adopted one of Viola's sons, who was still young when his mother remarried, as well as his wife's daughter's daughter, who was born a few years later.

Sarah was full grown when her mother married Ben Junior and was living on another island when her child was born. It was not Sarah's marriage but the adoption of her brother and daughter that asserted Ben Junior's *pūluna* relationship to Charles's family. Adoption was the return

Figure 7.8
Adoption and Intermarriage: Keanae, Kailua, and Hana

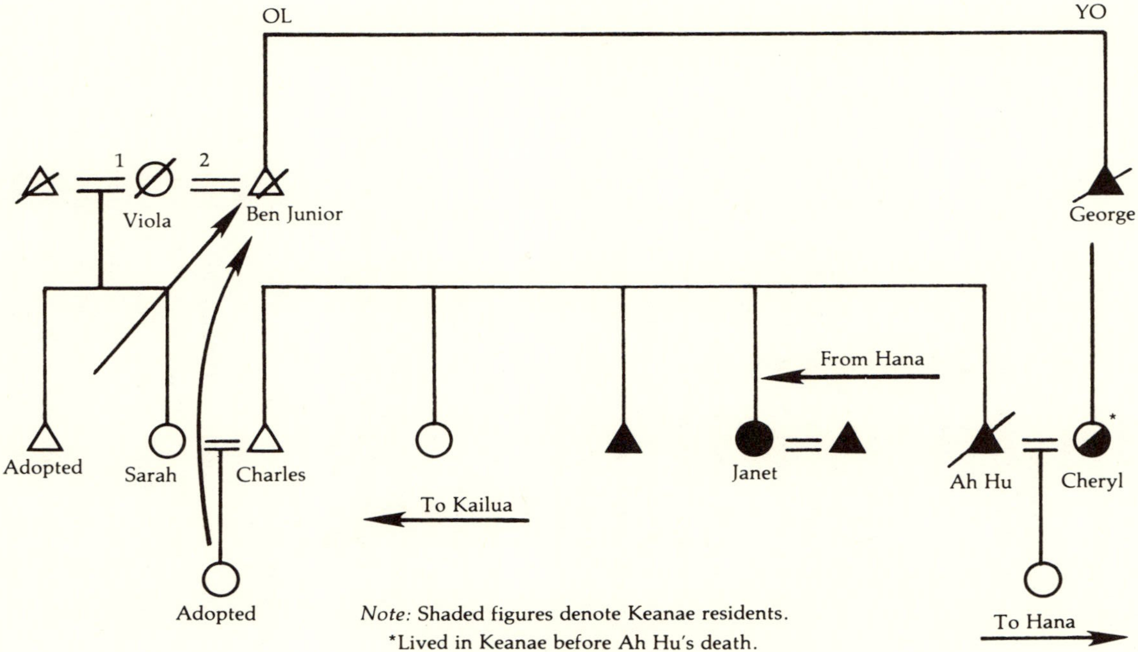

Note: Shaded figures denote Keanae residents.
*Lived in Keanae before Ah Hu's death.

on the exchange. The child's return to the maternal grand-parents defined Ben Junior's status as a parent-in-law, a wife giver. The adoption of the *mo'opuna* sealed the relationship between the two families.

The marital histories of Charles's siblings also show reciprocal intermarriage among Keanae, Kailua, and Hana. Sarah was from Peahi, where Ben Junior's family also owned land. A sister of Charles married into Kailua, the locality to which Ben Junior's family "belonged." Another sister, Janet, remained in Keanae and married a Hana man; they built their house on land given by Janet's father. Ah Hu's daughter married into Hana.

The premise of this chapter has been that marriage creates alliance. Most of the points that have been made about Hawaiian marriage refer to the enduring union that predominates among Keanae Hawaiians. Cohabitation is rarely lasting and does not create long-term relationships. Hawaiian marriage is an exchange between families: an exchange of *kuleana*s, of claims or rights. The exchange is normatively symmetrical, defining expectations of equivalence between affines and establishing a basis for generalized reciprocity. The exercise of the *kuleana*—the return on the exchange—may take several forms. It may be fulfilled by the service of a devoted *hūnōna* or daughter-in-law. A classificatory sister exchange accomplishes symmetry within the same generation. The adoption of a grandchild has the same effect; the return is merely delayed a generation.

As the conjunction of two families, marriage recruits children for both. According to the Hawaiian theory of relatedness, the offspring of a union are considered members of both parents' families; they are *mo'opuna* to both sets of grandparents. But in practice, affiliation with the two families is rarely equal. Relatedness creates equal options, but the options are not equally exercised. Since most marriages are exogamous, the children will not have equally frequent contact with both families. In practice, recruitment to a family depends on residential proximity and active exchanges, both verbal and material. Thus property succession and postmarital residence are important factors in family affiliation.

I have stated that nineteenth-century and modern adoption statistics do not bear out the norm, cited by Kamakau (1964:26), that boys are taken by the father's family and girls by the mother's. The discrepancy raises the question: what is this normative statement about? Previously, I related it to male and female lines of inheritance for real and intangible property. But inheritance affects place of residence, which figures importantly in the family affiliation of a couple's children. Kamakau's statement is about exchange among the people on the land: about binding marriage and normative property relations. As such, it reflects the ideals of patriliny and virilocality. Since men are jurally favored, a man is likely to remain in this father's home locality; his children are likely to be associated with their father's family. The normative premise is that men receive land and women marry out.

Since women marry out of the village more frequently than men, daughters and their children are more often dissociated from the family. The maternal grandparents' claim on their daughter's child is intelligible in the context of village exogamy and virilocality. This normative model does not account for landless junior collaterals, who constitute a traditionally problematic category. Figure 7.9 diagrams the ideal pattern. As described in Chapter 5, the structural and sentimental focality of women runs counter to jural norms. Although women are symbolically central, it is women who more often leave their natal land. Property transmission through women, a significant alternate pattern, appears to violate the norm that land should be transmitted through a line of males, but, as shown earlier, women usually convey land to men. Women are links in a chain of patrilineal succession; the land's destiny is still the same. Women are stable figures but on their husband's land or in the locality where they married.

Although repeated affinal ties between Hawaiian fami-

Figure 7.9
Normative Property Transmission, Virilocality, and Adoption

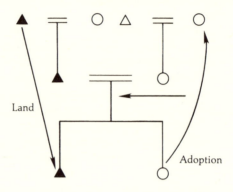

lies are relatively common, rarely are there more than two marriages between sibling sets. Most marriages link previously unrelated families, so that alliances are dispersed. It is advantageous to have affinal relationships with several families, thereby widening the network within which amicable reciprocity is possible. If the incidences of village endogamy and exogamy were reversed, most people in the village would be related to one another within a few generations. Since kinship is reckoned cognatically, finding an unrelated, marriageable person within the community could become a problem. But this difficulty could occur only with an entirely different system of land succession. High village exogamy is a corollary of impartible inheritance, which dictates that most siblings must marry out. The land will not be partitioned into tinier and tinier parcels to accommodate all members of the family. It is Western law that has created the debacle of a hundred heirs to a single piece of property. In former times, the problem of the wandering junior sibling was partially resolved by attachment to landholding households. Landless Hawaiians could live as dependents under those with land. According to elderly informants, household groups in Keanae were larger even in the early part of this century and included a variety of relatives. In recent years, however, more and more Hawaiians have departed the country for life outside.

High village exogamy continually imports strangers, who, while "family to" some residents, are unrelated to others. Neighbors, those who are neither relatives nor in-laws, are in Keanae because they married in within the past few generations. There is a dynamic at work here, a structurally generated drive toward disunity and fragmentation at the local level. The theory of generalized reciprocity, of giving without thought to the net balance, anticipates that everyone is either a relative or an affine. But the Hawaiian combination of cognatic kinship, impartible land-holding, and village exogamy introduces ambiguity into social relations in the person of inmarrying affines. Those who are neither family nor "family to us" are most likely to be suspected of acting high, for generalized reciprocity varies with social distance. Gift giving is both the barometer and the creator of social amity. Even between affines, a continuous one-way flow would strain the relationship. Like good friends, in-laws observe the ethic of equivalence and allow reciprocities to balance out over time.

Chapter Eight

IMPORTANT PEOPLE

I have spoken of Hawaiian big-men, entrepreneurs who attain prosperity and positions of influence without appearing to act high. There is both historical and formal justification for likening the important people in Keanae today to Melanesian big-men. The society of commoner Hawaiians, from whom Keanae villagers claim descent, was egalitarian. Historically, the people on the land were internally undifferentiated. Local authorities, the lower-level *konohiki*s, were appointed from outside by the chiefs and higher-level *konohiki*s. The people lived under the chiefs and owed tribute to them, but the commoners' relations to one another were not defined by hereditary rank. Within the village, social relations were egalitarian—as they are in Keanae today. But even among commoners, there were important people, people with land and many relatives, and they consolidated their position in the community with the same mechanisms as those used by present-day village big-men: with land acquisition and marriage alliance. This chapter explores the dimensions of the Hawaiian big-man's role in the traditional contexts of land, service, and alliance.

The archetype of the big-man is found in tribal societies lacking not only hereditary ranking but also economic stratification. Economic inequality certainly exists in Keanae; household income varies substantially within the village, from a widow's Social Security check to the income brought in by five able-bodied adults. The connection with the outside economy has long since introduced the material grounds for stratification. Nevertheless, the ethic of village society stipulates equality and symmetry in exchange. Social standing—and social amity—depends on the observation of this ethic, on how successfully an individual maintains equivalent reciprocities with other villagers. Since public opinion in Keanae censures ambition and economic success, the Hawaiian big-man appears to be a paradox. But such a person is not rich; overt prosperity is antithetical to Hawaiian criteria for esteem. An individual who displayed personal wealth in Keanae would be a stranger by definition. And the neighbor who reminds another of a debt or otherwise attempts to act high is made a stranger by general avoidance, which effectively levels most pretensions to superiority.

THE BASES OF PRESTIGE

In the absence of inherited rank and overt economic wealth, the only recognized bases of prestige are age and personal character. Here the Hawaiian big-man resembles his Melanesian counterpart, for "the indicative quality of big-man authority is everywhere the same: it is *personal power*" (Sahlins 1963:289; emphasis in original). The classic examples of big-men are found in societies such as Siuai (Oliver 1955), where leadership is achieved through personal mobilization of supporters and resources. Sahlins (1965:162–163) has summarized the distinctive characteristics of the big-man's role: "Pivotal local leaders come to prominence without yet becoming holders of office and title, of ascribed privilege and of sway over corporate political groups. . . . The process of gathering a personal following and that of ascent to the summits of renown is marked by calculated generosity."

Melanesian phrases that are particularly appropriate to the Hawaiian context are "man of importance" and "man of renown" (Sahlins 1963:289). The corresponding Hawaiian phrase is *kanaka ko'iko'i*, "important people" (Thrum 1865:XXI, 38). A nineteenth-century text states that "if the parents were honorable, and distinguished (*hanohano, a ko'iko'i*), or related to chiefs, and those of like kind," they might consecrate their child to be a *punahele*, a favorite destined to marry up into the ranks of chiefs (Kekoa 1865:40). *Hanohano*, meaning "dignified, distinguished, honorable"

(Pukui and Elbert 1971:54), stresses temporal achievement and earned esteem rather than inherited rank. *Ko'iko'i* conveys the notion of honor as well as influence; one gloss is "persons of integrity" (Andrews 1865:286). *Ko'iko'i* also has the meaning of emphasis and weightiness (Pukui and Elbert 1971:148). Describing the classes of Hawaiian society, Samuel M. Kamakau (1964:8) wrote: "Among the *maka'āinana* were chiefly people (*po'e ali'i*), those of some chiefly rank (*po'e kaukauali'i*), men of property (*ko'iko'i*), or prominence (*hanohano*), and children who were brought up as 'favorites' (*keiki punahele*) by their parents." Although belonging to the common people, such persons were implicitly set above the multitude. It is significant that Mary Pukui translates *ko'iko'i* in the Kamakau passage as "men of property," for property is indeed a distinguishing feature of these important people. The modern Hawaiian bigman has a historical precedent, for some of the large household groups evidenced in nineteenth-century materials must have belonged to such distinguished people.

But the origin of the present-day big-man's status differs from that of his prototype. Today's person of influence builds his position with personal effort. Historically, many of the important people living on the land were originally *konohiki*s or their descendants. Placed on the land as overseers, many *konohiki*s sought to settle in the local community, on land they acquired as individuals rather than through their office (Sahlins 1974). According to one *konohiki*'s testimony in the Mahele, the advantage of settling on the land was that "it would end the weariness of moving about because of the 'master' [chief]" (NT 1:118–119; quoted in Sahlins 1974). The *konohiki*'s status in the community was founded on an authority designated from above, but he used customary Hawaiian methods to integrate himself and his family into the local level. He acquired and developed land in his own right, without calling on the local people, hence without exercising the authority of his office (Sahlins 1974). He brought relatives with him and placed dependents under him on the land.

This core of persons intermarried with other landholders, creating a network of brother and brother-in-law relationships that is similar to the pattern of ties among Keanae people today. With the benefit of his land and relatives, the former *konohiki* remained more prosperous than other residents. An excavation of the house site of a *konohiki* who settled in an *ahupua'a* on the north shore of Oahu indicated that it was indeed more complex and materially more varied than the average (Kirch 1979:52).

The influential people in Keanae today are esteemed for being sober, humble, and industrious. Neighbors call them "down-to-earth" and "hard-working"—phrases that reveal a major contrast between the Hawaiian and Melanesian cases. The mien of the Hawaiian who is *ko'iko'i* is the inverse of that of the Melanesian big-man, for if he were to act big he would suffer desertion, a denial of status. The Hawaiian big-man's role is notable in its understatement and in the public denial of any special status to him. The successful Hawaiian entrepreneur maintains social viability by projecting an unassuming and disarming persona. Although overt ambition is self-defeating, it is possible for an individual to become truly high, admired by his peers rather than censured. In the opinion of other villagers, such a person has good character but never acts high.

The Hawaiian man of influence resembles the Melanesian big-man in the "personal manufacture" (Sahlins 1963: 289) of his position. His household is more prosperous than most, although, in keeping with the ethic of egalitarianism, his homestead is modest. One Keanae big-man quarters his family in a World War II army barrack. On one side, however, he has built a carport the height and breadth of a small airplane hangar, constructed of steel girders and corrugated iron. His work vehicles consist of a four-wheel-drive wagon and a Jeep panel truck. Since he is a foreman for the irrigation company, he has use of a company vehicle, another four-wheel-drive wagon. His wife's son, also living in the household, has a pick-up truck, and a late-model station wagon serves as the family's "good" car.

The recruitment of a faction is central to the Melanesian big-man's position: "leadership is a creation . . . of follow-ership" (ibid. : 290). The Hawaiian man of influence has cli-ents in the village who are obligated to work for him with-out pay, and he develops his faction in similar ways, by offering informal assistance to his neighbors. The influen-tial person in Keanae takes full advantage of the gift's in-strumental power and engineers his position by means of "calculated generosities, by placing others in gratitude and obligation through helping them in some big way" (ibid. : 292). He plays on the gift's intrinsic meaning in Hawaiian social relations. By timing and gauging his gifts and favors, the Hawaiian big-man creates a network of open-ended obligation. The gift is usually just within the bounds of friendship; the return may be solicited as a favor, with no suggestion of indebtedness or superiority. Nevertheless, the "something" engendered by the unrequited gift is an imperative, no less so for the appearance of solidarity.

The Hawaiian big-man engenders subordinate relation-ships while preserving the demeanor of friend and equal. The return for his favors is nonetheless mandatory, al-though it is requested as the free and spontaneous gift of friendship. The big-man's standing depends on the non-economic form and seeming solidarity of his relationships with other villagers. The *ko'iko'i* man, the person of impor-tance and integrity, is a traditionalist as well as an entrepre-neur. He evokes long-established notions of obligation while not appearing to violate the egalitarian ethic of ex-change in the village. Because of Hawaiians' sensitivity to status differences created by indebtedness, the big-man's position is particularly tenuous and requires a great deal of tact in calling on outstanding obligations.

Important people traffic in labor more than things. Work is the primary resource with which the Hawaiian big-man increases his household production in everything from taro farming to guava picking. Service is the return gift that he most frequently demands. The ability to call on out-standing obligations is a distinctive feature of his status.

Other villagers may be respected for their knowledge and experience but exert no particular claims on their neighbors. I do not categorize them as important people because they cannot use the leverage of indebtedness to call on the services of others.

The Hawaiian man of influence is also not simply prosperous. There are land-wealthy villagers who are excluded from the circle of everyday exchange relations and subjected to de facto ostracism. They may have shingle roofs, but they are not important people in the estimation of other villagers. The influential man in the village is well liked in spite of his economic prosperity. The measure of his success is the degree to which he maintains amicable reciprocities with his neighbors, for friends then become potential helpers.

Nevertheless, 'the big-man tries as much as possible to fill his labor needs from the ranks of his relatives and affines, who can be recruited under the mantle of generalized reciprocity. Typically, the man of influence is related by marriage to several other families in the village. He utilizes the expectations of the brother-in-law relationship for his own benefit. As in the Melanesian archetype, the core of the Hawaiian big-man's faction is "his own household and his closest relatives. . . . He capitalizes . . . on kinship dues and by finessing the relation of reciprocity appropriate to close kinsmen. Often it becomes necessary at an early phase to enlarge one's household. The rising leader goes out of his way to incorporate within his family 'strays' of various sorts, people without familial support themselves. . . . Additional wives are especially useful" (Sahlins 1963:291).

Certain characteristics of early Hawaiian society were conducive in this regard to the emergence of important people at the local level. Among Hawaiian commoners there have always been ample strays with whom to build up a household work force, most notably disfanchised junior siblings. The alternative for landless individuals was phrased as living "under" a landholder. The easy practice of adoption also readily permitted the recruitment of orphans and unwanted children, whether related or not. The person who recruited dependents for his household in these ways played on their subordination to enhance his own position.

As stated earlier, the size of the available work force is the most significant factor in household income. One Keanae big-man lives in a household of five adults, three of whom hold salaried jobs. While in Melanesia an additional wife is "especially useful," this man has an additional husband in the household. In the days when there was a prison camp at Keanae, he sponsored a trustee to come work for him. The man later married the big-man's wife's sister, and the two couples lived in the same household.[1] The wife's sister became interested in the big-man, and his marriage dissolved. The big-man's wife left Keanae, leaving him, his former sister-in-law, and her husband residing together in a polyandrous household. Although the latter are legally married and have two children, the big-man has also fathered children by this woman. The former trustee clearly occupies a subordinate role in the household; he rarely speaks and tends to his chores. Since the big-man is well liked in the community, other villagers usually refrain from commenting on the situation except to note, "That's the boyfriend, that." In Hawaii as in Melanesia, the most easily recruited clients are low-status individuals without familial support. The former trustee is from another island; he has no known family and no ties to Keanae people. As a stranger and a social outcast, he has no defenders in the village. He also has much to be grateful for since the big-man gave him a home and found him a job with the irrigation company for which he works; as foreman, the man of influence is his superior at work as well as at home.

1. Although at the time of fieldwork no married couples lived together in Keanae, several households housed more than one nuclear family in the past, as noted in Chapter 4. Usually these consisted of married offspring living with their parents. In a common cycle of family development, these households frequently dissolved by fission after the father's death. Extended families composed of married siblings tend to be unstable, as this example illustrates.

Outside his own family, the Hawaiian big-man can commandeer service only indirectly. Unlike the Melanesian leader, he has no power to command unrelated individuals, not even low-status villagers. In an important point of departure from the Melanesian model, he is not an acknowledged leader; he does not have an organized faction, but he does have people who owe him things and cannot refuse his requests. He cashes in on obligations with suggestions rather than demands. For this reason, I use the term *influence* rather than *authority*. By virtue of his gifts and favors, the Hawaiian big-man has weight but not the power to order people about. He builds relations of reciprocity but not compulsion.

Part of his personal skill is his ability to make it easy for people to repay him with service without appearing to be lower in status. He invites them to luaus where they will be expected to work; he repairs a fence while his relatives are visiting. And anyone who comes to spend the night at week's end will lend a hand in the taro patches, pulling for the order. As Hawaiians are wary of lower status, the successful *ko'iko'i* man must artfully balance influence with understatement. The Hawaiian big-man does not have a clearly defined faction of self-identified followers because of the Hawaiian emphasis on egalitarianism. The influential person's subordinates never openly admit their clientship; even though they are obligated to work for him, the continuing service relationship depends on preventing people from feeling that they are being used. The big-man's skill is that he manages to remain a "nice guy" while exerting influence. His clients stay with him because they are not forced to acknowledge their subordinate position; they do not advertise the fact that they may work for free.

LUAUS

I have stressed the obligations of the big-man's followers, without specifying what benefit they derive from the association: what obligates them in the first place? The big-man's clients receive many small favors and some not so small. If they have no car, they receive rides outside. He may treat them with trips to other islands, which they could not otherwise afford. They eat at his house and are incorporated into his household milieu, which imparts a sense of belonging and security to social strays who have few relatives in Keanae or an unhappy home situation. The Melanesian big-man develops a faction through "informal private assistance" and celebrates his renown with "great public giveaways" (Sahlins 1963:291). He advertises his greatness by "amassing goods, most often pigs, shell monies and vegetable foods, and distributing them in ways which build a name for cavalier generosity" (ibid.:291). The Hawaiian form of public distribution is the luau. The man of influence gives luaus more often than other villagers, and he avoids having to repay his neighbors by recruiting most workers from within his family. Hawaiians look forward to luaus, to the excitement, the crowd, and the food. It is fun to be associated with someone who gives luaus often, even if one has to work.

But the ethic and the status implications of the Hawaiian luau differ from those of Melanesian feasts. The generosity exhibited in the luau is too cavalier for most Hawaiians to accept without qualms—unless they have assisted in the preparations and consider it their just due. Villagers simply ignore the event if they feel that attending would threaten their equivalence with the host. During fieldwork, neither of the individuals whom I considered big-men in Keanae gave grand-scale feasts, although they were frequently involved in family luaus and at times took a peripheral role in other villagers' luaus, such as providing *kūlolo* for an affine's feast. The big-man may avoid large public events partly because of the work force needed to prepare an elaborate luau. One is after all indebted to the neighbors who are recruited to assist. The big-men in Keanae managed to give luaus that were within the means of the household and could be handled by relatives and clients alone.

Indeed, not giving ostentatious public distributions is part of the understatement of the Hawaiian big-man's position. This may seem a paradox, but the denial of special status accords with Hawaiian egalitarianism. A large luau calls attention to the host, opens the giver to public scrutiny and potentially to criticism. For a land-wealthy, prosperous man to give a large-scale luau to which all his neighbors were invited might be interpreted as acting high. The general resentment and talk stink that could result would jeopardize the big-man's influence in the community.

THE TARO AGENT

Although I speak of Keanae as one community, each of the two neighboring taro-growing areas, Lower Keanae and Wailua Valley, has a taro agent who acts as a middleman between the growers and the poi company. It is important to note that the agent is seen as an intermediary, not as a boss. He meets with his growers once a month at the Keanae School, and informants stressed that everyone can attend—the growers, their spouses, and any other family member with a stake in taro production. The agent's main function is to relay the company's orders to his planters and to see that the weekly quota is filled. Once a month the agents meet with the poi companies in Honolulu; Keanae poi is sold to Honolulu and Molokai, while Maui's poi comes from another taro-growing area on the island. The agent receives an order for a specific number of bags each week, and he divides it among his growers according to their desires and capabilities. He devises a rotation schedule to take into account individual fluctuations in supply since many growers have a large part of their crop ripening at once. Each week, the agent trucks the bags of taro outside to the pier, whence it is shipped by barge to Honolulu. The taro checks, one made out to each grower according to the amount of taro sold, are delivered to the agent, and someone in his household hand delivers them to the planters.

Although villagers consider the agent to be a go-between, he is an important person in the community, and his role exemplifies the personal attributes required of a Hawaiian big-man. The agent largely determines the allocation of the weekly order, potentially a subject of dissatisfaction, but I never heard a taro farmer complain about his or her share. The agent after all asks the growers for their preferences in the monthly meeting, and if the weekly order is inconveniently large or disappointingly small, that is the fault of the company and the vagaries of an impersonal market, not the agent. The agent tells his growers how much taro to supply and gives them their money. The fact that, to my knowledge, neither agent was ever accused of acting high is testimony to their powers of tact and conciliation.

Here again, the Hawaiian big-man upholds his position not by shaming another potentially important person but by maintaining a reputation as a "nice guy." He does this by quietly helping his taro-patch neighbors and by assisting his growers when they are in need. For example, one agent pulled for one of his growers when the man's wife was sick. The agent may have needed to make up his order, but he also indebted this man to him by ensuring that he would receive taro income for the week. The taro agent does not help people at inappropriate times, nor with any too-great assistance. The role is a convenient one for an aspiring big-man, for the taro agent can offer aid somewhat more readily than other neighbors without risking censure. Villagers understand that by helping his growers he is helping them all fill the company's order.

Both taro agents have achieved near immunity from talk stink, and, in a community rife with gossip, the general absence of talk stink about a person is tantamount to public esteem. The agent's growers are not *clients* as I have used the term thus far; they are not part of his household work force, nor do they regularly provide him with service. They work for themselves, not for the agent. Nonetheless, the agent's assistance creates a diffuse indebtedness among many of his growers and protects him from talk stink.

The Melanesian archetype of the big-man emphasizes the rivalry between men of renown. Competition is overt, and big-men challenge one another with the scale of their public giveaways. But just as important people in the Hawaiian village must understate their status, so competition between them is not expressed publicly. The prosperous man's good reputation is less a result of his importance vis-à-vis someone else than of his personal finesse. Yet both of the men whom I considered successful big-men in Keanae were taro agents, and there is competition for growers between agents. The Keanae agent had four growers in Wailua, out of eight who sold taro through him. The agent for Wailua had nine growers, with three in Keanae. An informant claimed that the Keanae agent had lost some growers, for unspecified reasons. During the period of fieldwork, none of the growers changed agents. Taro agents usually hold the job for many years, and they are not deserted in wholesale fashion. The Wailua agent's father held the position before him, and villagers consider it proper that the son took over the role. Growers may defect individually over the course of time but more because of ties to the other agent than because of a falling-out with their own.

The consolidation of a Hawaiian big-man's following is a long-term process, and the allegiances, once formed, are relatively stable. At the time of fieldwork, the two taro agents did not appear to be competing in any sense. Keanae growers have sold through two agents for some time, and villagers approve of the arrangement, giving the rationale that a single agent would not be able to handle all the business. Once the two agents recruited growers, a truce was drawn. Quite simply, there is also not much competition for the taro agent's job. The agent must be prepared to travel to Honolulu each month; he must possess a good-sized truck and be able to keep it maintained—as well as having enough strong arms available every week to fill it with bags of taro. He must time his social activities around the weekly order, a sacrifice of freedom that few Hawaiians wish to make. Perhaps most importantly, the taro agent must have the weight and the skill to deal amicably and authoritatively with the growers. Personal character is the most significant factor in the agent's—and the big-man's—role.

AMBITION AND INFLUENCE

It must be remembered that Hawaiians do not value power and material gain. Although anyone who works full time and also farms taro is hardly a shirker, few villagers seek out extra work. Most consider that they work to get by, to pay for food and other necessities, and to finance occasional luxuries such as interisland trips. There are successful taro farmers in Keanae who maintain good relations with their neighbors, but they do not have the ambition to influence others. Their goals may be more characteristically Hawaiian in that they are centered around life's essentials, around family and fish and poi.

Other villagers may be economic entrepreneurs and are prosperous enough to qualify as influential people, but they do not have the personal qualities needed to maintain amicable relations with their neighbors. They may have pursued their goals too obviously or too ruthlessly, or otherwise violated Hawaiian standards of behavior. At the time of fieldwork, one man known to be ambitious was elderly, alcoholic, and ostracized by most of his neighbors. But, in his youth, he had been a large-scale taro grower who hired unemployed village men to work for him. He had inherited no land from his parents, although four of his siblings were bequeathed parcels or interest in parcels. By buying up the interests of others, he acquired four parcels, for a total of 4.582 acres, and undivided shares in eight others. With an additional, leased taro plot, the total land area to which he had access was 13.435 acres. In an area where most landholdings are measured in fractions of an acre, this is a substantial estate. A typical Homestead Lease Award in Keanae, in contrast, consists of two and a half acres. This man also married a woman who had land in her own right. He gave a house lot to his son-in-law, who thereafter worked in his taro patches, but his only other client was a hard-drinking village ne'er-do-well.

Despite his economic prominence in former times, this landowner was shunned by other villagers in his later years. It was said that he only wanted his wife's land and had abused her until she was driven into indefinite hospitalization. At the time of fieldwork even his daughter and son-in-law visited him infrequently. He lived alone, with few social contacts except a group of local "hippies" who were allegedly plying him to sign over his land. His neighbors called him greedy and deplored his avarice and callousness. This man had been a company foreman in the past and was known to have "high retirement" income, but it was not his economic standing that doomed him in public opinion. In the estimation of other villagers, his unconcealed ambition and ill treatment of his wife were un-Hawaiian. Such a man has few friends and never receives spontaneous assistance from his neighbors. His only regular workers were his son-in-law, who was obligated by the gift of land, and a few low-status villagers whom he paid for taro-patch labor. In contrast, the mark of a big-man is that he has people to work for him for free.

ALLIANCE

Marriage and relatedness figure significantly in the making of a big-man's following; the agent/grower relationship is not a volatile one partly because it often coincides with a tie of kinship or affinity. One way to deal with another influential man is to forge a marriage alliance with him. Figure 8.1 shows one taro agent's relationships to his growers. The agent, Billy, is related to Abraham, the land-rich man described above, in two ways: they are classificatory brothers-in-law (*kaiko'eke*) and also *pūluna*, co-parents-in-law by virtue of the marriage of their children to each

Figure 8.1
Relationships Between a Taro Agent (Billy) and His Growers

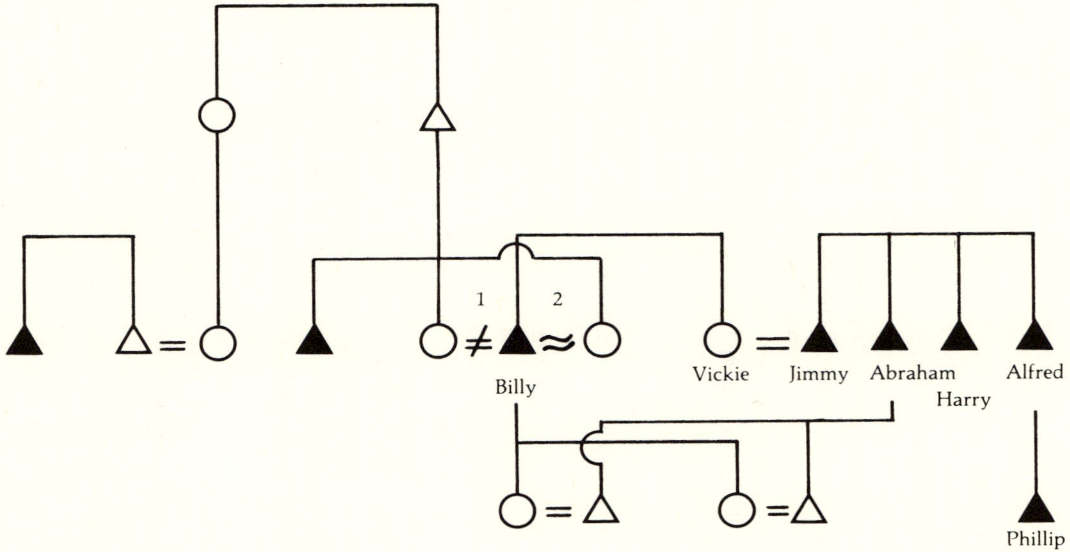

Note: Shaded figures denote growers.

other. Both of Abraham's sons were adopted in infancy; one has been designated his heir.

Abraham's affinal ties to Billy suggest his one-time importance in the village. From Billy's perspective, the relationship with Abraham is advantageous in several ways. He has recruited a major grower and created additional links with his family, to which he was already allied as a brother-in-law. Billy is the Keanae taro agent, but Abraham, Harry, Alfred, and Phillip live in Wailua. All are active growers and might otherwise sell through the Wailua agent. Billy and his sister Vickie are quite close; to use the traditional phrase, she is his *kuleana* in her husband's family. With the marriage of his daughter to Abraham's heir, Billy has acquired a son-in-law who will one day also be land wealthy and will live in Keanae after his father's death. Billy will then have a daughter and *hūnōna* living in the village and available for assistance requests. His grandchildren will be associated with Abraham's large family.

These marriages constitute an alliance between two important Keanae families. Of the large sibling set represented by Jimmy and Abraham, four brothers and four sisters have remained in the village—unusual among Keanae families. One brother is dead; another lives outside and leases his land to a brother living in Keanae. They pride themselves on being among the few "pure" Hawaiians in the village. The four brothers market taro, one on a full-time basis. But for one sister, all the siblings living in Keanae own land. Their landholdings are not impressive in area, except for Abraham's. Keanae lands have been so fragmented since the Mahele that it is rare for any one individual to amass a sizable area. Most large landholdings are the product of deliberate accumulation by individuals such as Abraham. Although small in size for the most part, their landholdings are impressive in their distribution, in the number of different parcels and interests held.

It is impressive and unusual also that five of the ten siblings received some land through the family and were thus encouraged to remain in Keanae—largely through their mother's actions in dividing the family estate. Four others secured land by various other means. Three of the brothers received undivided interests in a Land Commission Award from their mother after their father's death, but the chain of title is broken, and I was unable to trace how this land came to the parents. One sister received a homestead from her mother; another inherited her husband's lands through survivorship. Three of the siblings purchased Homestead Lease Awards in Keanae.

The family's inheritance illustrates the destiny of a *konohiki*'s land and descendants. As shown in Figure 8.2, the siblings are descended from the family of Kaniho, a *konohiki* who received land in the Mahele and settled into the Keanae community. Although not notably prosperous except for Abraham, the former *konohiki*'s family has nonetheless managed to acquire enough land and, in the current generation, to dominate the local scene by sheer force of numbers. Although neighbors remark that there are "plenty of them around here," the family is not remembered as having any special status. Their father is listed as a taro planter in commercial directories as early as 1910, but he apparently married into Keanae from Huelo. An informant even claimed that the family was "not from 'round here," reflecting the fact that the father was from the Huelo area. (See the preceding chapter for affinal ties between Keanae and Huelo.)

Kaniho was the *konohiki*, the chief's land agent, for Wailua. Before the Mahele, Wailua belonged to the chiefess Keohokalohe (Dorothy B. Barrère, personal communication), and Kaniho was evidently her agent on the scene. Twenty-three out of thirty-two claimants cited him as donor in their testimony before the Land Commission. Some said that they received land from him as early as the time of Kamehameha I, meaning before 1819. Kaniho testified that he received his own land from another *konohiki* in 1842. Both Keanae and Wailua were declared crown lands in the Mahele; thus the entire area not awarded to commoners eventually became public lands from which Home-

stead Awards were apportioned. Kaniho claimed six parcels in the Mahele and was awarded four, for a total of
8.758 acres. He had no children of his own and lived with
his younger brother's son Kamali. Kaniho died at Wailua in
1868, leaving his property to his wife and his brother's son
Kini (P-668, 2nd c.c.).

As is evident in Figure 8.2, Kaniho's land descended to
Alfred and Keola through mostly patrilineal links. Kamau-
koli inherited half of Kaniho's land, as well as a Royal Patent Grant from a classificatory father and another Land
Commission Award that his father, Kini, had acquired. Ka-
maukoli had no known sons and conveyed his lands to his
grandchildren Alfred and Keola. Keola sold one parcel of
Kaniho's award to his brother Abraham, who later conveyed it to his son; today cows graze on what was once the
konohiki's fish pond. Significantly, Abraham once deeded
this piece to Billy, his *pūluna*, for use as taro land. The price
was one dollar, a token compensation that usually marks a
transaction as a gift between relatives but might also signal
an agreement to sell in the future. Whether there were
other considerations in this sale I do not know. Four years
later, Billy conveyed the land back, and Abraham bequeathed it to his son, reserving a life interest. These transactions underscore the effects of marriage alliance. Such
cooperative exchanges of land commonly occur between
close relatives. Here two important men and their families
are linked by marriage in a solidary relationship. These influential people use long-established Hawaiian methods to
consolidate a position in the community: marriage alliance
and land accumulation.

As shown in Figure 8.1, Billy is affinally related to seven
of his eight growers. The eighth is a young haole who lives
in Keanae and farms taro. Five of the growers are *kaiko'eke*,
actual or classificatory brothers-in-law. While Billy's growers are associated with him through marriage, the core of
the other taro agent's following is made up predominantly
of blood relatives. As shown in Figure 8.3, only one of
Kimo's growers is a brother-in-law. Kimo farms taro jointly

Figure 8.2
A *Konohiki's* Family

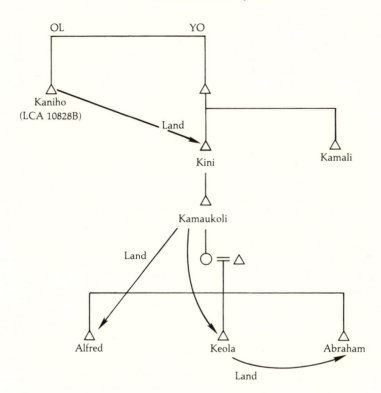

with a younger brother; their father was taro agent before
Kimo. The younger brother occupies the Keanae home,
but most of the land is in the elder's name. Nine households market their taro through Kimo. He is related in
some fashion to five of his growers; two are not included in
the genealogy because their relationship is too distant to be
specified.

These contrasting modes of relationship between the
two taro agents and their growers reflect the different ways
in which they acquired the position. In a de facto sense,

Figure 8.3
Relationships Between a Taro Agent (Kimo) and His Growers

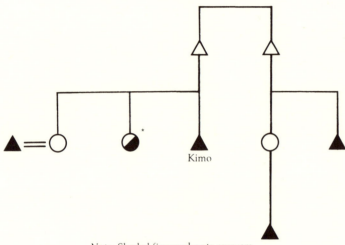

Kimo

Note: Shaded figures denote growers.
*Former grower.

Kimo inherited the agent's job, while Billy won his. Marriage alliances are the mark of an entrepreneur. Billy's father died when he was a boy, leaving him substantial, landholdings but few relatives in the village; except for a sister, he has no kin in Keanae. The family has no collateral ties to other villagers, and the only relatives with whom Billy has frequent contact are his sisters, the rest of the family apparently having died out or dispersed. Kimo is descended from Chinese-Hawaiian rice planters, and his family is linked by kinship and marriage to other Keanae residents. Billy is an entrepreneur but also a traditionalist. He recruited his growers through alliance, while Kimo benefited from past family associations and relationships. If Billy's offspring assume the agent's role and his growers' families continue the marketing relationship, the affinal links that he has fostered in his own generation will produce much the same pattern of ties as shown in Figure 8.3, for marriage creates kin in the next generation. The agent would be related to his growers as cousin, uncle, and nephew.

LAND AND LABOR

Both taro agents are themselves large-scale growers. A big-man's household typically garners income from taro marketing as well as from salaried employment. Land and labor are the crucial variables in profits from taro farming, and influential people are able to muster both. The ideal is to have enough land for taro to be harvested continuously rather than having salable crops only intermittently. The strategy is to "plant as you pull," but to do so a grower needs land for planting as well as time and workers for harvesting. As one of the taro agents explained, "If you only work part time and have a small place, you may not be able to help it. But if you get big place, you can rotate, keep pulling all year round." The critical variable here is not land ownership but access to land. One may grow taro on land in which one has only a partial interest if the other owners live outside or do not use the land. Kimo has considerably increased his taro acreage by leasing land from the state. He has interests in eleven parcels, three owned jointly with his younger brother, and leases another seven. Although the land that he owns totals only 3 acres, and more than half of that is a house lot, his leased lands comprise 8.85 acres. Kimo also pastures cattle on abandoned taro land, another sign of prosperity.

A major aid for large growers has been the tilling machine, which five or six taro farmers own. The machines save time and labor, for they turn the roots and the "rubbish" into the mud as a natural fertilizer before replanting. This considerably shortens the interval between harvesting and replanting; otherwise the grower must turn the soil by hand. But the machines are expensive, around a thousand dollars with attachments at the time of fieldwork, and only large-scale producers have the capital to invest in them. Both taro agents own tilling machines.

Billy's landholdings are impressive, both in area and in the fact that he owns most of them exclusively, without the ambiguity of undivided interest. He inherited four parcels from his father and purchased three others, for a total of 19.739 acres. The lands he bought are taro patches in Lower Keanae, and only one is held as an undivided share. The other interest holder is his wife's brother, who lives outside; Billy's undivided interest effectively gives him additional taro land to use with the assent of his *kaiko'eke*. His first wife also had a Homestead Award in her own name, but this land was lost to him when they were divorced. Billy also leases prime taro land and a banana plantation in Lower Keanae from a widow in the village. The banana plantation is his pride and joy; he grows several varieties and is always eager to obtain seedlings for new ones. But his tender care of the banana patch resembles the old woman's avarice for fish, which she herself disliked. The family can eat only so many bananas. The bananas are primarily for exchange not for home consumption or sale. When ripe, the bunches are broken up and distributed to friends and relatives.

Billy's largest parcel is an eleven-acre portion of *hui* land running "from the mountain to the sea." This phrase, often applied to the *ahupua'a* land section, implies a full range of environmental opportunities. He pastures cattle on the property and tends a few taro patches for home use near the headwaters of a spring on the land. A nearby gulch is planted in watercress and is partly leased to an outsider. Watercress is another special food that the family takes outside to friends and relatives. The half mile of ocean front overlooks deep water and is a fertile private fishing spot. Billy's wife is an expert fisherwoman and regularly takes in large catches, which she dries and stores. Again, the fish are partly for the family but partly to give away.

Billy's household is the one previously described as polyandrous and composed of five adults. With three salaried workers and a high weekly taro order of ten bags, I estimate that annual household income was well over thirty thousand dollars in 1975, counting only salaries and taro marketing. There are also a number of supplementary economic activities that a household such as this can—and does—take advantage of. Much of Billy's prosperity is due to his ability to enlist additional help when needed, even though he originally had few kin in Keanae.

I have called Billy an entrepreneur who inherited substantial lands but was poor in relatives compared with other villagers. His only close kin within easy driving distance are a sister in Keanae and another sister in Wailuku. Their father died young and had no siblings in the area. Billy's "grandmothers" were said to belong to an old and distinguished Keanae family, but none of their descendants are left alive in the village. His mother was the granddaughter of a Royal Patent Grantee, but her haole father conveyed away all the land interests after her mother's death. The relatives on the mother's side have apparently died or dispersed. Nonetheless, Billy has built a network of relationships and associations in Keanae. As the oldest sibling and the only son, he inherited his father's lands but gave equal half-acre parcels to his two sisters, as diagramed in Figure 8.4. The sisters gave the land in turn to their own children, both of whom were building houses there at the time of fieldwork. For a small gift of land, one acre out of a twelve-acre parcel, Billy has consolidated his family's position in Keanae and ensured the residence there of a niece and nephew who are indebted to him. Although Ella's first obligation is to assist her own mother in the taro patches, she occasionally helps Billy when he is pulling a big order. Thus Billy adds to the family pool of possible workers.

The exchange of land for service is a long-established Hawaiian concept and was the basic principle underlying chiefly land redistribution. The recipient is obligated to repay the land giver with assistance and loyalty. This kind of exchange is a frequent theme in Hawaiian legends, as when a son-in-law serves his wife's father who has

Figure 8.4
Land Giving by a Big-Man

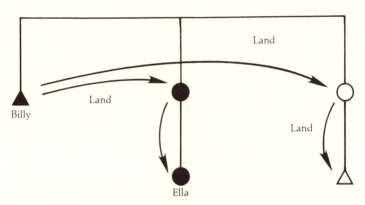

Note: Shaded figures denote Keanae residents.

provided him with land. In Keanae, control of land certainly helps to make someone *ko'iko'i*; land is desirable not only for its material returns but also—and perhaps more importantly—for its potency as a gift.

Large landowners often hire unemployed and low-status villagers to work for them. But influential people can enlist workers who help them without pay. To illustrate the big-man's use of indebtedness to recruit labor, I will relate a cycle of events involving Billy and an unrelated client. This young man was a rather disreputable character, known for his lying and occasional thievery, and was disliked by many villagers. Although in his twenties, he lived with his elderly mother and did no work for anyone except Billy. He had a long-term service relationship with Billy's household. He regularly worked in Billy's taro patches and occasionally received five dollars for his labor; the going rate for taro-patch work at the time was fifteen dollars a day. The young man also fixed fences, helped with the cattle, and did other odd jobs around Billy's homestead. He was not paid for these chores. At times he seemed a fixture in Billy's household; he ground poi with Billy's wife and daughter, accompanied them on fishing trips, and considered it his personal *kuleana*, his right and responsibility, to drive Billy's wife on her errands and fishing expeditions.

A social deviate in several respects, the young man was a storehouse of Hawaiian oral traditions. He spoke fluent Hawaiian, a rarity among people his age, and could debate the nuances of words with his elders. He knew fishing lore and could build an *imu* and *kālua* a pig properly. The *akule* fishers regularly used his yard to sort their equipment. For this convenience and for the use of his boat, they always gave the young man and his mother a larger-than-average share of the catch. Billy's daughter would call them, even from outside, to quiz them on the day's fishing plans. If the prospects were good, she would offer to come and make lunch for the crew, a sure way to guarantee a share of the catch. Since the young man had no source of income of his own and no car, Billy often treated him to trips outside, where he stayed with Billy's sister and nephew.

To all appearances, this client was like a member of the family; the important difference was that he had to work for them in exchange for the association and was consistently cast in service roles. For example, Billy paid his way to Hilo for a family luau. Like other members of Billy's household, the young man eagerly looked forward to the event, but as his aunty indignantly commented, "He had to work, only go for work." The luau was buffet style, and he had to serve and work behind the food table. Billy's sister's son wanted to pay his way to Honolulu for another party, but the young man's aunty felt that the offer was transparent. "It's only because they want him to work for them," she claimed; "I hate that, when they give you something only so you'll work for them."

For another luau, Billy enlisted the young man to *kālua* the pig. Billy's sister and daughter came to the client's mother and offered to "buy" some of her sweet potatoes. As the old woman pointed out afterward, how could she take their money when they had paid her son's fare to Hilo? The offer of payment was an obvious ploy, a cashing-

in on an obligation. Billy's family thus extended the relationship of subordination to their client's mother. While
the pig was baking, the young man and Billy's nephews
were put to work fencing and were ignored until it was
time to open the *imu*. Even then, Billy expected the young
man to come when called and to complete the task he had
begun. Angered at this treatment, the boy remained at
home when called to come eat. His subordination had
been made too obvious; he had been commanded like a
servant when he had done the work as a friend, at least in
his own eyes. "I tired," he said; "I no like go." By working
for Billy and then refusing to eat the fruits of his labor,
he made himself "more high," albeit temporarily. He had
given something and refused to accept the symbolic repayment. As explained earlier, eating another's food can imply
lower status.

But, as the young man's mother related, "Billy did the
right thing: he came and begged him for go. Then he went
to the taro patches and came back and twice begged,
begged him to come eat, come eat." It was only when Billy
begged him repeatedly that the boy felt appropriately
thanked and consented to go eat. Billy's demeaning himself to thank his client constituted recognition of his service
and a public statement that it was he who was obligated
to the young man not the other way around. At least temporarily, his begging canceled out his client's subordinacy. The big-man thereby retained a follower by making him feel higher than himself and by allowing him to
save face. The young man's mother, however, did not attend the luau. As she described it, the acceptance would
have made her obligated, and subordinate, to them. The
family urged her to come only casually without begging in
a fashion that would allay her doubts. To preclude the possibility of lower status, she preferred to avoid contact with
Billy's household.

After the luau, the young man was nonchalant about his
participation. He said that he "might" accept their offer of
a trip to Honolulu, although there was little doubt that he
would go. He felt that he was entitled to it, but tending an

imu was hardly worth a fare to Honolulu. As his aunty complained, "If he goes he'll only have to work, work for them, break his back. . . . Bullshit!" The ambiguities of this commerce hooked the young man into the big-man/client relationship. When putatively spontaneous gifts and favors are the stuff of exchange, one can never be sure that two gifts are equivalent or that the transactions have canceled out.

In the aftermath of the luau, the young man's service relationship with Billy's household continued as before. Billy's begging was a ritualistic assertion of mutual equality, a ceremonial gesture that resolved a situation so that relations could remain the same. Shortly afterward, when the *akule* fishers had been in, Billy's wife and sister came to ask the young man for some because the fishermen had refused to sell any. According to his mother, he had to give them part of his own share, no matter how little he had, because of all that they had done for him. By continuing to give their client gifts, Billy's household maintained his indebtedness and subordinacy. A few weeks after the Honolulu trip, Billy's daughter and niece stopped by the young man's house on their way outside. His mother asked them to bring back poi and cigarettes. The weighty implications of accepting food, and particularly poi, created the irony of the taro agent's daughter buying poi outside at the supermarket. The girl refused to take any money and refused again on returning, a gratuitous gift that both the young man and his mother resented. If at such times the spontaneous gift appears motivated by self-interest as much as by aloha, it is not because Hawaiians are particularly calculating. The disingenuousness of giving simply reflects an essential truth about exchange: there is power in the gift.

INFLUENCE AND AUTHORITY

The existence of locally important people may seem to contradict the Hawaiian concern for equivalence within the community, but I have argued that big-men in Keanae succeed precisely because they understate their importance in dealings with other villagers. Billy and Kimo are figures of influence rather than authority. In some respects, the modern big-man's attributes and strategies can be traced to cultural precedents set by the *konohiki*s in pre-Mahele times, but there are also crucial differences. The taro agent is analogous to a lower-level *konohiki* in that he is the intermediary between the village and an external demand. Although he does not set the quantities, the agent communicates production goals to the growers and determines how they will be met. But the agent is supposed to be a middleman, not a boss. He has nothing to do with allocating land or organizing irrigation-ditch maintenance, tasks historically the province of local *konohiki*s. When the Mahele established private property, the *konohiki*s lost their special status, and some lost the land on which they lived. Those who did receive land could settle in the communities that they had administered. But the loss of the *konohiki*s created a void in local-level authority. Although present-day important people draw on the precedent of the *konohiki*'s role, they are not *konohiki*s. The big-man's status is neither defined by an external authority nor publicly acknowledged, and for this reason he has no power to command. The critical difference is that individuals who are *ko'iko'i* are distinguished by general respect and the esteem of their neighbors, not by obedience.

I have stressed that the Hawaiian big-man achieves his position through his own effort: through hard work, land accumulation, and marriage alliance. It is not accurate to assume that such distinguished people in the village are actually descended from former *konohiki*s. Hawaiian genealogical memories are short, and Hawaiians repudiate notions of inherited rank; witness the scorn that greeted visitors who claimed *ali'i* (chiefly) blood. But land and a large family convey a potential importance in village affairs. To the extent that a *konohiki*'s family settled on the land and prospered, the descendants could become *hano-*

hano, a ko'iko'i—not as the recognized descendants of *kono-hikis* but as landholders and relatives of landholders.

Against the Hawaiian ethic of egalitarianism, the modern big-man balances a real but understated influence, founded on a network of open-ended obligation. In keeping with Hawaiian-style social relations, the distinguished man maintains a profile of modesty and good character. He suggests rather than orders; he obligates rather than commands. By denying any special personal importance and asserting that he is no higher than his neighbors, the Hawaiian big-man espouses the principle of symmetry in exchange and strengthens his position in the village further. The truly influential man is an entrepreneur but also a traditionalist. The person who acquires land and money while violating Hawaiian standards of behavior is merely an entrepreneur, not *ko'iko'i*, not a man of integrity.

Chapter Nine

ON HISTORY, THE PRESENT, AND THE FUTURE

The aim of this study has been to explore the meaning of *Hawaiian* in a fashion that incorporates an understanding of the past; the persistence of prior cultural categories has been a recurring theme. At least superficially, Hawaiians are perhaps the most acculturated people in Polynesia. Hawaiian society was remarkable for the lack of resistance it presented to outsiders and for its seeming readiness to incorporate alien elements. Their indigenous lifeways apparently destroyed long ago, many modern Hawaiians are recruited by the tourist industry to participate in the manufacture and sale of "Hawaiian culture" for commercial ends. Certainly the pursuit of a real Hawaiian tradition is difficult in this context, where authenticity seems so easily invented, and the premise of continuity may seem far-fetched in the face of wholesale change. But the ways that modern Hawaiians—at least in Keanae— classify things and people are rooted in past symbolic schemes; analogues and precedents can be found in pre-Christian Hawaiian ideology and in other Polynesian cultures. These prior values and categories are most evident in Hawaiian notions of family, relatedness, and exchange.

Keanae Hawaiians categorically separate commercial relationships with the outside from social relationships with people inside. This distinction constitutes the crucial difference between Keanae and non-Hawaiian communities. With friends and relatives, interactions take the form of exchange-in-kind. Long-established categories define the terms of this commerce. The commodities exchanged derive their significance from a set of values that can be traced to the pre-Christian era. The gift in Keanae creates an obligation and thus can serve as a weapon, an instrument for raising one's status over another. Mainland Americans, too, are uneasy about outstanding obligations, about not paying back gifts and social invitations. But here exchange is not a total social phenomenon, whereas gift giving forms the dynamic of social relations in Keanae. The driving ethic is generalized reciprocity, the open-ended expectation of some future return. In short-term cycles of neighborly interactions, this ethic bears such fruit as bananas, taro shoots, and other small favors—the stuff of everyday exchange. These casual and apparently minor gifts significantly affect the balance of a relationship. But the imperative of reciprocity also drives long-term cycles of exchange among Hawaiians, as marriage and adoption join families and localities in a network of relatedness.

THE PAST IN THE PRESENT

I have discussed Hawaiians' current minority status and their recent mobilization as an ethnic group tangentially because my primary interest has been the social world inside. But the setting makes this focus appropriate; it might be less appropriate for a study of Hawaiians in Nanakuli or Honolulu. Keanae villagers are identified and perceive themselves as "people on the land," descendants of the *maka'āinana*, not as displaced or ubanized Hawaiians. Yet even in Keanae, it is impossible to ignore the interaction of the inside and the outside. Keanae residents do not live in pristine isolation; their experience of tradition is shaped by the wider social and political context. Is Hawaiian tradition as it is represented in Keanae authentic and real? Yes— according to the current conception of Hawaiian tradition.

But the relationship between past lifeways and the culture of Keanae Hawaiians today is not a simple one. One can discover correspondences to the past, but there are also obviously constructed elements in Hawaiian tradition, even as it is represented in Keanae. I am not suggesting that Hawaiians, or any other group, consciously and calculatingly manipulate their social reality—that they distort received "facts" to their own ends; rather, I argue that tradition is a symbolic category, not an objectively definable body of artifacts and customs handed down from the past. Social groups always use tradition to define themselves vis-à-vis others; Keanae Hawaiians are both living, and living up to, a model of the past by which they distinguish themselves from non-Hawaiians.

Viewing tradition symbolically, as a system of meanings, has two implications that run counter to our common-sense understanding of the relationship between the past and the present. One is that tradition is always changing, not simply because of internal or external social change, but because it is interpreted anew in each generation. Every generation uses a model of the past to define itself, and this image is inevitably invented to some extent because it is formulated in the current social context. The other somewhat unsettling implication is that there are no unequivocal "facts" to be discovered in the relationship between past and present. Rather, our informants' models and interpretations are the most significant determinants of social behavior, and our own models are simply analytic attempts to explain that behavior rather than descriptions of objective truth.

This interpretation does not invalidate the reality, or even the authenticity, of modern Hawaiian tradition. The point is simply that such authenticity is always contextualized, always defined in the present. Tradition comprises that which is interpreted as being traditional in the present. The past is never received mechanically, without reflection and without alteration. If we discard the notion that tradition refers only to practices with demonstrable links to the aboriginal past, then calling someone "aunty" and playing the ukulele are just as traditionally Hawaiian as building an *imu* or adopting a grandchild. All these practices are part of what is presently understood as Hawaiian tradition, although they have varying relationships to the customary practices of the past.

KEANAE'S FUTURE

Ironically perhaps, Keanae's identity as a traditional Hawaiian place has been enhanced in recent years by quite modern political developments; the changing self-perception of Hawaiians in general—their awakening as an ethnic group—has made it likely that the village will survive and that it will remain a distinctively Hawaiian community. At the time of fieldwork, Keanae's survival seemed by no means certain to me. The preponderance of elderly residents suggested that the village was vulnerable to an influx of foreigners who would buy up Hawaiian lands. Population had declined dramatically since the opening of the Hana road, and many homesteads were abandoned. In the absence of recognized local authorities, I thought it possible that villagers might not become alarmed about the trend until it was too late. The level of internal dissension—talk stink—in the village also seemed ominous for Keanae's future. The end of the chiefs' and *konohikis'* control over the local level created a vaccum that has never been filled. After the Mahele, disharmony among the people on the land increased. As a "child of the land" complained in the 1860s, "The common people are *konohiki*s now. . . . Everybody that has a *kuleana* of his own is a *konohiki*" (E-305, 1st c.c.). In pre-Mahele times, the *konohiki*s managed the maintenance of the irrigation system. Now each taro farmer cleans his or her own section of ditch but not necessarily without complaining about neighbors who may not do their share.

Keanae informants said that formerly local people had fishing *hui*s, cooperatives, to catch *akule* and other school fish, but these dissolved because of petty bickering and disputes over money. An elderly resident explained the cause of the *huis'* demise: "Somebody says he had this expense and that expense, and wants to get paid, and then they don't want to pay. I told my husband to give it up. Too much trouble, not worth it." Another villager concurred: "No more the days when you argued at the wharf! That was terrible then." Hawaiians have a stated ethic that people who are working together should not fight. They become visibly upset at public quarrels. Informants related how a young man disgraced himself by publicly cursing at a neighbor when the fish were being brought in; by his act, he shamed himself and everyone in hearing. Yet Hawaiians seem inevitably drawn into the sort of "grumbling and dissension" that marred the voyage of the double-hulled canoe Hokule'a to Tahiti in 1976 (see Finney 1979). At the time of fieldwork, Keanae villagers seemed to be avoiding communal activities altogether. According to one informant, the last *hukilau*, or communal fishing party, had been held in 1966. In 1975, in the absence of local fishing groups, a crew of Japanese and Filipino fishermen from outside used Hawaiian methods to catch *akule* in Keanae.

It is always difficult to say, on the basis of one stint in the field, whether the level of talk stink in a small community is a threat to its existence or a functional mode of social relations. Such disharmony is, after all, found in peasant societies that have survived for centuries and even millenia. Despite apparent internal disunity, rural communities still manage to present a solidary front to the outside.

On brief return visits to Keanae in 1981 and 1982, I was impressed by the appearance of renewed vigor, even a new solidarity in the community. More land was planted in taro than in 1975; a villager said that a crew of local boys now fished for *akule*. During the period of fieldwork, there had been signs that replacement of the grandparental generation was taking place, and the process was even more evident several years later. Many young couples had settled in Keanae; several houses were newly built, others were under construction. My favorite aunties were dead, but their homesteads were occupied by young Hawaiians, and their taro patches were open. The daughter and son-in-law of a village big-man were newly settled on a small, precipitous lot that he had given them, thus further consolidating his family's position in the community. The continuity of Hawaiian landholding in Keanae bodes well for the destiny of "the taro place." Land succession in Keanae continues to follow the traditional pattern; most siblings leave the valley, but one usually returns to reside on the family land.

But the key to Keanae's survival is not merely the continuity of long-established practices. The village's renewed vitality is due at least partly to an evolving sense of solidarity among Hawaiians in general—a political development that originated outside but that has penetrated the consciousness of Hawaiians living inside as well. Assuredly, the increasingly positive valuation attached to traditional Hawaiian activities has imbued the lifestyle of Keanae residents with new meaning. The Hawaiian cultural renaissance, the voyage of the Hokule'a, the occupations of Kahoolawe, Hawaiians' growing reverence for the '*āina* have all enhanced Keanae's public visibility and its symbolic status vis-à-vis the outside society. Villagers in turn have experienced a new self-awareness as upholders of "the real old style," with the result that they may consciously seek to enact activities that they perceive as distinctively Hawaiian, such as giving a luau or fishing for *akule* and distributing part of the catch to all who assist. The village's survival is thus made even more likely by the present-day social and political context. One also cannot ignore the escalating market price of poi as a factor encouraging renewed interest in taro growing.

There is one other bugbear to be considered in this discussion of Keanae's viability. If there is a threat to Keanae's future as a Hawaiian place, it may be an economic one. Now that Keanae is dependent on external employers, markets, and social agencies, real economic disparities must be weighed against the ethic of egalitarianism. Is it possible for internal solidarity to deteriorate further as material inequities increase within the community? As in other rural villages, talk stink in Keanae is a leveling mechanism, often directed at those who violate the ethic of equivalence and seek to be higher than their peers. Economic disparities are possible within a market economy as they were not in a village of subsistence farmers. It is possible that, as material differences between neighbors become more pronounced, the ethic of exchange will be strained to reconcile real inequities with the ideal of egalitarianism. The danger is that the strangers in the village will become more numerous as more people become economically high.

But I do not believe in this possibility because the market economy penetrated Keanae over a hundred years ago and yet the egalitarian ethic of village social relations has persisted. Keanae's Hawaiianness will prevail as long as a community of neighbors and relatives survives; and it will survive if residents refuse to alienate their lands. The possibilities for wealth in Keanae are, after all, limited to the income from taro marketing and salaried work inside. More importantly, economic differences continue to be subordinate to Hawaiian values and priorities. The big-man's household is more prosperous than the widow's, but this disparity alone does not bring him prestige. The widow's needs are modest, but she too once had a big family and a household full of workers. The material differences between them are appropriate to their life situations; as an elderly "mother" in the village, the widow is in fact more likely to be esteemed than someone who is merely prosperous. The key to Keanae's future as a Hawaiian place is that residents have chosen a lifestyle that they recognize as traditional and have committed themselves to Hawaiian ideals. Those who are ambitious in a Western sense leave the village. Those who remain choose to live in the style of *kama'āina*, children of the land.

PERSISTENCE AND CHANGE

Terms such as *persistence* and *change* seem to imply mutually exclusive processes. Yet social scientists know that this either/or implication is false and have devised a variety of rubrics to describe the dialectical relationship between the force of the past and the impact of the present: structure and history, structure and event, reproduction and transformation (Sahlins 1981), convention and invention (Wagner 1981)—all represent analytic attempts to effect the wedding of stasis and change. A crucial problem for this pursuit has been the ethnographic variety of responses to foreign contact. For example, some Oceanic societies, such as Samoa, seem to have retained their indigenous culture to a great extent in spite of colonization—indeed, to have insisted almost aggressively on cultural preservation. Hawaii contrasts as an apparent example of total cultural transformation, historically aided and abetted by the society's own leaders, the chiefs.

I have shown that in one Hawaiian community, there are demonstrable correlates with the past, customs that follow precedents found in pre-Christian and precontact Hawaiian society. Cultural persistence in Hawaii cannot be traced in material artifacts or even stated rules. The surviving links to the past are less tangible than grass houses, shell valuables, or native clothing, and they rarely reflect explicit norms such as "We marry our mother's brother's daughter" or "We give mats to our in-laws at marriage." The institutional framework of Hawaiian society is gone; the makeup of the world outside the village has been transformed.

The greatest impact of foreign colonization was perhaps the loss of the indigenous authority structure. Throughout the nineteenth century, native Hawaiian authorities surrendered or were relieved of their power. The process began with Captain James Cook's arrival and the Hawaiian chiefs' rush to adopt foreign symbols of high status (see Sahlins 1981), and continued with the displacement of the *konohiki*s during the Mahele and the overthrow of the monarchy at the end of the nineteenth century. But even this decapitation of the society was not unprecedented in Hawaiian legend and cultural history, nor did it effect a wholesale transformation of the political hierarchy. Marshall Sahlins (ibid.:30) has pointed out "the Hawaiian symbolic proportion—chiefs are to the people as the Europeans were to Hawaiians in general." The categorical relationship between chiefs and people was transformed in the nineteenth century, but it was also reproduced: the salient social opposition became Hawaiian/haole rather than commoner/*ali'i*. Certainly there are good historical reasons for the hostility that some Hawaiians feel toward haoles today, but their current relationship is also motivated by the cultural past.

What is the key to different societies' experiences of foreign contact? As Sahlins has shown for Hawaii, a culture's response to the contact situation is ordered by prior cultural values and categorical relationships. Hawaiian culture placed a high value on innovations from outside and thus incorporated the potential for transformation within its indigenous ideology (ibid.:29–30). Even today, Hawaiians are always eager to adopt a better idea, whether or not of native origin. I encountered this trait on several occasions. Once after I had purchased some fishing tackle outside, I mentioned to a Keanae friend that the Japanese store owner had shown me a knot for tying the hook to the line. My Hawaiian fishing companion was eager for a demonstration, for it was just possible that a foreigner might have a method superior to hers.

Modern Hawaiian society illustrates both persistence and change. The principles that guide social relations inside have withstood the transformation of the community's relationship to the external society; Hawaiian culture reproduces itself in the crucial categorical relations between commodities and between people. Indeed, the premise of different transactional rules has become part of the social opposition between inside and outside, Hawaiian and foreign—a contrast simultaneously ancient and modern.

Cultural reproduction is always selective. What changes and what stays the same is a matter of values—what a society considers important, desirable, and high. This cultural valuation derives in part from indigenous ideology but also acquires meaning in the present. It is not happenstance that the luau, exchange-in-kind, and the centrality of women are the most salient examples of Hawaiian cultural persistence. These are all parts of a complex of relationships that was symbolically marked and weighty within the prior value system but that is also meaningful in the modern social and political context. Hawaiians build an *imu* and tie *laulau*s by splitting the stem of the cordyline in part because their parents did so, but also because today they perceive these activities to be quintessentially Hawaiian. Even exchange-in-kind is not an unselfconscious holdover from the past since residents can point out that giving, as opposed to selling, differentiates their community from the outside.

The notion of structure emphasizes the reproduction of prior categorical relationships, such as the movement of commodities and people between blood relatives and affines. Structure may transform itself through its own internal dynamic or be transformed through an interaction with historical events. Cultural reproduction is never perfect, but neither is cultural transformation entire or complete. Both the nineteenth-century contact history and the state of Hawaiian culture today are evidence of this fact. What of tradition in this light? I have called tradition a model of the past rather than an objective inheritance. A conscious category that is continually being revised in the present, tradition is the level at which past symbols are reevaluated and reinterpreted in light of present-day distinctions and meanings. The reformulation of tradition is one aspect of culture change—the locus of symbolic creativity or "invention" (Wagner 1981). Tradition is both structured and meaningful and thus incorporates both the past and the present. Keanae villagers today reflect on their traditions, reenact them, and also change them, recognizing the present-tense significance of their activities when they say, "We Hawaiians do this."

Ha'ina mai ka puana. My song is ended.

GLOSSARY

ahupua'a. Ancient land division running from the mountain to the sea.

akule. Mackerel.

ali'i. Chief.

aloha. Affection, love.

'aumakua. Guardian spirit.

'awa. *Piper methysticum* or kava, used ceremonially in other Polynesian societies. An intoxicating drink is made from the root.

hānai. Adoptive; literally "feeding."

hanohano. Honored, distinguished, honorable.

haole. White person, foreigner.

haupia. Coconut pudding, a standard luau dish.

heiau. Temple of the old Hawaiian religion.

ho'āo pa'a. Binding marriage as opposed to cohabitation.

hui. Corporation, society, cooperative group.

huli. Taro tops, shoots for planting.

hūnōna. Son-in-law.

imu. Underground oven.

kahuna. Expert in Hawaiian healing methods, sorcerer; originally priest.

kālua. To bake in the underground oven.

kama'āina. Old-time resident; literally "child of the land."

kanaka. Man, mankind.

ko'iko'i. Important, weighty; people of integrity.

konohiki. Landlord, headman, land agent.

kuleana. Claim, right; also, Land Commission Award.

kūlolo. Taro-coconut pudding baked in the *imu*, a luau dish.

*laulau*s. Bundles of meat and greens wrapped in *ti* leaves, a luau dish.

luau. A Hawaiian feast; taro leaves.

maka'āinana. The common people.

mo'opuna. Grandchild.

'opihi. Sea limpets, a delicacy served at luaus.

pau. Done, finished.

po'e. People.

poi. Taro paste, the traditional staple food of Hawaii.

pōki'i. The youngest child.

ti. Cordyline terminalis, a plant used ritually in the old Hawaiian religion and still valued by Hawaiians for ceremonial and medicinal purposes.

WORKS CITED

Adams, Romanzo
  1937   *Interracial Marriage in Hawaii*. New York: Macmillan.
Andrews, Lorrin
  1865   *A Dictionary of the Hawaiian Language*. Honolulu: Henry M. Whitney.
Anonymous
  1868   "The Story of Kanewailani." *Ke Au Okoa* 2 February–2 April. Bernice P. Bishop Museum Library. Typescript.
Barnes, J. A.
  1967   "The Frequency of Divorce." In *The Craft of Social Anthropology*, edited by A. L. Epstein. London: Tavistock.
Barrère, Dorothy B.
  1959   "Glossary." In *Fragments of Hawaiian History as Recorded by John Papa Ii*, translated by Mary Kawena Pukui. Honolulu: Bishop Museum Press.
Bates, G. W. [A. Haole, pseud.]
  1854   *Sandwich Island Notes*. New York: Harper & Bros.
Beaglehole, Ernest
  1937   *Some Modern Hawaiians*. Research Publication No. 19. Honolulu: University of Hawaii.
Burridge, Kenelm
  1969   *Tangu Traditions*. Oxford: Oxford University Press.
Campbell, Archibald
  [1822] 1967 *A Voyage Round the World from 1806 to 1812*. Facsimile edition. Honolulu: University of Hawaii Press.
Carr, Elizabeth Ball
  1972   *Da Kine Talk*. Honolulu: University Press of Hawaii.
Carroll, Vern, ed.
  1970   *Adoption in Eastern Oceania*. Honolulu: University of Hawaii Press.
Clare, Alice, and Jack Morrow
  1930   "Maui: A Few Facts About the Valley Isle." Ms., Maui Public Library, Wailuku.
Cohn, Bernard S.
  1980   "History and Anthropology: The State of Play." *Comparative Studies in Society and History* 22:198–221.

Corney, Peter
    1896   *Voyages in the Northern Pacific*. Honolulu: Thomas G. Thrum.

Coulter, John Wesley, and Chee Kwon Chun
    1937   *Chinese Rice Farmers in Hawaii*. Bulletin 16:5. Honolulu: University of Hawaii.

Cross, W. A.
    1912   "The Story of Rice in Hawaii." *Mid-Pacific Magazine* 3 (April):345–351.

Dibble, Sheldon
    1909   *A History of the Sandwich Islands*. Honolulu: Thomas G. Thrum.

Ellis, William
    [1827] 1917 *Narrative of a Tour Through Hawaii*. Honolulu: Hawaiian Gazette Company.

Finney, Ben R.
    1979   *Hokule'a: The Way to Tahiti*. New York: Dodd, Mead.

Forster, John
    1959   "Acculturation of Hawaiians on the Island of Maui, Hawaii." Ph.D. diss., University of California, Los Angeles.

Gallimore, Ronald, and Alan Howard, eds.
    1968   *Studies in a Hawaiian Community*. Pacific Anthropological Records No. 1. Honolulu: Bernice P. Bishop Museum.

Goldman, Irving
    1970   *Ancient Polynesian Society*. Chicago: University of Chicago Press.

Gonzalez, Nancie L. Solien
    1969   *Black Carib Household Structure*. Seattle: University of Washington Press.

Goodenough, Ward H.
    1951   *Property, Kin, and Community on Truk*. Publications in Anthropology No. 40. New Haven: Yale University.

Handy, E. S. Craighill
    1940   *The Hawaiian Planter*. Bulletin No. 161. Honolulu: Bernice P. Bishop Museum.

Handy, E. S. Craighill, and E. G. Handy
    1972   *The Native Planters in Old Hawaii: Their Life, Lore, and Environments*. Bulletin No. 233. Honolulu: Bernice P. Bishop Museum.

Handy, E. S. Craighill, and Mary Kawena Pukui
  1972   *The Polynesian Family System in Ka-'u, Hawai'i.* Rutland,
          Vt., and Tokyo: Charles E. Tuttle.
Howard, Alan
  1971   *Households, Families and Friends in a Hawaiian-American
          Community.* Working Paper No. 19. Honolulu: East-
          West Population Institute.
  1974   *Ain't No Big Thing.* Honolulu: University Press of
          Hawaii.
Howard, Alan, R. Heighton, Jr., C. Jordan, and Ronald Gallimore
  1970   "Traditional and Modern Adoption Patterns in Ha-
          waii." In *Adoption in Eastern Oceania,* edited by Vern
          Carroll. Honolulu: University of Hawaii Press.
Huntsman, Judith, and Anthony Hooper
  1975   "Male and Female in Tokelau Culture." *Journal of the
          Polynesian Society* 84:415–430.
Ii, John Papa
  1959   *Fragments of Hawaiian History as Recorded by John Papa Ii.*
          Translated by Mary Kawena Pukui. Edited by Doro-
          thy B. Barrère. Honolulu: Bishop Museum Press.
Judd, Henry P.
  1938   "Riding Round East Maui (c. 1908)." *Paradise of the Pa-
          cific* 50 (August):5–6.
Kamakau, Samuel M.
  1868   "Some of the Practices of the Hawaiians." *Kuokoa*
          8 August. Translated by Mary Kawena Pukui. Ms.,
          collection of Dorothy B. Barrère.
  1961   *Ruling Chiefs of Hawaii.* Honolulu: Kamehameha
          Schools Press.
  1964   *Ka Po'e Kahiko: The People of Old.* Translated by Mary
          Kawena Pukui. Edited by Dorothy B. Barrère. Special
          Publication 51. Honolulu: Bishop Museum Press.
Kanepuu
  1867   "The Story of Kana." Translated by Elspeth P. Sterling.
          Bernice P. Bishop Museum Library. Typescript.
Keesing, Felix M.
  1936   *Hawaiian Homesteading on Molokai.* Research Publica-
          tion No. 12. Honolulu: University of Hawaii.
Keesing, Roger M., and Robert Tonkinson, eds.
  1982   *Reinventing Traditional Culture: The Politics of Kastom in
          Island Melanesia. Mankind* Special Issue 13(4).

Kekoa, E.
1865   "Birth Rites of Hawaiian Children in Ancient Times."
        Translated from *Kuokoa* by Thomas G. Thrum. Thrum
        Collection 23. Bernice P. Bishop Museum Library.
Kelly, Raymond C.
1977   *Etoro Social Structure: A Study in Structural Contradic-
        tion.* Ann Arbor: University of Michigan Press.
Kirch, Patrick V.
1979   *Late Prehistoric and Early Historic Settlement-Subsistence
        Systems in the Anahulu Valley, Oahu.* Report 79-2. Hono-
        lulu: Bernice P. Bishop Museum.
Kuykendall, Ralph S.
1938   *The Hawaiian Kingdom: 1778–1854.* Honolulu: Univer-
        sity of Hawaii Press.
1953   *The Hawaiian Kingdom: 1854–1874.* Honolulu: Univer-
        sity of Hawaii Press.
1967   *The Hawaiian Kingdom: 1874–1893.* Honolulu: Univer-
        sity of Hawaii Press.
Lamphere, Louise
1974   "Strategies, Cooperation, and Conflict Among Women
        in Domestic Groups." In *Women, Culture, and Society,*
        edited by Michelle Z. Rosaldo and Louise Lamphere.
        Stanford: Stanford University Press.
Leach, E. R.
1958   "Concerning Trobriand Clans and the Kinship Cate-
        gory 'Tabu.'" In *The Developmental Cycle in Domestic
        Groups,* edited by J. R. Goody. Cambridge Papers in
        Social Anthropology No. 1. Cambridge: Cambridge
        University Press.
Lévi-Strauss, Claude
1969a   *The Elementary Structures of Kinship.* Translated by
        James Harle Bell, John R. von Sturmer, and Rodney
        Needham. Boston: Beacon Press.
1969b   *The Raw and the Cooked.* Translated by John and Doreen
        Weightman. New York: Harper and Row.
Lind, Andrew W.
1959   "Community Types in Hawaii." *Social Process in Hawaii*
        23:5–19.
Linnekin, Jocelyn
1983a   "Defining Tradition: Variations on the Hawaiian Iden-
        tity." *American Ethnologist* 10:241–252.

1983b   "The *Hui* Lands of Keanae: Hawaiian Land Tenure and the Great Mahele." *Journal of the Polynesian Society* 92:169–188.

Linton, Ralph
1943   "Nativistic Movements." *American Anthropologist* 45: 230–240.

Lorden, Doris
1935   "The Chinese-Hawaiian Family." *American Journal of Sociology* 40:453–463.

Lueras, Leonard
1975   "Keanae: The Hawaii That Used to Be." *Honolulu Advertiser* 18 December: A1.

Malo, David
1951   *Hawaiian Antiquities*. 2nd ed. Translated by Nathaniel B. Emerson. Honolulu: Bishop Museum Press.

Mathison, Gilbert F.
1825   *Narrative of a Visit to Brazil, Chile, Peru, and the Sandwich Islands*. London: Charles Knight.

Mauss, Marcel
1967   *The Gift*. Translated by Ian Cunnison. New York: W. W. Norton.

Morgan, Lewis Henry
1909   *Ancient Society*. Chicago: C. H. Kerr & Co.

Neal, Marie C.
1965   *In Gardens of Hawaii*. Honolulu: Bishop Museum Press.

Oliver, Douglas
1955   *A Solomon Island Society*. Boston: Beacon Press.

Otterbein, Keith F.
1966   *The Andros Islanders*. Lawrence, Kansas: University of Kansas Publications.

Protect Kaho'olawe 'Ohana
1981   *Aloha 'Āina* (newsletter). Winter.

Pukui, Mary Kawena
n.d.   Interview transcripts, collection of Dorothy B. Barrère.

Pukui, Mary Kawena, and Samuel Elbert
1971   *Hawaiian Dictionary: Hawaiian-English, English-Hawaiian*. 3rd ed. Honolulu: University Press of Hawaii.

Pukui, Mary Kawena, E. W. Haertig, and Catherine A. Lee
1972a   *Nānā i ke Kumu* (*Look to the Source*). Vol. 1. Honolulu: Hui Hānai.

1972b   *Nānā i ke Kumu* (*Look to the Source*). Vol. 2. Honolulu: Hui Hānai.

Redfield, Robert
1956   *Peasant Society and Culture.* Chicago: University of Chicago Press.

Ritte, Walter, Jr., and Richard Sawyer
1978   *Na Mana'o Aloha o Kaho'olawe.* Honolulu: Aloha 'Āina o na Kūpuna, Inc.

Rosaldo, Michelle Z.
1974   "Women, Culture, and Society: A Theoretical Overview." In *Women, Culture, and Society,* edited by Michelle Z. Rosaldo and Louise Lamphere. Stanford: Stanford University Press.

Sahlins, Marshall D.
1962   *Moala.* Ann Arbor: University of Michigan Press.
1963   "Poor Man, Rich Man, Big-Man, Chief: Political types in Melanesia and Polynesia." *Comparative Studies in Society and History* 5:285–303.
1965   "On the Sociology of Primitive Exchange." In *The Relevance of Models for Social Anthropology,* edited by Michael Banton. London: Tavistock.
1974   "Historical Anthropology of the Hawaiian Kingdom." Research proposal submitted to the National Science Foundation by the Bernice P. Bishop Museum. Typescript, files of the author.
1981   *Historical Metaphors and Mythical Realities: Structure in the Early History of the Sandwich Islands Kingdom.* ASAO Special Publication No. 1. Ann Arbor: University of Michigan Press.

Schneider, David
1965   "Some Muddles in the Models: Or, How the System Really Works." In *The Relevance of Models for Social Anthropology,* edited by Michael Banton. London: Tavistock.
1968   *American Kinship: A Cultural Account.* Englewood Cliffs, N.J.: Prentice-Hall.

Shepard, F. P., G. A. MacDonald, and D. C. Cox
1950   *The Tsunami of April 1, 1946.* Berkeley and Los Angeles: University of California Press.

Smith, M. G.
1962   *West Indian Family Structure.* Seattle: University of Washington Press.

Smith, R. T.
   1956   *The Negro Family in British Guiana*. London: Routledge
            and Kegan Paul.
   1974   "The Matrifocal Family." In *The Character of Kinship*,
            edited by Jack Goody. Cambridge: Cambridge Univer-
            sity Press.
State of Hawaii
   1974   *The State of Hawaii Data Book*. Honolulu: Department of
            Planning and Economic Development.
Tanner, Nancy
   1974   "Matrifocality in Indonesia and Africa and Among
            Black Americans." In *Women, Culture, and Society*,
            edited by Michelle Z. Rosaldo and Louise Lamphere.
            Stanford: Stanford University Press.
Territory of Hawaii
   1895   *Laws, Special Session*. Honolulu: Robert Grieve.
   1929   *Indices of Awards Made by the Board of Commissioners to
            Quiet Land Titles in the Hawaiian Islands*. Honolulu: Of-
            fice of the Commissioner of Public Lands.
Thrum, Thomas, ed.
   1865   "Ka Ho'omana Kahiko." Selections from *Kuokoa*. Ber-
            nice P. Bishop Museum Library.
   1877   "Notes on the History of the Rice Culture." *Hawaiian
            Annual*, pp. 45–49. Honolulu: Thomas G. Thrum.
Thurston, Lorrin A., ed.
   1904   *The Fundamental Law of Hawaii*. Honolulu: Territory of
            Hawaii.
University of Hawaii.
   1965–1967 *An Economic Study of the County of Maui*. Honolulu:
               University of Hawaii Economic Research Center.
Wagner, Roy
   1981   *The Invention of Culture*. Rev. ed. Chicago: University
            of Chicago Press.
Watson, Leslie J.
   1932   "Old Hawaiian Land *Huis*—Their Development and
            Dissolution." Ms., University of Hawaii Library.
Webb, Malcolm C.
   1965   "The Abolition of the Taboo System in Hawaii." *Jour-
            nal of the Polynesian Society* 74:21–39.
Wenkam, Robert
   1970   *Maui: The Last Hawaiian Place*. San Francisco: Friends
            of the Earth.

Wyllie, Robert C.
  1855   "Answers to Questions." In *Annual Report, Minister of Foreign Relations (1849)*, pp. 49–95. Honolulu: Polynesian Press.
Yamamura, D. S.
  1941   "A Study of the Factors in the Education of the Child of Hawaiian Ancestry in Hana, Maui." Master's Thesis, University of Hawaii.

INDEX